48.60

Bis

TOWARDS A COMPETENT WORKFORCE

Dedication

This book is dedicated to the memory of
Bob's mother, Norah Patricia Penn (formerly Mansfield)
and
Lindsay's father, Derek Frank Hobbs

Royalties

All royalties from this book will go to
The Carmel McAnespie Trust Fund
Carmel, a member of staff at NCVQ, died at the age of 30 from cancer.
The Trust Fund will be used to help fund cancer care for young women.

TOWARDS A COMPETENT WORKFORCE

Bob Mansfield and Lindsay Mitchell

Gower

Published by
Gower Publishing Ltd
Gower House
Croft Road
Aldershot
Hampshire GU11 3HR
England

Gower
Old Post Road
Brookfield
Vermont 05036
USA

British Library Cataloguing in Publication Data

Mansfield, Bob
  Towards a competent workforce
  1. Vocational education – Great Britain   2. Vocational education – Planning – Great Britain
  3. Labor economics – Great Britain
  I. Title   II. Mitchell, Lindsay
  370.1'13'0941

ISBN 0 566 07699 3

Library of Congress Cataloging-in-Publication Data

Mansfield, Bob.
  Towards a competent workforce / Bob Mansfield and Lindsay Mitchell;
  consultant editor, George Webster.
      p.   cm.
  Includes bibliographical references and index.
  ISBN 0-566-07699-3
  1. Vocational education – Great Britain – History – 20th century.
  2. Occupational training – Great Britain – History – 20th century.
  I. Mitchell, Lindsay.   II. Webster, George.   III. Title.
  LC1047.G7M36   1996
  370.11'3'094109045–dc20   96–3977
                                                                    CIP

Typeset in Century Old Style by Bournemouth Colour Press and printed in Great Britain by Hartnolls Ltd, Bodmin.

Contents

List of Figures

List of Tables

Preface

Towards a Competent Workforce traces the development of Vocational Education and Training (VET) in the United Kingdom from 1982 to 1995. Readers who are not familiar with the existing VET system, its institutions and technical language should read the Note on occupational standards and National Vocational Qualifications (pages xxiii–xxiv) which gives an overview of the main features.

The book tells a story. The story is not a novel, rather it is a history of a number of ideas. The ideas are simple – but making them work proved complex. We were involved in the processes and development which helped bring them into fruition between 1982 and 1995. They centre on the phrase we chose as the title to this book: towards a competent workforce. They are:

- an effective and efficient economy needs motivated, educated and well-trained people;
- many groups of people have a stake in the economy – this gives them rights, and responsibilities to each other and to wider economic aims;
- modern economies are characterised by rapid change;
- people working in modern economies need to be able to change their work and working methods – rapidly;
- systems designed to educate and train people should be changed to meet these economic needs – and should result in people who are well motivated, educated, trained and able to change.

These ideas are our interpretation of the policy imperatives which guided a radical change in the system of VET in the United Kingdom. The nature of the change can also be characterised by four key features:

1. The vocational curriculum (what people should learn to prepare for work) changed from descriptions of the skills and knowledge needed to descriptions of what people need to achieve – ie work expectations.
2. Recognition of achievement was to be based on demonstrated competence rather than attendance at a course of learning for a fixed period of time.
3. Access to education, training and certification (in the form of qualifications) was extended to cover all occupations.

4. There has been a recognition of what we have always known – that people can learn by doing and that the workplace can be a valuable learning environment and resource.

The development of these ideas and the methods and processes which emerged from them has given us the VET system we know today.

The telling of this story is the structure of the book. It is told in four parts, each of which is presented from a slightly different perspective. The perspectives are:

- rhetorical;
- theoretical;
- technical (concepts);
- technical (applications).

RHETORICAL

Part I is rhetoric – the art of using language to persuade. These first two chapters state our position on the nature of education and the changes which have occurred in the economy which demand an imaginative response from the VET system. We outline the key factors which have brought about important changes and offer our interpretation of them to advance our central claim: that the economy has changed so radically that we need a new approach to VET, based on a new understanding of the nature of work and the competence needed by individuals. Part I asks the question, 'What is the competent workforce?'.

THEORETICAL

Part II contains the theory – largely other people's theories, as it happens, interpreted and modified by ourselves. We chart the development and history of models of occupational competence, suggesting that these come from two broad traditions with different ways of describing the competent workforce.

The first is characterised by a control philosophy which assumes that people are not worthy of trust, nor capable of working without the imposition of strict controls over the work process. Work is differentiated by the type of work – and, more significantly, along the lines of social class which have dominated the British attitude to work and working people. The work undertaken by the many – variously referred to in history as the 'labouring classes', the 'proletariat' and the 'working class' – has been defined and organised, through the mediation of power relationships, as minimal routine tasks. This in turn has led to methods of skills analysis and vocational training which implicitly follow this control model, from the imposition of dehumanised work practices through work and method study to didactic forms of instructional training.

In this model the competent workforce is the managerial class; those who do the work are the compliant workforce.

The second tradition is enabling rather than controlling. It recognises that all people have many capabilities which can be enabled – or encouraged to emerge – through the provision of opportunities for learning and the proper recognition of achievement (which includes appropriate levels of reward for contributions to wealth creation). It also recognises the social nature of work. Work and the patterns of working practice and working relationships are not determined by any natural laws of economics or human nature; rather, working relationships are negotiated over time and are constantly changing. Work is a defining human activity, so it should be shot through with human attributes – the abilities we have as a species to question, conjecture, imagine, create and improve. Work is also carried out within a society which, in the UK, claims to be a developing democracy, so work, too, should be infused with the very principles and values which underpin democracy – the values of participation, representation, account-ability, fairness and justice.

In this model the whole workforce is the competent workforce.

We are proponents of the latter tradition. We find the former unsavoury, anti-democratic and extremely limited in its vision of both work and the people who are engaged in it. But simply stating our adherence to a tradition of thought will not make things happen. This tradition of philosophy, of sociology and of historical interpretation needs to be developed to produce a new way of describing the work role which provides a clear alternative to the view that work, for most people, involves little more than simple reflexes in response to imposed procedures. This we offer in the form of the Job Competence Model, a model developed in the context of a particular training initiative with a limited focus but now applied to all work roles at all levels in all occupations – a universal model of the competent workforce.

Having a description of the nature of competence is a starting-point, but it is only part of the story. What is also needed is the expression of that model in methods and techniques which can be used to represent occupational com-petence in a way which will enable us to:

- describe work roles with precision;
- form qualifications which recognise capability and competence;
- design participative learning systems which will enable learners to develop their competence;
- develop open, fair and just systems of assessment.

These methods emerged during the 1980s in the form of occupational standards and National Vocational Qualifications. They were imperfectly formed because, we believe, the empowering ideologies which underpin them did not find favour with the policy makers. They remain imperfect, but still retain the potential for emancipating people from narrow and confined jobs into enriched and recognised work roles.

Part II also traces the history of the development of the Job Competence Model and occupational standards from their origins in the Youth Training Scheme. The history is not a retrospective justification of any positions we held then or hold now. It is there to provide a context and a backdrop against which the reader may understand the powerful forces, views and opinions, many of which are still unresolved, which merged together to form our current VET system.

TECHNICAL

Parts III and IV together constitute a technical manual on how to use **functional analysis** and **occupational standards,** two of the key methodologies used to define and describe the competent workforce. These are the chapters which we have been pressed to write since 1989 by people who, flatteringly, asked us to produce the definitive statement on these two methods. At that time both methods were insufficiently rigorous to be called 'methods', and we were not happy to publish anything about the methods without being able to explain fully our rationale. What we offer is not necessarily definitive, but is **our version** of both methods, which we were closely involved in developing, backed by nearly eight years of solid practice in which we have refined our approaches and techniques.

We believe what we have to say is, although not definitive, authoritative. It is not definitive for two reasons. First, the agencies which oversee the implementation of VET policy, the Department for Education and Employment and the National Council for Vocational Qualifications, are not likely to agree entirely with our version of the methods. What we have to say is close enough to the official line to be clearly recognisable, but we often go further and are more assertive in some of our statements than either agency would choose to be.

Second, what we have to say is not definitive because there are other versions of functional analysis and occupational standards in the field. This is a cause of much confusion and legitimate criticism. Having seen public statements which claim that occupational standards and National Vocational Qualifications are broad based, concerned with whole-role performance, express best practice and anticipate future requirements in work roles, people are astonished to come across standards which are narrow task descriptions describing activities which are simply a series of disconnected routines, focused very clearly on minimal organisational requirements in the here and now. They criticise the standards programme for not delivering what was intended. If they come across such standards and qualifications **without** having seen the public statements, they are equally critical – but in addition they see this as characteristic of the entire approach.

The same is true of functional analysis. It is, as we show, a method which emerged as an alternative to task analysis, a holistic approach which expresses broad work roles within an occupation based on a participative process of negotiation. However, if people have been exposed to the lists of routinised tasks which pose as 'functional analysis' then we are not surprised if they reject the approach as being reductionist, behaviourist and part of the very tradition that it tries to replace. A method cannot be held responsible for those who misuse it.

In part, we are trying to set the record straight. We are often identified as two of the key contributors to the development of functional analysis and occupational standards. This is **our** opportunity to describe what we think they are, how they are developed and what they are intended to achieve. We wish to place a clear distance between our interpretation of the methods and the misuse which we encounter and for which, to some extent, we are held responsible.

We do not cover the extremely practical questions of how to enable organisations to prepare to meet the challenges identified in Part I. Standards need to be consistent with the underpinning values and aims of organisations, and our specification of standards will make sense only to organisations which have the same commitment to a future-oriented vision and which value the people who work with and for them. If organisations want routine task descriptions the better to control and systematise routines and procedures, they do not need our version of occupational standards – a task analysis will do nicely. In Chapter 15 we offer a method of examining whether standards do have benefits to offer organisations.

The clearest and most obvious use of occupational standards is in the design of National Vocational Qualifications. For the sake of brevity, we use in this book the term National Vocational Qualifications (NVQs) to cover Scottish Vocational Qualifications (SVQs) and the National Council for Vocational Qualifications (NCVQ) to include the role of the Scottish Vocational Education Council (SCOTVEC) as an accrediting body for SVQs. Although the Scottish system has many unique features, NVQs and SVQs were intended to be equivalent qualifications.

One of the problems in the evolution of the VET system is that 'the competent workforce' has been interpreted as 'the qualified workforce', without regard to any links which there might be between our model of occupational competence and the qualifications which have been developed. In many quarters some NVQs have been criticised for being too narrow, routine and technically focused, so we would encourage organisations to fight a rearguard action, to develop demanding and challenging descriptions of competence which are fit for purpose in strategic, forward-looking organisations. Although these issues are very important and pressing, we have no room left to consider them in this book. They will have to wait for a later publication.

Finally, despite our general enthusiasm about the systems and processes which lead to occupational standards and National Vocational Qualifications, we do not wish to be seen as apologists for a system which we believe to be fundamentally flawed and distorted by a number of frankly political interventions.

We believe that there are two significant constraints on the achievement of all the potential which *The New Training Initiative* (Manpower Services Commission, 1981) envisaged and which the standards programme tried to implement. These are the issues of bureaucratisation and ownership.

BUREAUCRATISATION

The last person to deliver a revolution is a bureaucrat – yet bureaucrats are precisely the ones who are charged with delivering both occupational standards and NVQs. At every level in the system, classic bureaucracies control both the development and implementation processes which have led to an increasing welter of procedures, administrative systems and overwhelming paperwork. Employers, candidates, assessors and scheme managers are protesting wildly and, in our view, legitimately.

It is not just that, by their very nature, these controlling bodies are bureaucracies. It is that they act like the worst kind of bureaucracy, committed to creating a well-ordered and efficient homeostasis, dedicated to smoothly running systems where information is often collected but little used. This stifles the dynamic processes of change and innovation which was the hallmark of the development process when the first tentative steps were taken in the early 1980s.

These bodies often take as their organisational model the traditional Civil Service. Committees are spawned by the dozen and generate subcommittees, each with a remit, another working subgroup, a secretariat and a reporting structure. Reams of paperwork land on the desks of willing but unsuspecting contributors to the development process. Confusion expressed within the system is met by a barrage of even more paper. Even in critically important technical documents like the NCVQ guidance document 'NVQ Criteria and Guidance' we find that nearly half the informative text describes procedures and paperwork systems.

Little attention is paid to the needs of the users of standards and the recipients of materials. Standards are complex technical documents which are, essentially, reference works. They are not a book, they have no plot, and to anyone other than the professional programme designer or assessment specialist they offer little in the way of a good read. Yet they are distributed by the hundreds to laypeople who have never seen them before and who are immediately put off by their apparent complexity, formal and structured language and the repetitious nature of the layout. This underlines another characteristic of bureaucracies – communicating solely through written documents. Bureaucracies produce documents, they distribute them together with more documents to interpret the original documents, collect feedback through documents and respond to problems and difficulties in using the documents by commissioning and issuing yet more documents.

Of course, this is a caricature. Many of the organisations involved in standards development are more dynamic and organised as change agents than the above picture suggests. But we are extremely wary of a general tendency in which the original purpose of the standards programme is rapidly becoming obscured by the weight of paperwork and the administrative requirements of bureaucracies.

OWNERSHIP

The issue of ownership, unless resolved, threatens to alienate important stakeholders in the VET system. The issue centres on who the NVQs are designed to benefit and who owns – or, more accurately, defines – the occupational standards on which the NVQs are based.

The issue is expressed most clearly in the composition of Lead Bodies. These were originally set up along the lines of the tripartite system which was the model used for the Manpower Services Commission. In this model three interest groups, or stakeholders, were balanced: employers, employees (usually represented by trade unions) and educational practitioners.

Lead Bodies are no longer required to conform to this model. Originally described as employment led, they are now often referred to in Department for Education and Employment literature as employer led. This effective domination of the employer interest has led to grave disquiet and has affected the credibility of the programme in some quarters where it is accused of setting standards and defining qualifications which meet the immediate and narrow needs of current employment.

The processes of standards development are also affected by the issue of ownership in the sense of who is consulted, who has a say in the structure of the standards and what methods are used for consultation. Our preference has always been for a development process in which different stakeholders are invited to contribute, where comments are clearly recorded by participants, then processed and used directly to develop and modify the standards before presenting them again in another round of consultation. This is, potentially, a profoundly democratic process – but we are not convinced that it is the norm in standards development.

We are not suggesting here that employers are part of some sinister conspiracy, nor that trade unions on Lead Bodies would always represent the real needs of candidates. What we draw attention to is the picture this may give to the rest of society: that standards are designed by employers to meet their needs. It is not too far from this position to argue that standards are little more than new ways of ensuring compliance and imposing authority.

SUMMARY

In summary, then, we propose that an approach which had the strengths of being both profoundly democratic and innovative is in danger of becoming inert and authoritarian. In this book we seek to describe how the standards programme came about, its roots and aims. We hope that, having read the book, readers will be in a better position to judge the merits of the approach to determine whether it is capable of delivering the competent workforce.

Bob Mansfield
Lindsay Mitchell

Acknowledgements

A book of this type cannot be the sole product of just two authors. Many people have contributed to the ideas and methods which have gone into this work, and it would be impossible to acknowledge them all. We record below the key people who have inspired us and worked with us since 1982 and without whom this book would not have been written.

TO THOSE WHO INSPIRED US ...

Inspiration is a funny thing for the simple reason that you may be inspired by a piece of work or a particular writer and end up developing in a different direction. This makes it difficult for the source of the inspiration to recognise the debt you owe them, because what you have done does not concur with their view of the world or the directions that they might have taken. This has been the case with an important source of our ideas.

A powerful influence on our thinking and the development of the methods we describe in this book was the project conducted by the Institute of Manpower Studies in 1982 which resulted in the seminal work *Training for Skill Ownership*. In particular the two main authors, Chris Hayes and Nickie Fonda, continued to provide encouragement and support for the approaches we were developing. We are aware, however, that both Chris and Nickie became concerned about the direction our work eventually took, and might not be particularly happy with our claim that functional analysis was derived, essentially, from their pioneering work on Occupational Training Families and the Work Learning Guides. Nevertheless it was, and we acknowledge both their profound influence on our early thinking and our debt to them.

The other key inspiration comes from the work of the Work-Based Learning Project, which grew from the ESF Core Skills Project, also started in 1982, to provide a new curriculum model for the Youth Training Scheme. The director of the ESF Project, Margaret Levy, provided a source of inspiration for ourselves and for many other researchers in this field. Margaret is a woman of intense enthusiasm, and is now a valued and much-loved friend as well as a respected colleague. It was her support for our work and her unceasing drive radically to change VET which inspired our own search for methods and approaches which would help achieve her far-reaching vision.

Finally, an inspiration from an author we have never met and who knows nothing of our existence: Will Hutton, the Editor of the *Observer* and author of *The State We're In*. We are not economists, but many of our approaches are based on a view of the economy and of economic and social change. These views have been strongly influenced by Will Hutton's weekly articles on the nature of the British economy and the political changes that are needed to develop an economic system which combines the wealth-creating imperative of the market with the human imperative of justice.

TO THOSE WHO WORKED WITH US

We have worked with hundreds of people since 1982 – research colleagues, project workers, officers of the Department for Education and Employment (and its precursors, the Manpower Services Commission, the Training Commission, the Training Agency and the Department of Employment), the National Council for Vocational Qualifications and the Scottish Vocational Education Council, clients from Lead Bodies and Professional Bodies, contributors to working groups, colleagues and friends in our own company. All have contributed to the development, formulation and articulation of our ideas and the methodology to which we have contributed. Even when profoundly disagreeing with us and criticising our methods and approaches, they have helped us fill in gaps in our thinking, motivated us to strengthen our arguments and encouraged us to bring coherence to the methodology. We thank them all.

Some people have been important co-workers who have contributed substantially to our work and who have provided us with considerable support and help. David Mathews, who co-authored the original Job Competence Model, has been a colleague and friend since the early days of the ESF Core Skills Project. He is responsible for originating and clarifying many of the analytical models which underpin occupational standards, the process of functional analysis and the practical use of standards. Gilbert Jessup has been a colleague since the ESF Core Skills Project in which he contributed to the emerging ideas about assessment. Since then his career has included setting up the unit which took on the issue of developing a sound methodology to underpin the standards programme, leading the research programme for NCVQ and, finally, becoming Deputy Chief Executive of NCVQ. Our relationship with Gilbert has sometimes been intellectually stormy, particularly on those occasions when he has disagreed with our position and methodology. But Gilbert has always had an unfailing talent for spotting the next critical stage in development and the shortcomings of existing methods – and it is this for which we thank him.

It remains for us to thank all the people who have lived through the painful emergence of this book. Since it was first mooted in 1989, the unfailing support and constant nagging of our co-directors, Tom Caple and Nanci Downey, has helped the work see the light of day. Nanci is, by her own admission, not a researcher. Her interest lies in the implementation of occupational standards and the practical use of standards and models of competence. In this she has been both our fiercest critic and our greatest support – not in the sense of disagreeing with our position and methodology, but in pointing out to us where and in what ways it simply does not work. Her important work in developing standards, developing evidence specifications and designing assessment systems has explored and given life to our sometimes rather theoretical position. She has thrown up difficulties and problems – and solutions – to help us bring the methods and systems together and cover gaps in the emerging model of competence. Nanci spots the inconsistencies – and also provides the sound management support to the company which allows us the time to bury ourselves in writing. Tom, by his reading and commentary on drafts and his contributions to our work on the practical use of standards, provides both intellectual rigour and flashes of comedy. We were very taken with a recent fax from him in which he expounded the origins of the word 'science' – mostly in Greek!

Our company, PRIME Research and Development, is modest, in size and influence, but we are proud of it and all the staff who have worked with us over the years, most of whom have moved on within the VET system to make their own important contributions. We thank Shirley Taylor, Alan Leigh, Martin Christie and Jackie Sturton, all of whom have their own companies – still involved in VET – and Mike Chitty and Lesley Dunlop, who currently work with us and provide both professional support and intellectual stimulation. We also thank Shirley Swift, Tina King, Gill Firth and Liz West – administrative staff who have supported us over the years.

Conventionally, authors thank the people who transcribe and correct the manuscript. But PRIME doesn't work like that! Since all members of the company input and edit their own material, we are the originators and transcribers; so we thank each other for many valuable years of intellectual support, development and friendship.

Our thanks are also due to George Webster, consultant editor to Gower Publishing, who helped the book reach the light of day. George introduced us to Gower and helped in the early stages when we were faced with knitting together hundreds of pages of papers, reports, research documents and disconnected draft chapters into a coherent whole. George and his colleagues at Gower gave us sound advice on the structure – always delivered with great tact – including the helpful suggestion that chapters which varied in length between 7,000 and 30,000 words required some urgent rethinking.

ACKNOWLEDGEMENTS

Finally, we must thank our two partners, Nanci Downey and George Boak. Perhaps the saying 'a policeman's life is not a happy one' should read 'an author's life is not … '. Both Nanci and George have been supportive and encouraging. They, as much as us, will be glad the book is finished. As for the next one …

B M
L M

A note on occupational standards and National Vocational Qualifications

The national standards programme, which is promoted and sponsored by two government agencies, the Department for Education and Employment (DfEE) and the National Council for Vocational Qualifications (NCVQ), aims to create nationally recognised vocational qualifications which are relevant to the needs of competitive organisations in a modern economy. The process of standards development involves industries and occupations identifying the level of competence people need in the work environment – work-role expectations. These expectations are expressed in a commonly agreed format of units and elements of competence, associated performance criteria and range statements. (Elements of competence are also called occupational standards.)

The title of an element of competence describes an occupational *outcome* (what people are expected to achieve). The performance criteria describe critical performance indicators (how you would know that someone can do what is described by the element to expected standards). The range statements describe the circumstances or contexts to which the standard applies. The element title, performance criteria and range statements, taken together, are an *occupational standard*. The standards, or elements, of competence are grouped into units of competence which are used to structure National Vocational Qualifications.

DEVELOPING STANDARDS

Industries and occupational groups are represented by Lead Bodies which can be statutory training authorities, employer organisations, professional bodies or employer/employee consortia. Lead bodies are recognised and partially funded by the DfEE and have the authority, under the standards programme, to define standards for an agreed occupational area. Increasingly, Lead Bodies within each occupational area are encouraged to form Occupational Standards Councils which are intended to provide greater coherence in the provision of qualifications. The use of the standards and the qualifications is voluntary, but the government believes that market forces will encourage employers to recognise them.

Sets of occupational standards are developed into vocational qualifications by selecting those which are relevant to particular work roles and attaching to them an assessment process which is capable of providing valid, reliable and cost-effective evidence that the standards have been achieved. The complete qualification (the standards plus the assessment process) is then submitted to the National Council for Vocational Qualifications for accreditation. The Council matches the qualification against a number of criteria which are concerned with structure, relevance, coherence, open access and industry acceptability. The Council does not award or administer the qualification – this is done by a separate Awarding Body.

A qualification accredited as a National Vocational Qualification (an NVQ) forms part of a complete framework of qualifications which is intended to cover all occupations at five achievement levels. The qualification is then available for use. The standards and assessment processes are used to develop learning programmes which directly address the requirements defined within the standards.

An alternative route is to use the standards directly within organisations to contribute to human resource development and management. The standards can also be used to inform learning design without direct reference to NVQs. These processes are shown in Figure N1.

Developing agreed standards, based on the needs of employment, is intended to develop qualifications and associated learning programmes which are more relevant to industry needs.

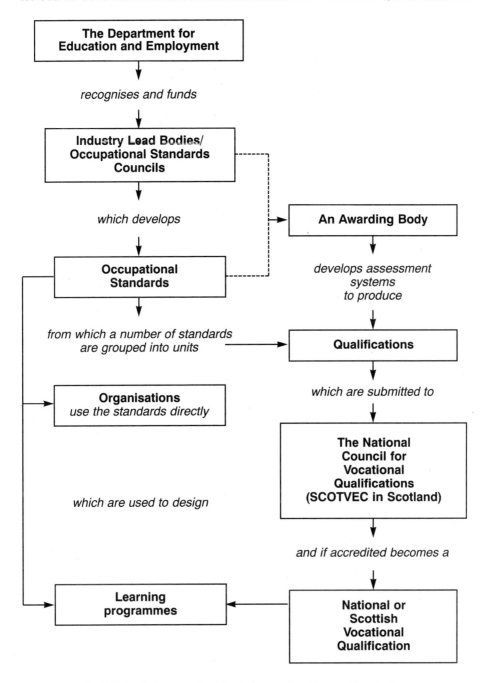

Fig. N1 Developing occupational standards and National Vocational Qualifications

Part 1
WHAT IS A COMPETENT WORKFORCE?

1 Education, training and the changing economy

WHAT IS EDUCATION – OR WHAT IS IT FOR?

The question 'What is education?' is not an issue for this book. Such issues are usually resolved by attempting to provide definitions or specifications to do with the nature of education. Our concern is how educational systems and processes can develop the levels of competence required to achieve agreed socio-economic goals. Consequently we are more interested in the **role** and **purpose** of education than in a debate about its fundamental nature.

The role and purpose of the systems and processes of education can be described as:

1. to prepare people for independent economic activity – we may call this the instrumental purpose, a means to an end;
2. to empower people to play a full part as citizens in a democratic society – this purpose is to do with access, choice and equality of opportunity;
3. to enable every person to develop their natural talents and capabilities to the fullest extent – this purpose is to do with individual progression, improvement and self-fulfilment.

Seen in this way, it is easy to assume that vocational education and training is solely concerned with the instrumental purpose – independent economic activity. This would suggest that Vocational Education and Training (VET) is merely a subset of broader or general education, but such a view is extremely narrow and difficult to sustain.

Vocational education should incorporate all three purposes and can do so as an implicit and integral part of the system – for example, the adoption of democratic and group-based learning processes and open-access policies supports empowerment and democratic access (see (2) above). In the past these processes and policies were often absent from VET, largely because our view of democracy was markedly different. Authoritarian and élitist views influenced both general and vocational education on the assumption that teachers and trainers were an élite cadre of experts to be attended to and copied, without question, by pupils and trainees. The pupil or trainee in such systems can be likened to an empty bucket into which knowledge and skills are poured by the teacher or trainer until the bucket is full. Learning is one way, processes are didactic.

A more liberal consensus, which is still an uneasy truce in many quarters, has largely replaced the authoritarian, didactic view of educational processes. The liberal consensus proposes a view of learning which stresses the **relationship** between the learner and the provider of the learning resource (the teacher/ trainer). In this model the learner has something to offer and, given the appropriate resources and motivation, can activate their own learning capability, thus achieving independence from the authority of the teacher. We may see this as an advance in our concepts of democracy. The powerful restatement of democratic processes which produce the concepts of empowerment, local decision making, devolution and consultation, impacts on our educational system as well as our wider democratic institutions.

There have also been explicit attempts to insert the concepts of the liberal consensus into the heart of educational processes. The development of additional soft or process skill inputs to VET curricula is a conscious attempt to modify and dilute the purely instrumental nature of vocational training by deliberately inserting curriculum content concerning the individual's relationships within wider society. These initiatives are most well developed in the liberal studies and social and lifeskills programmes which were designed to parallel vocational skills training in the further education sector.

These attempts to broaden the scope of VET have themselves been contentious, often leading to conflicting accusations – proving that the liberal consensus can by no means be assumed. On the one hand, interest groups whom we might call economic pragmatists, have argued that nothing other than specific skills training is relevant to the work environment for which the individual is being prepared. On the other hand, interest groups predominantly associated with educational provision have argued that narrow, specific skills training is short-sighted and neglects the individual development and access opportunities which a broader educational focus can offer.

To some extent this argument is history. Employers in modern enterprises are not so short-sighted as to deny the contribution of broader-based education to the quality of their workforce. In many companies general education is promoted and financially supported on the grounds that educated people are competent people and competent people make for successful organisations.

The multi-purpose model of education is also inherent in our newly reformed systems of VET. The body which sets the criteria for the implementation of UK VET – the National Council for Vocational Qualifications (NCVQ) – explicitly refers to the importance of equality of opportunity in the provision of education and training. Access to qualifications, and progression between them, is fundamental to the structure of the framework of National Vocational Qualifications (NVQ).

Policy in VET, therefore, has already recognised the importance of the three purposes of education. A competent workforce, the concept which this book tries to define, is not the skilled workforce which previous generations would have recognised. We have moved away from a view of work which isolates it from the totality of human action and experience and restricts the description of skills to the manual reflexes which are the bare minimum required to meet immediate needs. The nature of work and the nature of competence are part of the very fabric of our democracy.

Although the VET system and the political institutions which give it legitimacy have recognised the importance of a broader view of work and competence, there is however a gap between this recognition and the willingness and ability to implement these worthy policies which set the strategic direction of VET. We have suggested that education cannot be parcelled up and shared between the general education sector and VET. There is, and there should be, overlap. A general system of education which failed to provide any foundation for economic activity would be a monstrous waste of social resources. Indeed, most advances in the scope of, and access to, educational provision have been based on the need to prepare people more effectively for work. Equally, a VET system which ignored the humanistic values of equality, access and individual progression would be rightly accused of producing little more than factory or office fodder and of cynically ignoring the legitimate interests and democratic rights of all individuals in society.

WHOSE VOICE?

VET needs to meet the three purposes of all education and training systems and to do this it needs to take into account the legitimate interests of three different groups: the State – which represents society as a whole, employing organisations and individuals. Only then will a balanced, effective and democratic VET system be achieved. Claiming supremacy for one of these groups in isolation will not achieve the three purposes. Each group has a legitimate interest which, as in all mature democracies, requires recognition and balance. As well as rights, each group also has responsibilities.

- The state has the right to set policy, but with this right it carries the responsibility of setting policy which meets the identified needs of the whole economy, both now and for the foreseeable future, and which meets the needs of all individuals in society as should be expected in a mature democracy.
- Employing organisations have the right to expect competent people to enter employment who are fit for work. Employing organisations also have the right to expect their immediate general and vocational skill needs to be met arising from their direct and indirect funding of the system. But they also have the responsibility to invest in their own long-term future and that of their employees by recognising wider social and economic needs and the rights of the individuals whom they employ.

5

- Individuals have the right to equality of access to the VET system, progression within it and the right to develop to their fullest potential so that they can exercise choice. This is a right based on the individual's contribution to the funding of the system and a legitimate expectation for a member of a democratic society. The responsibility for individuals is to develop their capabilities to meet new and emerging demands as society and economies change. They also have the responsibility to contribute to the system so that others can benefit as well.

These balances suggest a number of strategic imperatives. We need:

- a VET policy which is clearly related to the needs of the economy – so we need to know how we can create an economy which meets the needs of all citizens;
- to articulate the roles and responsibilities of all those who have a stake in the development of vocational education and training;
- to enable those stakeholders to play their part effectively by putting into place empowering processes for the development and implementation of VET.

A strategy for VET therefore needs a view of an effective economy with a view of competence which translates the strategy into VET processes and systems that fit the economy, employing organisations and individuals for the future. We need a competent workforce at every level. But to achieve this we need to articulate what we mean by occupational competence and then gear our vocational education and training system to deliver it. Despite the rhetoric and the exhortations, this has not yet been done.

RESPONDING TO THE CHALLENGE – A COMPETENT WORKFORCE

Our argument is simple. There is no clear strategy in the UK at present – apart from worthy rhetoric. There is no clear view of what competence means now or what might emerge in the future – apart from revisions of systems and approaches which are well past their sell-by date.

What the UK has done is to cobble together a jumble of skills and task analysis, bolt on a series of personal competence constructs and call this 'competence'. What it has also done is to set in place a potentially complex and radical system – occupational standards and National Vocational Qualifications – which fundamentally confuse the terms 'competence' and 'qualification'.

The public debate has not been about a competent workforce, but a qualified one. In seeking a measurable index for the success of the brave new VET system, we have settled for the number of NVQs which the population achieves – a benchmark based on **quantity.** A **quality** benchmark would require that NVQs represent a future-focused and broad view of occupational competence and that individuals who achieve NVQs actually develop their competence. All too often

NVQs are firmly based on current practice which, by definition, is inadequate, and many NVQs are awarded on the basis of existing competence alone – ie they accredit candidates for what they can already do, rather than encourage or require them to improve. This numbers game may satisfy bureaucrats and politicians, but without rigorous quality assurance, constant scrutiny and evaluation it will not make individuals more competent and our economy more competitive.

NVQs were designed to **raise** overall occupational competence to a level where British industry could compete more effectively with foreign competitor nations and companies. This suggests that NVQs should be uncompromisingly strategic and forward looking in content, reflecting the best current practice and antici-pating emerging practice. It also suggests that an NVQ candidate should be able to do more when they have achieved their NVQ than they could do before.[1] These commitments are a critical feature of the NVQ criteria document[2] and are re-iterated in many public pronouncements from government, agencies and organisations like the Confederation of British Industry and the Trades Union Congress.

If we do develop strategic NVQs then few people will be able to access them in the short term since current practice is so far behind the standards we need to achieve. This problem is compounded if we continue to encourage the view that access to qualifications is based on people's current jobs. What this suggests is that NVQs are a retrospective confirmation of skills and jobs which already exist – the very skills and jobs which are holding back our industrial and economic development.

We believe that NCVQ should promote as a priority those qualifications which represent the most demanding standards in the world. If our industrial recovery is to be led by qualifications and the standards programme then nothing less will do. Qualifications should model the real changes which we know are affecting our industries along with the industries of other nations. In addition, they should model the broad-based qualifications and training programmes which are the hallmark of success in many progressive companies and countries. The implications for this kind of policy are immense. They could mean a drastic reduction in the number of NVQs available to leave just those which are able to provide demanding and challenging targets for our current and future workforce.

This position potentially conflicts with the requirement for NVQs to have covered a percentage of the workforce by 1995, but we would ask, what does 'cover' mean? If 'cover' is interpreted as 'set strategic targets for ...' then a smaller number of more demanding NVQs could meet the requirement. If, however, 'cover' means applicability to current jobs (which we believe to be the driving force of the initiative) then we will merely reinforce the status quo, already known to be woefully inadequate.

Our charge is that many NVQs, and the standards on which they are based, are inadequate. Many are based on narrow, job-specific skills and lack any recognition of future capability. Others are so generic in focus that they fail to capture occupational realities and lack credibility. Standards and NVQs have arisen from a series of unconnected initiatives rather than a coherent strategy which recognises the realities of economic change and then empowers the VET system to anticipate and meet those changes. An important first step, therefore, is to examine those economic changes which we should expect a VET strategy to address.

THE NEW ECONOMY – FROM RHETORIC TO REALITY

The UK is not short of statements which describe the effects of the new economy on work organisation and the need for a broader view of competence. Here are some of the worthy public statements which usually seek to start, or restart, the same debate.

Then ...

> Britain needs a flexible, adaptable workforce to cope with the uncertainties which cloud the future. The technological revolution and the need to become more competitive present real challenges for as far ahead as we can see. Markets and prices for products, processes and services will continue to fluctuate. Firms and individuals must either adapt to change or become its victims.[3] (Manpower Services Commission, 1981.)

And then again ...

> To succeed in business and a career, people will need to be highly flexible and adaptable about where they work and how they work and to replenish constantly the range of skills and abilities they use at work. Even where jobs do not demand of workers a high level of technical skill, they will certainly need greater flexibility in approach, greater breadth of experience and greater capacity to take responsibility.[4] (Department of Employment, 1988.)

And again ...

> The education and training which employees will require will need to be broadly based, promoting not just a narrow technical understanding of the job but competence in the broader work context. This broader occupational competence is concerned with adaptability, management of roles, responsibility for standards, creativity and flexibility to changing demands.[5] (Confederation of British Industry, 1989.)

And again and again and again ...

> All Britain's major competitors understand that a major factor in economic success and social stability is the qualifications levels of their workforce ... The TUC firmly believes that the future of this country depends on raising the skills of the workforce and giving them a greater say in their work.[6] (Trades Union Congress, 1992.)

Now ... (1)

UK business needs to compete successfully in the global market if the quality of UK society is to be maintained and raised. To improve competitiveness and turn techno-logical and economic change to the UK's advantage, a competent and adaptable work-force is essential. To achieve this it is necessary to raise the skills level of the workforce.[7] (Confederation of British Industry, 1994.)

Now ... (2)

The UK faces a world of increasing change; of even fiercer global competition; of growing consumer power; and a world in which our wealth is more and more dependent on the knowledge, skills and motivation of our people. These changes present both opportunities and challenges. To prosper in this rapidly changing world, we have to improve our economic performance across the board. We must raise our productivity and adapt our skills, the way we work, and our products to meet new circumstances and opportunities. In future, the most successful nations will be those which develop high quality, skilled and motivated workforces and make good use of them.[8] (Department of Trade and Industry, 1994.)

Now... (3)

To compete internationally the UK needs a highly motivated and well qualified workforce. We need young people who are well prepared for work, employers who see the importance of developing the skills of their employees, and people in the labour force who take their development seriously.[9] (Department of Trade and Industry, 1995.)

White Papers and public reports are traditionally strong on rhetoric and scant on detail. But what is intriguing is that the messages – ranging over 14 years – are almost exactly the same. There is clearly no shortage of rhetoric or realisation that our economy is undergoing fundamental change.

The statements are easy to summarise since they repeat the same basic themes. We are in a competitive economy, which is becoming more competitive. Many things are changing and changing fast. We need flexible people and flexible organisations to compete successfully. The similarities in the language of the various public statements quoted previously can lull us into the sense that they are all talking about the same economy with the same work processes, technology and requirements.

The need for flexibility and adaptability is even greater now than in 1981 when *The New Training Initiative* was written. In the 15 years since, there has been an enormous acceleration in the advance of technology, whilst markets and economies have become more turbulent and unpredictable.

In 1981, shortly before the publication of *The New Training Initiative* (NTI), Clive Sinclair launched the Sinclair ZX81 home computer. It boasted 1k (one kilobyte) of random access memory (RAM). For the technologically challenged, one kilobyte is 1,012 'bytes' or pieces of information. For convenience, think of one byte as a single character. A megabyte is 1,012,000 bytes.

The ZX81 used a domestic tape recorder to store data, and could, at a squeeze, hold nearly a page of text at a time if you had the patience to wait for ten minutes for the primitive word processor to load. Unfortunately it didn't have a printer, so your words of wisdom were only ever available in flickering characters on your domestic TV. It also cost over £100 – without any storage or display facility at all. It sold like hot cakes.

In 1991, just ten years later, an early draft of a paper which became this chapter was prepared on a computer which loaded a word processor in four seconds from a hard disk capable of storing 80 megabytes of information (about 50,000 pages of text). The computer had four megabytes of memory (4,072 times that of the ZX81) and was connected to six others by a network which gave access to another 240 megabytes of storage. A laser printer produced the first version of this chapter – at a quality which put previous dot-matrix and daisy-wheel printers to shame.

As we prepared the final drafts in 1995 we were riding the exponential curve of new technology. We have new computers – they seem to last for about 18 months these days as new models crash in price and outstrip previous performance. On each new machine, the 4-megabyte memory has been replaced by 8, the 80-megabyte hard disc by a 350-megabyte disc and the network now gives access to an additional 1,200 megabytes of storage. We have access to two printers: one is a 600 dot per inch laser which gets us even nearer to typeset quality. The old survivor from 1991 was recently traded in as part payment for a colour bubble jet printer. One of our 1991 model computers, with an upgraded hard disc and additional memory, is a communications centre, attached to a modem which operates as a fax and gives us access to the Internet and e-mail.

To make a fair comparison, our machines are business computers, not home computers, but in comparison to many on the market and in general use they are quite modest machines. Readers in two or three years time will no doubt marvel at the antiquated equipment used in the far-off days of 1995. Does this mean increasing costs? Far from it.

In 1981 the few business computers on the market cost over £4,000 (over £6,500 in 1995 values) and offered disc storage of 150 kilobytes and an internal memory of 32 kilobytes. Each of our new computers cost £1,500 – so the 1995 computer offers over 2,300 times more storage and over 250 times more memory for under one-quarter of the relative cost.

What does a change like this mean to the manufacturing systems which produce such equipment and the administrative systems which use it? What does it mean for the people who design, make and use such equipment? Changes in technology, equipment, systems and methods are now incremental – they accelerate at rates which are not within our imagination to contemplate. All we know is that there will be change and that it will continue to accelerate – there are no brakes and no means of stopping the flight. We may as well just grin and bear it or, more constructively, accelerate along with and ahead of it.

Changes of this type put some meat on the bones of the worthy rhetoric of White Papers and other public statements. Relating change to the real things happening around us emphasises that the infrastructures which support economic and social change, of which vocational education and training is a key contributor, must, of necessity, have to change and adapt just as fast – if not even faster – to keep up with the competition.

Computers, of course, are an easy and very obvious example. They are equally easy to reject as a single and unrepresentative instance in a world which has, in reality, changed little since the heady days of full employment in the 1950s and 1960s. Lest we fall into this seductive trap, take another look around at the environment.

Consider the buildings which are in the process of construction in every town centre and the office and retail parks which follow the ring roads of our major cities. Two things should strike us. First, they are increasingly built with complex steel frames to which are attached prefabricated panels with a brick infill. The second thing we should note is that the buildings are usually offices, with perhaps some shop fronts at the ground floor. On the industrial estates they tend to be warehouses. If the building is for retail use it is likely to be a huge modern shopping mall with covered walkways, fountains, indoor gardens and all the paraphernalia which denotes the triumph of the consumer society. What do we learn from this? We learn that our economy is changing from a manufacturing to a service and consumer base; and that the signals should be telling us that building methods and systems are changing – yet we seem to be training joiners and bricklayers as if the brick-built semi of the 1930s was still with us.

Look at the new cars on our roads, or go to a showroom to enquire about buying one. One manufacturer has four separate ranges, of which one range has 17 style options – engine type, capacity, trim, number of doors – and within each of the 17 styles there are more options: paint colour, upholstery fabric, extras such as radio cassette players, four channel stereo, compact disc players. Many manufacturers regularly introduce limited editions. Starting in the late 1980s, Ford offered an Escort option which involved the customer choosing from a range of accessories to further personalise their car. A BMW can be designed by the potential owner from a vast range of options. Nissan has over 400 variants on one model, most of them passing through the production system within a single week.

Drive your new car into a housing estate. You remember housing estates – rows and rows of identical houses, the 'little boxes' of Pete Seager's song of the 1960s. Now the identikit boxes are replaced by a mix of styles, shapes and options. Bijou cottages sit next to grand detached residences, a mews appears nestling behind a small block of exclusive apartments. Decorative brickwork is reappearing, on warehouses, factories and offices as well as houses.

If you have recently bought a house, note what happens when you come to fit a telephone. There was a time, not so long ago, when the range of telephones was restricted to black or white. In the 1960s some new colours appeared. Then came the Trimphone, the warble of which was quickly imitated by starlings, and which was so light that the dial could not be used unless the telephone was firmly held down to stop it turning with the dial. Now there are telephone shops where you can choose a can of coke with the dial in the base, Mickey Mouse with a receiver arm, a racing car, mobile phones, wall phones, phones with memories and built-in answerphone systems with fax facilities, shopping reminders and last number redial. There are even facsimiles of the 'traditional' phone – available in black or white!

The mass production philosophy so dear to Henry Ford, and applied to everything from houses to matchsticks, is fast disappearing under a range of choices and options which defy description. Our manufacturing economy is evolving into a fast-reacting, market-driven and customer-oriented system of ever-increasing complexity and diversity, driven by the need to be different with more and more models and options. Product differentiation has gone wild. Some of the differences are simply variations on a very common theme, but the effect on the manufacturing systems is fundamental. In the next chapter we examine how these changes have resulted in a fundamental shift in the nature of work and the organisations in which work takes place.

NOTES

1. A case study of good practice described in the Confederation of British Industry report *Quality Assessed* reported the implementation of NVQs in a major vehicle manufacturer. As part of the evaluation of the programme, participants were asked whether they had developed any new skills as a result of achieving the NVQ. Of the 14 candidates, only three answered 'yes' to the statement 'I am better at doing the job' and five answered 'yes' to the statement 'I have gained some new skills'. By contrast, all the candidates thought that the qualification was worthwhile and 12 were pleased that their skills had been recognised. Despite the obvious motivational benefits to the individuals and the company, we would question whether an NVQ which fails to improve current performance for nearly 80 per cent of candidates and offers no new skills to 65 per cent of candidates offers any sustained added value.
2. National Council for Vocational Qualifications, *NVQ Criteria and Guidance.*
3. Manpower Services Commission, *The New Training Initiative.*
4. Employment Department, *Training for Employment.*
5. Confederation of British Industry, *Towards a Skills Revolution.*
6. Trades Union Congress, *Bargaining for Skills.*
7. Confederation of British Industry, *Quality Assessed.*
8. Department of Trade and Industry, *Competitiveness, Helping Business to Win.*
9. Department of Trade and Industry, *Competitiveness, Forging Ahead.*

2 Demands on competence – the changing nature of work

CHALLENGING COMPLACENCY

Despite the obvious changes taking place all around us, complacency still reigns in many quarters. We are still told that the Japanese can't develop anything new – they only copy what we clever and inventive Westerners invent. The caricature of the wily Oriental busily copying British designs in opium-filled sweat-shops still lingers in our national consciousness. How else, after all, could the Japanese have become so successful if it were not for cheating – for not 'playing the game'.

Our prophets, whom we revere at the dinner table and the business seminar, are ignored and treated with dangerous complacency in the boardroom. Tom Peters, the US theorist, is both charismatic and frighteningly right, yet people react with suspicion to his analysis of Western economies. What they ignore when rejecting his observations on the grounds that eloquence hides naivety is that his analysis, interpretation and prescriptions are backed by countless real and living examples.

Peters does not make up the companies which have thrived, survived or collapsed in the new industrial age, yet people are able to confidently reject his approach on the grounds that a sausage manufacturer in the USA is not an adequate model for an engineering company in the UK. The 'not invented here' approach of British companies is a major contributor to our increasing failure to meet the demands of the world economy. Quality assurance systems which rely on the commitment and contribution of the workforce are firmly rejected on the grounds that they are Japanese in origin and British workers would not match the caricatures of the apparent docility and conformity of Japanese workers. Perhaps someone should have warned Nissan when they moved into Sunderland or Toyota when they commissioned factories in Derbyshire and North Wales.

A year or so ago a letter in the *Independent* castigated a feature on the Latin economies which had based many of the observations on the well-known laziness and the 'mañana' culture of the Iberian peninsula. The letterwriter simply pointed out that, at the time Spain and Portugal had the highest economic growth figures in the whole of the European Union – over 6 per cent in that year. Hispanophiles will know that the practices of Spanish business and industry leave much to be desired, but even so they managed 6 per cent growth before their current economic crisis. No doubt we will be able to blame this affront to our national pride on unfair European Union grants, lower costs and standards of living or any other convenient excuse which allows us to creep back into our corner of complacency on the top left-hand corner of a far away land called Europe.

So what is happening to send us into the tail spin from which we badly need to recover? The homilies of changing markets as far as we can see and the need for flexibility and adaptability are real. The changes are all around us, in every newspaper every day, on the news, in our factories and offices. We need only to look up and take notice.

For VET to be successful it is essential that we look beyond the rhetoric to clarify how the world of work is changing and determine what is happening in the economy and the broader environment, in organisations and the nature of work. This is not difficult, for there are many reliable sources on the nature of economic change. What is important, however, is to translate these changes into the consequent demand on the competence needed to meet the change – and the challenge.

CHANGING MARKETS, ECONOMIES AND INDUSTRIES

We see a globalisation of markets and a shrinking world economy. Green beans from Kenya are as common as potatoes from Jersey and new forms of telecommunications make a fax or e-mail from Hong Kong an unexceptional event. The scope of markets widens: more goods and services are available to more people as trade barriers collapse under the pressure of the expanding European Union, the democratisation of the Eastern European block and the GATT agreements. More multinational companies emerge and small companies spring up to service specialised home markets and the locally based internationals.

The industries which traditionally provided mass-production based, semi-skilled jobs are either upgrading their skill requirements with changing production methods or exporting labour-intensive production systems to less-developed countries where the balance of investment between labour and capital is still geared towards labour. This year alone saw the demise of the last UK-based Bryant & May match factory in Merseyside, and a polythene bag factory in Telford closed down as the equipment was dismantled and exported to China where labour costs were a fraction of the UK's. The more developed industrial economies require a highly skilled and adaptable labour force to run the increasingly flexible industries. Increased labour costs are met by increased added value. Skill shortages in our economy are almost always for highly skilled workers, technicians and specialists.

International awareness is catching on – particularly in the capability which is so lacking in the UK, foreign languages. No longer able to hide behind an empire in which all the natives are expected to speak English, we now have to learn other languages to keep up in global markets.

Colleges are starting to offer traditional trade training in a European language. Numerous initiatives encourage trainees and students to spend part of their study time in another country. The foundation and professional training directorates of the European Union bristle with initiatives to support exchanges between companies and educational institutions. Local colleges are working in Poland, Hungary and Russia. European universities have set up a Masters programme for professional trainers which offers placements in two other member state countries and calls for **three** foreign languages as an entry requirement.

As the economy globalises concerns emerge about resource availability, the pollution of the entire planet and overpopulation; concerns about consumption are balanced with worries about sustainability. This affects widely diverse occupations.

Architects design for the entire life cycle of a building, taking into consideration the use, potential change of use, eventual demolition and restoration of the site. Engineers no longer evaluate technical problems in terms of scientific and engineering principles alone. Products are seen in terms of their impact on the environment and the ability of materials to be recycled. All these implications are taken into account at the design stage.

CHANGES IN THE NATURE OF WORK

In organisations the most obvious change is the technology we now use to process data and information. In offices, laborious manual charting and 'ready-reckoner' calculating are replaced by computer-based spreadsheets which require higher levels of competence and ingenuity to set them up, devise and programme the formulae, de-bug faulty operations, interpret results and make sense of the vastly increased sources of information which the technology makes possible.

Typewriters now belong in museums as word processing, text editing and desktop publishing threaten to engulf us with reports, memos and display materials which, up to five years ago, would have required a full design, origination and printing facility to produce. Desktop publishing systems are capable of generating text and artwork which is within an ace of professional systems, costing less than £8,000 and requiring little more than a modest office for accommodation.

Databases now store more information about us than we can imagine. The Internet links over two million computers. Files with millions of records can sort, extract and retrieve information in seconds. Ten years ago the time-scales required to do the same job would have been apocryphal stories about the entire Chinese nation marching past one point in single file. We are now offered the complete banking service with electronic transfer through telecommunications and database development.

The technologies we now employ change the very interface of work. In factories, offices and hospitals we are seeing an incremental shift from direct manual control of operations to process monitoring and control – because technology is replacing the manual control of operations, previously undertaken by people. The physical turning of wheels and dials to control machine tools directly is replaced by computer-controlled systems which rely on human skill and ingenuity to plot tool travel, plan effective sequences of operations, commission and set up the complex machines, monitor and intervene when things go wrong and undertake complex problem solving.

This, in turn, changes our entire view of manufacturing operations. In the days when raw manual skills were required to operate the machine tools we divided factory sections into the tooling types, each of which required different operators to control them; thus we had turning sections and milling sections. Now we can identify common processes – calibration, set up, monitoring and control – and can change our systems from the specific machine to the process and product, what the factory is there to produce. Now we find the small components section, the x product section and, in the skill requirements necessary to work in this new structure, flexibility becomes reality.

In all aspects of our lives the micro-processor revolution is distancing human beings from direct control, generating more complex and accurate information and making systems more complex. We have reached the point where expecting to understand any one system is an impossible aim. People have to move away from 'doing' to 'managing the systems which do the doing'. We are no longer the system, we must become system managers.

CHANGES IN PRODUCTS AND SERVICES – DISCOVERING THE CUSTOMER

Products and services in the modern organisation are designed to meet the existing and anticipated needs of customers and users. Although this seems obvious now it was by no means the pattern of industrial development in the past. The customer often had to put up with what the system could produce and what the designer felt like designing. The design engineer would sit down and produce the most technically elegant solution to a problem regardless of customer demand or need, even if this were known.

The trick which gives the competitive edge in modern manufacturing and service provision is for the customer to feel that the product or service which they receive is designed and produced not just with them in mind but personally for them. The term 'mass customisation' has been coined to describe this process whereby stock items are produced which are capable of quick and simple modification to produce individualised products. This is not really a trick in the sense of wishing to delude the customer. What it represents is the extent to which the customer is offered a product or service which has been adapted to meet their individual requirements and needs.

One consequence is that our industries are changing their production and process systems from multiple batch and continuous production techniques to 'small batch' or 'batch of one' approaches in the headlong drive to differentiate the product and customise, to meet ever more refined customer needs. The factory systems on which Ford and Taylor built their mass production techniques, based on the atomisation of physical tasks, are in terminal decline.

We see this trend in education and training with institutions as well as with private companies offering the fully bespoke training design service – tailoring the programme to meet client needs – rather than offering a place on a mass-produced course. We see it in vehicle manufacture where a car company can have as many as 400 substantial variations in a single model, all on the line at the same time, as companies adopt the policy of making to order and work towards another demanding target of responsiveness: 'sell one – make one'. Manufacturers capitalise on this tendency in their public advertising: 'everything we do', say Ford 'is driven by you'.

The trend continues in financial services. No longer are we visited by the 'man from the Pru'. He, or increasingly she, is now a 'financial adviser' or 'consultant', committed to helping you select the product which can be tailored to fit your precise financial needs.

In community care the focus (some would say the rhetoric) is on packages of care which the service user should be able to perceive as a seamless service. Professionals are meant to adapt to client needs and not the other way round. If the client has multiple needs then service providers should be able to provide for those needs in the most efficient and effective way, preferably by multiskilling. There are shifts to commissioning packages of care for individual clients, a far cry from when clients took what was available and were expected to adapt to the provision on offer. This is not just customer centredness. Customer centredness is not really new. We are accustomed to polite telephone greetings instituted by customer care consultants which take nearly a unit of telephone time for the hapless operator to deliver.

A clear customer orientation is a much more serious matter. The needs of the end user are implicit in every activity; they are not confined to sales staff and delivered by vacuous and token expressions like 'always smile at the customer' and 'the customer is always right'. The penetration of the customer philosophy is profound. A few years ago we asked a senior trade union convenor about the union response to team working environments in a West Midlands factory. The convenor replied 'the job of this company is to get quality products to our customers on time. The job of management is to act as our interface with the customer – to negotiate the deal and to get the finished product moving quickly. The needs of the customer are everybody's business.' The convenor, by the way, was the cousin of Red Robbo, the trade union leader who headed a number of wildcat strikes in the 1970s.

Apple Computers adopted a customer logic when they designed the Macintosh computer in 1982. The design job was given to users. Teams of computer users throughout America were brought together and asked to specify a human-friendly computer. The result was the 'Mac', which has dominated hardware and software design ever since.

Meeting the real needs of the customer results in a massive increase in product differentiation (more and different products) and a parallel decrease in product life cycles (a fast response in design, production and service delivery). More telephones and more models of car increase the need for design and development skills, marketing skills and adaptability in the manufacturing system. These changes require **real** flexibility and adaptability. People need to be able to change quickly to new production methods, new products, changing standards. The TV series 'Troubleshooter' featuring Sir John Harvey Jones showed a worker in a ceramics factory who had been hand stamping the backs of plates for 16 years. Sir John commented that this kind of mindless activity is declining and will continue to decline as a model of factory work. Factory workers will work in complex environments dominated by sophisticated technology which will be able to meet the challenges of ever-increasing differentiation in the marketplace. Training systems geared to developing single skills and efficiency in performing atomised tasks will be replaced. What we need now and for the future are multiskilled people who have the additional process skills of being able to learn and relearn constantly throughout their working life.

CHANGES IN ORGANISATIONS

These identifiable trends have had a significant impact on organisations. Some organisations, which we refer to as 'enterprises of the future', have welcomed and thrived on economic change and we record below some of the characteristics of their culture and strategic approach.

CHANGE AND INNOVATION STRATEGIES

Change is now the way in which the environment is described and understood. It is, moreover, welcomed because the ability to anticipate change and respond rapidly to new challenges, new technologies and new markets is the competitive advantage which characterises the enterprise of the future. This impacts on the research and development function in organisations which becomes ever more important as the environment is constantly scanned to identify trends and new developments which can be turned to advantage.

Innovation is becoming the greatest source of added value, replacing engineered mass production systems. The importance of the research and development spend shows itself in company results and company growth. The

Apple Computer Company spends a larger percentage of turnover on research and development than any other computer manufacturer and returned (albeit reduced) profits in the early 1990s when other companies (including IBM) were showing losses and many computer companies were collapsing. The construction industry in Japan is buoyant: the five largest Japanese construction companies spend more **each** on research and development than most European **countries**.

As one measure of the speed of innovation we can examine patent applications – a barometer of innovation. Will Hutton, writing in the *Guardian* (16 September 1991) reported that in 1979 nearly 11,000 patent applications were made throughout the European Community. In 1991 that number of applications was made **every two months** – a six-fold increase in the rate of innovation. At a recent conference a manager from a Dutch electronic manufacturer reported that 80 per cent of the products in manufacture were developed within the last two years.

NETWORKS NOT HIERARCHIES

Many previous models of organisations assumed that the overall purpose of an enterprise was to achieve internal stability and to force stability on the surrounding environment – to achieve a state of homeostasis which effective management and fine tuning would keep well balanced. Many offices still have aphoristic posters on the walls which speak with sarcasm of the perils of reorganisation and change.

These old models of stability are falling by the wayside. In some organisations a regular labour turnover is seen as healthy, bringing in new blood and new ideas whilst establishing new networks around the goodwill of previous employees.

Traditional roles and job descriptions are collapsing to form broader responsibilities which are flexible, adaptable and subject to constant and rapid change. Whole layers of management disappear as companies 'flatten' to make the most of people and to give them as much responsibility for quality, work processes and outputs as is possible. Service and support jobs are bought in as required on contract to allow organisations to concentrate on their core business.

As new roles are defined, status divisions disappear as they are no longer appropriate and are contrary to modern organisational values. Single-status organisations replace formal hierarchies dominated by size of desk, quality of carpet, provision of dining facility. Works and staff divisions are gone. The clocking in machine is donated to an industrial museum. Operatives become 'associates' and receive salaries, sick pay, pensions, private health insurance. With responsibility comes reward.

The modern enterprise has no place for rigid functional specialisms based on traditional job demarcation and academic disciplines. Team working is no lofty rhetoric but a reality as individual operatives are regrouped into manufacturing cells and teams with considerably enhanced responsibilities. Teams and internal networks replace departments which previously vied with one another to attribute blame and claim ascendency.

These changes are imperatives. In Japan, engineering graduates operate CNC machinery. Visiting UK executives were known to snigger at the very thought. 'Graduates operating machinery on the shop floor – what a waste of talent!' At least, they sniggered until they also noticed that there were no quality controllers, work study engineers, progress chasers, supervisors, production controllers or first-line managers. The graduate engineers had incorporated all these jobs, planning, setting up, commissioning and monitoring their own production facility in its entirety – collapsing levels of hierarchy into flat and fast organisations capable of responding to changing requirements in a moment.

Goods coming in to the new enterprise are not checked and tested – they are assumed to be right first time from the supplier, with whom a new relationship has developed. Only the minimum amount of stock and work in progress is tolerated. The old practices of setting suppliers against each other to drive down costs are replaced by close supplier relationships in which suppliers are developed and nurtured. In this way the roles of the purchasing, buying and costing functions have been changed. People in these roles have to manage co-operative development between supplier and purchasers and negotiate agreements with 'preferred suppliers' who are guaranteed orders for the future. Networks expand to cover both suppliers and distribution agencies, with the entire process from raw materials through manufacture to delivery to the customer seen as one continuous flow. The process is a whole system which is fully integrated – it is called 'integrated materials management'. The same is true for large retail outlets where computerised systems mean that goods go straight to the shelves without being checked or being kept in storage.

Design is no longer seen as a function to be performed solely by important people called designers. In manufacturing environments the design team will comprise design engineers, materials and logistics controllers, suppliers, production and manufacturing engineers, environmental engineers and operatives, all working together from concept to manufacture. In a recent visit to a car manufacturer we noticed a group of assembly workers away from the line working on an upturned car. When we asked what they were doing we were told that they were working out the optimum routing for the braking system for a prototype four-wheel drive model. We assumed that the assembly workers had been assigned to undertake a small project to help the design team. Wrong. They were **members** of the design team.

In the past, design was a function which existed apart from all other functions. A design was conceived and then passed to estimators and cost clerks to see how much it would cost to manufacture. It was passed to production engineers who would work out how to make it. It was sent to suppliers to get outline costings and delivery schedules. All too often it was sent back to design because it cost too much, couldn't be made economically and was beyond the capability of a supplier to deliver. Designers blamed the lack of ingenuity of manufacturing engineers. Everyone else blamed designers for having their heads in the clouds. Now, all these processes happen concurrently. All critical design parameters are built in to design processes from day one with shared imperatives and shared responsibilities between networked team members.

PROCESS AND OUTCOME ORIENTATION

Organisations of the past were actively engaged in monitoring and controlling the processes and inputs to systems. In manufacturing, stock and materials inwards, and manufacturing processes, were rigidly controlled, measured and inspected. The work was measured and checked by an overseer or controller as those producing it were considered to be either unable, or not to be trusted, to check the quality for themselves. The new enterprise measures outcomes – the effective **results** of activity – leaving human ingenuity to provide the effective processes which make the system work. This new form of organisation assumes that everyone is responsible for quality and that this is an integral part of their role.

Production work is increasingly measured by the results achieved – not the time taken to undertake work activities, which was the basis of piece-rate systems. This change can create strains and tensions. A large manufacturing company introduced output/outcome measurement into one plant, together with team-work systems with shop-floor responsibilities for quality improvement and work methods. The result was a stiff note from the accountants. The measured work system, still in operation, was recording considerable non-productive down time, suggesting gross inefficiencies in management and control of production. The system was recording team meetings, quality improvement circles, time spent on training and managing the work processes as 'non-productive'. At the same time production had risen by 50 per cent but the measured work system was not designed to evaluate outcomes, only inputs and processes.

Piece rate systems themselves are fast disappearing under the influence of the mighty Japanese car manufacturers who have single-status employment, no clocking in (measuring the inputs of work) and no piece rates (measuring the length of processes). With this change comes a change in the conception of work. Previously seen as the productive time spent actually engaged in the activity, work is now expanded to include the management of operations, training, quality assurance and quality improvement, all of which are seen as positive contributions, not unproductive down time.

Traditional roles and functions disappear in this environment. Production control changes radically, progress chasing becomes a shop-floor responsibility, as does in-line inspection and a host of traditional control functions. Quality is the responsibility of everybody whatever they are doing. Everyone is working towards a common purpose.

IMPROVEMENT – THE QUALITY VISION

Responsibility for the management and co-ordination of work processes devolves to 'fact holders' – those who actually do the job. Inspection and quality control is replaced by direct responsibility for quality and a final quality check. The capabilities of all employees needs to increase as semi- and unskilled jobs are phased out.

The widening of work roles also heralds the change from externally imposed quality **control** systems to total quality management and **assurance**, where individuals and key groups take full responsibility for product and service quality and work to 'right first time' standards.

In an enterprise of the future, improvement is the norm, not the subject of special projects or drives. Part of the philosophy of total quality management (TQM) involves the commitment to constant improvement, rather than doing as little as is necessary for minimum acceptability. In line with the constant improvement philosophy is the imperative to get things right first time and the recognition that doing it right first time to high quality standards is actually easier (and considerably cheaper) than low quality which has to be improved and repaired. The old British adage that 'quality costs' is replaced by Philip Crosby's optimistic 'quality is free'.[1]

The obsession with quality is not confined to the manufacturing sectors. Service providers, even in education and training, are flocking to register for BS/ISO accreditation as the assurance of quality products and services offering good value replaces the notion that the best is the cheapest. But there is a danger here: claims for quality can be based on very shaky foundations and supported by flimsy evidence. The assertion that 'our quality is the best' could become just as hollow as the claim that 'our prices are the cheapest' if not backed up by commitment to quality and a total quality approach.

Many of the examples of quality service are small and simple – 'delights'. For example, many service garages return your car cleaned, inside and out, with a feedback sheet for you to register your views about the service and signed by the mechanic who undertook the service.

Targets for production, service delivery and quality are everyone's business, and those targets are tangible and demanding. A case study developed in the 1960s describes a foundry where a particular component was proving extremely difficult to manufacture to specification – the foundry returned a consistent 95 per cent scrap rate on this item. Considerable ingenuity was invested in justifying this appalling figure – the nature of materials, the extreme tolerances required, the problems inherent in the manufacturing process. The components were closely monitored and the consistent scrap rate charted on impressive graphs. Everything was counted frequently, the processes were rigidly controlled, the message to operatives on the ground was to try and do better. No one considered asking the foundry workers to become involved in solving the problem.

In the defence industry, organisations were, in effect, paid to make mistakes. The 'cost plus' system meant that the cost of producing equipment and materials was calculated and the company profit margin added. If errors occurred, additional costs were charged and were usually forthcoming. The faults were put down to needs for modification and changes which had been made since the original costing.

Right first time and zero-defect concepts were alien to such environments. It required new enterprises to challenge the complacent view that 'nothing is perfect' and 'you can't get it right every time'. The new enterprises asked, 'Why not?'

Now, manufacturing and service delivery is geared to being right first time, every time. Hence the lack of inspection of goods and components coming into factories, since the expectation extends to suppliers and subcontractors as well. Suppliers have a further requirement: to deliver just in time, so that the component is in stock for the shortest time practicable.

Typically British was the response a colleague met when investigating the purchase and supply function in a large organisation. 'Do you practice just in time approaches?' she enquired. 'Just in time', blustered the senior purchasing manager, 'can be just too late – just another buzz-word.' Compare the cynical response to the utter confidence of a UK-based Japanese car manufacturer. The order for car seats is placed with the supplier as the body shell starts on the engine and trim assembly line. The body reaches the seat installation section two hours later – and the company requires a 20-minute lead time on delivery. This gives the supplier one hour and forty minutes to deliver the seat following the receipt of the order. Granted the supplier is on the same site, a deliberate policy on the part of the car manufacturer, but this kind of requirement forces adaptability and fast response down the line. This is a tricky balance. If delivery is late the line stops. 'Ha ha,' gloat the cynics, 'this proves the point.' But does it? The stoppage of an entire production line in a large car factory is everybody's business, including the managing director's, and it did not take too many direct phone calls from the managing director of the manufacturing plant to the managing director of the seat manufacturer for the systems to get into line.

Equally, the cynics speak of taxis rushing between plants to deliver components and delivery vehicles parking in the loading bay overnight to be on time for a delivery. But the organisations which require these tight schedules do not see this as their problem – and suppliers who are wasting resources on taxis and additional transport time have a very good incentive to get their own systems working just in time as well.

RESOURCES ARE VALUE – PEOPLE ARE VALUED

Resources in the enterprise of the future are seen as a constant chain of value, rather than precious assets to be guarded at all costs. Waste is abhorred and minimised wherever it occurs. Waste elimination is a facet of everyday life, not enshrined in major waste-reduction and cost-cutting jamborees. The Toyota model – '1,000 improvements of 1 per cent are better than one improvement of 1,000 per cent' – has taken hold as all members of the enterprise constantly evaluate and monitor waste in small ways so that all can be involved and feel that their contribution is important.

Materials resources – stock and work in progress – was described to us by a manufacturing manager as 'value in the right place'. And it should be in the right place only for as long as it takes to confirm it is there and then use it to add value. Some organisations have no stores and materials are delivered straight to their point of use by the supplier. The storekeeper – previously the guardian of the company assets, committed to avoiding giving anything away – now facilitates the speedy movement of materials.

Resources are also conserved. Enterprises of the future are keen to ensure that the future is protected. Professions as diverse as engineering, accountancy and agriculture have gone 'green'. They recognise the important balance of total systems and the importance of a long-term view of resource sustainability. BMW based an advertising campaign on the fact that the new 3 series is 80 per cent recyclable – environmental friendliness is a competitive advantage.

Most important, the human resource – people – is the most valued asset of all. The enterprise of the future does not believe that technology will replace humanity. We now know that all technology requires human ingenuity to make it work effectively. For every automated system there is a system design team, a commissioning team and a control and monitoring team to make it work. The investment in people in the enterprise of the future is serious and real. Vast sums are committed to training and development – much of which does not appear familiar to the trainers of the 1960s and 1970s since it involves on-job coaching, mentoring and structured work-based learning. Some companies are even considering placing the training investment on to the balance sheet of the enterprise rather than on the profit and loss account. This initiative is fundamental. It makes training a long-term investment in assets rather than a short-term cost which has to show an immediate return to be valued.

FROM SKILLED TO COMPETENT

To meet the new challenges faced by the enterprise of the future, new skills are needed – now. The requirements for change and innovation, new working methods, ever-increasing quality and the management and conservation of resources are not achieved by systems and bureaucracies. They require human ingenuity and a fundamental change in our concept of occupational competence. None of these challenges will be met by simply **stating** that people need to innovate, to be more flexible and adaptable, to take responsibility for quality, to co-operate in multidisciplinary teams, which is the focus of the public rhetoric.

People need to **learn** to do these things, which means that they need to have the opportunities to learn, develop and practise in a supportive environment which values and rewards them. There is a need to invest in the future and a need to recognise that such an investment will be challenging: challenging our notions of work and challenging the ways in which we have thought about people in the past. Innovation, flexibility and adaptability are not achieved lightly nor cheaply.

New skills are urgently needed – skills which are not confined to specific work roles but which are needed to cope with all the complexities of modern life. We need an increase in *numeracy and literacy* as new technology spawns ever more detailed management, control and assurance information. In addition, the management of the technology itself depends on the interpretation of complex manuals and technical instructions for setting up systems and problem solving. A skilled machinist who has read little more than the *Sun* for 20 years is almost illiterate in terms of modern manufacturing systems. One of the consequences of computer technology is that it increases the amount of information which has to be read and interpreted. Far from being the 'paperless office', we are now supplied with more information than we can use. Thus we need to be able to read, select, evaluate, interpret and use information effectively.

We need a massive increase in *general process skills* – planning, decision making, effective interaction and problem solving – as specialists decline, management hierarchies decrease and more responsibility is vested with the workforce at the sharp end. This is one of the major consequences of the realisation that the workforce does have brains which they can use. But we cannot expect people suddenly to manage complex systems when they have become accustomed to authoritarian management, close monitoring and supervision, and petty status divisions.

Consequently, *management skills* and attitudes need to change as well, towards encouraging people to contribute and empowering groups to take the new responsibilities which are key to organisational success.

Finally, we need to change the focus of our vocational education and training away from narrow skill- or task-based training towards broader, role-based approaches to developing competence.

To meet these new demands we need new standards to lead a drive towards incremental improvements in quality. We must improve the quality of our products, our services and, above all, the quality of the people who make and deliver them. This means that we must dramatically improve the quality of our vocational education and training.

NOTE

1. Crosby, *Quality is Free.*

Part 2
MODELS OF COMPETENCE

3 New definitions of competence – the search is on

In Chapter 1 we looked at the changing nature of work and the new demands which this makes on the competence of the workforce. In this chapter and the next we are concerned with how the concept of occupational competence has been described, defined and modified in the light of these changes. In particular we will be concentrating on a particular view of competence – the Job Competence Model – which was developed to describe occupational competence in a way which captures the new economic demands and the changing nature of work we described in Chapters 1 and 2.

First, a little history. Most of the changes in vocational education and training (VET) in the UK have been the result of important policy and legislative interventions – usually linked to a series of initiatives to promote the training of young people and adults. Perhaps the most important of these was *The New Training Initiative* (NTI)[1] which set the scene for the identification of 'new standards' which were intended to define what people at work should be able to do. This was in contrast to previous systems of VET which were based on time serving through traditional apprenticeships and on day or block release at local further education colleges – both based on curriculum models which owed more to traditional practice than current, let alone future, requirements. NTI was published by the Manpower Services Commission, the government agency charged with the delivery of VET policy.

NTI also identified a number of important targets for vocational training which were closely linked to targets being developed by other members of the then European Economic Community. These included an integrated provision of education and vocational training for young people, to replace the limited and rather haphazard arrangements which then existed, and the provision of opportunities for life-long learning for adults – an area which was not so much haphazard as non-existent.

The need for this change was quite clearly stated, and we quoted a significant passage from the NTI document in the first two chapters: we needed to change, claimed the authors of NTI, because 'Britain needs a flexible, adaptable workforce to cope with the uncertainties which cloud the future'.

The detailed text of NTI described, in embryo, all the features and processes which remain key issues for the UK VET system of the 1990s. The need for future-oriented, relevant occupational training, national schemes, the important role of qualifications, the need for training to be to standards were all aspects of the NTI vision.

A number of training initiatives aimed primarily at young people had preceded the publication of NTI, including the Training Opportunities Programme (TOPs) and the Youth Opportunities Programme (YOPs). However, with the clear policy direction and resources offered by NTI, the way was open for a national integrated programme of youth training geared to the principles of flexibility and adaptability in the light of new demands created by technology and markets. This was the Youth Training Scheme (YTS), launched in 1982 to offer all school leavers the opportunity to receive one year's integrated occupational training combined with real-work experience, leading to a recognised vocational qualification. Before long, YTS was increased to two years and combined with the guarantee that all young people would be provided with extended education or a training placement.

The original YTS was based on a number of fundamental principles which echoed the intent of NTI. YTS was to focus on the outcomes of learning and would offer:

- competence in a job and/or a range of occupational skills;[2]
- competence in a range of transferable core skills;
- ability to transfer skills and knowledge to new situations;
- personal effectiveness.

YTS also specified a number of important processes. Trainees were to be offered a combination of real work placements linked with relevant off-job training. In the first years of YTS, providers were expected to offer three work placements in order to give a practical foundation to the development of transferable skills which would create the 'flexible and adaptable workforce' of the NTI vision. There was also a gradual shift in YTS from local to national certification, consistent with the developments of the Review of Vocational Qualifications and the emergence of Lead Bodies and the National Council for Vocational Qualifications.

YTS was radical, but flawed. Expected to do too much too quickly, and overloaded with expectations which were beyond the VET system to deliver, it was also accused of being a cynical device to soak up rising youth unemployment and to achieve national training on the cheap. But the challenge of YTS was to develop not only the first national training scheme for young people in all occupations but also a new curriculum model, based not on what a curriculum committee thought young people should know but on what young people needed to be able to do, now and in the future. The curriculum model was also charged with the task of integrating learning – linking learning in the work environment with learning in colleges or other training organisations.

Relating this curriculum model back to the outcomes of YTS posed a number of problems. If young people were required to be competent in a job, then what did job competence mean, both now and in the future, where the structure and content of jobs appeared increasingly uncertain? If they were to achieve qualifications, or credits towards a qualification, where were the relevant, integrated qualifications which met current and future requirements? If they were to transfer skills to new and different work environments, what were the skills of transfer and how could future work demands be described? If they were to be competent in a range of core skills, what were the core skills they needed?

These questions generated a number of important development projects which sought to provide a structure for YTS which differed from a traditional educational curriculum. The YTS curriculum was not to be based on a description of what should be taught or learnt, the curriculum inputs, but on a clear elaboration of the outcomes – what should be achieved. This new principle of curriculum design spawned three important research themes:

- the concept of skill ownership;
- work-based learning;
- core skills.

And it is from these themes that most of the current structures, systems and methods of VET developed.

SKILL OWNERSHIP

The Training for Skill Ownership Project[3] introduced into the world of vocational education and training a number of important developments and concepts which were to have an influence only long after the project itself had concluded. The main influences were:

1. The introduction of the term '**occupational competence**' and its central importance as the fundamental outcome of vocational education and training. Competence was defined as 'the ability to use knowledge, product and process skills to act effectively to achieve a purpose'.
2. The need for new kinds of assessment to force a break from a reliance on examination or test passes and on the listing of experience without any description of its quality.
3. The notion of '**transfer**', the ownership of skills, described as 'the ability to redeploy learned skills and knowledge in new and unfamiliar circumstances'.
4. A stress on describing the outcomes of activity: what the learner is able to achieve at the end of a process of a learning rather than detailing the learning inputs (the curriculum). 'The test for success must be described in terms of how the trainee contributes to some overall purpose, how independent s/he has become in acting effectively and how s/he can use this competence in

unfamiliar situations ... because content and outcome concentrates on the person's effectiveness, it is primarily concerned with outcomes – what s/he can do, rather than with inputs.'

5. The need to focus on broad occupational roles described within Occupational Training Families (OTFs), and the proposition that new models of occupational competence need to include more demanding expectations than were traditionally expected of the workforce. The OTFs had an important influence on the description of occupational areas, including the horizontal axis of the NVQ framework. The families are shown in Table 3.1 matched against the closest equivalent NVQ Area of Competence.

Occupational Training Families	OTF Key Purpose	Closest NVQ Area of Competence
1. Administrative, Clerical and Office Services	Information processing	Providing business services
2. Agriculture, Horticulture, Forestry and Fisheries	Nurturing and gathering living resources	Tending animals, plants and land
3. Craft and Design	Creating single, or small numbers of objects, using hand/power tools	No equivalent
4. Installation, Maintenance and Repair	Applying known procedures for making things work	Embedded in engineering
5. Technical and Scientific	Applying known principles to make things work/usable	Embedded in engineering
6. Manufacturing and Assembly	Transforming metallic and non-metallic materials through shaping, constructing and assembling into products	Manufacturing Constructing Engineering
7. Processing	Intervening in the working of machines when necessary	Manufacturing
8. Food Preparation and Service	Transforming and handling edible matter	Embedded in providing goods and services
9. Personal Service and Sales	Satisfying the needs of individual customers	Providing goods and services
10. Community and Health Services	Meeting socially defined needs of the community	Providing health, social care and protective services
11. Transport Services	Moving goods and people	Transporting

Only three of the NVQ Areas of Competence are not covered by the OTFs:

1. Extracting and providing natural resources
2. Communicating
3. Developing and extending knowledge and skill

These are not covered because the OTFs describe occupations which are the target for young entrants, which is not a common entry route in these three areas.

Table 3.1 The Occupational Training Families, their key purposes and the NVQ Areas of Competence

6. A distinction was made between two broad aspects of occupational competence: the contribution to the main purpose of the organisation, such as product manufacture or caring for clients, and the contribution to the maintenance of the organisation itself.[4]

The methodological approach which the Training for Skill Ownership team used for analysing occupations involved the progressive separation of work roles, taking the key purpose of an occupation in the economy and using this as a starting-point from which to analyse the component roles which enabled the key purpose to be achieved. This approach resulted in Work Learning Guides, diagrammatic representations of the analysis which described all the work roles. An example of a Work Learning Guide is shown in Figure 3.1. This was the inspiration for the more formal and detailed methodology which became known as functional analysis, which we cover in Chapters 5–8.

WORK-BASED LEARNING AND CORE SKILLS

Partly arising from the work of the Training for Skill Ownership project, but also working in parallel on the YTS curriculum model, was the second major research and development initiative which profoundly influenced the VET system of the 1980s and 1990s. Jointly funded by the European Social Fund and the Manpower Services Commission, this project was designed to operationalise the concept of 'core skills' within a model of learning which deliberately exploited the opportunities for learning available in the workplace. It was called the ESF Core Skills Project and was directed by Margaret Levy who had also been involved in the commissioning of the Training for Skill Ownership work.

The principle of **work-based learning** is simple. We learn by doing, combined with supportive education and training which provides us with the skills, knowledge and understanding which we need to act. But it is the application of skills, knowledge and understanding in the real-work environment which is the primary and most powerful focus for learning. Learning is linked inseparably to the work role. The concept of work-based learning, as expressed by Levy,[5] was:

> linking learning to the work role of the learner *and* having three interrelated components, each of which provides an essential contribution to the learning process. These three components are:
>
> – structuring learning in the workplace;
> – providing appropriate on-job training/learning opportunities;
> – identifying and providing relevant off-job learning opportunities.

A more simplistic notion of work-based learning has a long history in the UK. Usually called 'sitting by Nellie' it was the method by which many young people learned: sitting next to an experienced worker and hoping to pick up the skills and tricks of the trade which would make them competent workers. Usually this

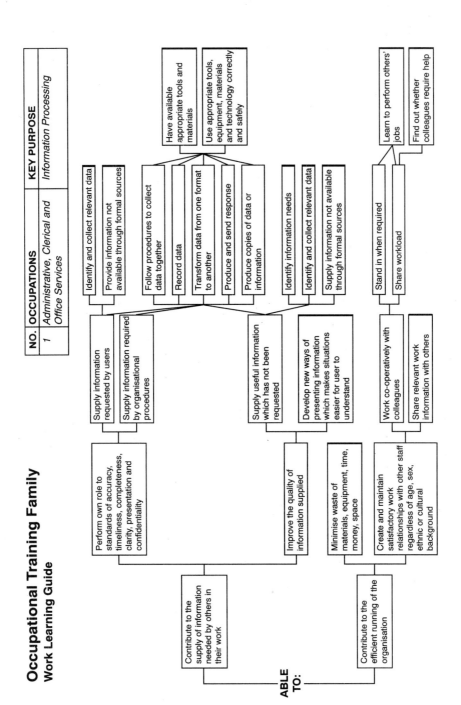

Fig. 3.1 An OTF Work Learning Guide

34

method was extremely inefficient. 'Nellie' could be incompetent and consequently pass on the wrong techniques or inadequate skills. 'Nellie' could resent the presence of the trainee and deliberately sabotage any learning that might take place. More often, 'Nellie' was an entirely competent worker, but did not have the skills to pass on their competence to another person. The method lacked structure, technique and clarity about what was required.

The work-based learning approach argued that trainees need a structure to define and facilitate learning.[6] The ESF Core Skills Project set up a number of satellite projects in different regions of the UK and worked closely with training providers and employers involved in the YTS. The approach entailed exploiting the facilities and resources of the work environment and combining these into structured **work-based projects** which capitalised on the learning opportunities offered by the workplace. To do this, the project designer had to describe the opportunities offered by the workplace in sufficient detail for them to be relevant to the trainee and their work supervisor, but in terms which were sufficiently general to apply to most of the workplaces within an occupation. This required a common set of descriptions for all work activity.

THE YTS CORE SKILLS

The **YTS core skills** had an empirical base derived from an extensive study of work activities. In this they differed from the other versions of core skills in use at the time which were, in the main, made up by well-meaning curriculum committees. The first stage of the ESF Core Skills Project involved the analysis and elaboration of the core skills, and the development team included Bob Mansfield and David Mathews (authors of the Job Competence Model) and Nanci Downey, who later contributed substantially to implementation methods for occupational standards which were a direct result of this work.

The core skills consisted of 103 separate core skills statements, expressed as learning outcomes, grouped into 14 **core skill groups**. The skill groups were organised into four **core skill areas**. Each skill group was associated with one or more **keywords** which were used to highlight the presence of a core skill in work activities. The core skill areas, groups and keywords are shown in Table 3.2.

The rationale for identifying a core of skills to support the YTS curriculum was twofold. First the core skills offered a common language to enable trainees and their trainers to identify the common aspects of different activities and different jobs – to help them identify opportunities for transferability. Second, they were used to analyse current activities to uncover and elaborate the complexities of work so that learning both on and off the job could benefit from a curriculum derived from a common language of skills. The core skills provided the important elaboration of the outcomes which had to be achieved and also attempted to change the way in which work was perceived. The core skill areas of Number,

CORE AREA/Core Skill Group	KEYWORD(S)
NUMBER	
1. Operating with numbers	COUNT, WORK OUT, CHECK AND CORRECT, COMPARE
2. Interpreting numerical and related information	INTERPRET
3. Estimating	ESTIMATE
4. Measuring and marking out	MEASURE, MARK OUT
5. Recognising cost and value	COMPARE, RECOGNISE VALUE
COMMUNICATION	
6. Finding out information and interpreting instructions	FIND OUT, INTERPRET
7. Providing information	PROVIDE INFORMATION
8. Working with people	NOTICE, ASK FOR ASSISTANCE, OFFER ASSISTANCE, REACT, DISCUSS, CONVERSE
PROBLEM SOLVING	
9. Planning – determining and revising courses of action	PLAN, DIAGNOSE
10. Decision making – choosing between alternatives	DECIDE
11. Monitoring – keeping track of progress and checking	CHECK, MONITOR, NOTICE
PRACTICAL	
12. Preparing for a practical activity	LOCATE, IDENTIFY, HANDLE, LIFT AND TRANSPORT, ADJUST, ARRANGE, CARRY OUT PROCEDURES, CHECK
13. Carrying out a practical activity	ADOPT SAFE PRACTICES, LIFT OR TRANSPORT, MANIPULATE, OPERATE, SET-UP, ASSEMBLE, DISMANTLE
14. Finishing off a practical activity	CARRY OUT PROCEDURES, CHECK, RESTOCK

Table 3.2 The core skill areas, groups and keywords

Source: Manpower Services Commission, *Core Skills in YTS: Manual Part 1,* Sheffield, Manpower Services Commission, 1984

Planning and Problem Solving, Communications and Practical Skills were held to be present in all work roles, with the important caveat that if they were not, then **for learning purposes they should be.**

This concept was fed into the work-based projects designed to structure work-based learning, with the project designers deliberately enriching work roles by the addition of activities related to the core skills. So, for example, a project based around the pricing of products in a supermarket would be enriched by adding additional activities. The trainee might be asked to:

- find out from other people how price changes were implemented and the company policy on changing prices for goods already in stock (oral communication, finding out information);
- calculate the average price of classes of similar products and chart the price range (use of number and producing graphical information);
- find out about common malfunctions in pricing guns (the main equipment used

at the time) and use the manufacturer's manual to dismantle and reassemble the machine (problem solving, practical skills);

- investigate at the college or training centre the latest advances in pricing: for example, bar-code readers, scanners (finding out information, new technology).

In these ways apparently routine and simple work tasks were exploited for all the learning potential they could offer.

THE NEED FOR NEW APPROACHES

These new approaches to curriculum development had common themes which generated a need for new approaches and methods. Most importantly, they required that almost all work activities be described in a common format which could structure learning and certification. This was the purpose of the Occupational Training Families and the Work Learning Guides. All the work roles appropriate to young people entering occupations were described in broad outcome terms.

At a more detailed level, the requirement to analyse work activities for common underlying core skills and to design learning systems around work meant that work activity had to be elaborated in some detail. Added to this, it was clearly necessary that some consensus be reached about what work expectations are – about what occupational competence is.

The concept of Occupational Training Families, the work-based project approach and the core skills had already started to hint at the possibility that the content of existing work was often unable to provide a sufficiently rich and demanding learning environment – it required enrichment. This is not too far from a position which argues that occupational competence should be described in a way which is more demanding than what is currently expected in the work environment, that the focus for VET should not be work as it is now but a wider vision that encompasses transfer to other kinds of work and adapting to different requirements in the future; in other words, the NTI vision in practice.

But the ESF Core Skills Project, which developed both the work-based learning model and the core skills was hampered by the existing technologies of occupational analysis and vocational training. What was available for analysis was what was there – existing work activity. And the methods for elaborating work activity were various forms of job and task analysis.

TASK ANALYSIS

Task analysis has a long history, not just in VET but also in methods engineering and work study. Task analysis uses one key process which is then linked to two major purposes. The process involves identifying in detail the components of work activity. The first purpose is to use the detailed components of activity in order to attach ideal cycle times to task components for the purpose of imposing external controls, the engineering of production, which involves removing inefficiencies which will get in the way of operator performance. This also provides a database for piecework payment systems. For the second purpose, the detail is used to structure training programmes. It is applied mainly to manual operations, because this kind of activity involves clearly identified sequences and actions and the results are tangible products.

Task analysis, when well practised, is entirely fit for its purpose. It can analyse observable work activities with precision and generate ideal descriptions of tasks which can be used to remove inefficiency and improve productivity. It is most appropriate in the environment in which it developed and which it supports – highly proceduralised, manually oriented, mass or continuous production systems. With some modification it can be applied with some success to jobs and occupational sectors which also feature highly proceduralised work but which are not strictly manual production, such as clerical work and routine service occupations such as retail. Outside these systems it has little to offer for no other reason than that it was not designed for any other system – just as the classification systems developed for teeth have little to offer if our purpose is to categorise limbs.

Despite these limitations, task analysis was the method used by the ESF Core Skills Project because it seemed to have the potential to provide common descriptions of work activity and no other suitable method existed. A modified version was developed within the project, called 'core skills analysis',[7] to provide a learning and assessment format for work-based learning. Initially, task analysis appeared to work, but this was nothing to do with the universal applicability of the analysis system itself. It was because the kinds of jobs and occupational sectors which were the target for YTS trainees tended to be those associated with routines, procedures and semi-skilled manufacturing – precisely the environ-ments where task analysis originally thrived and prospered.

The first problem to emerge from the application of task analysis was repetition and redundancy. In workplace after workplace, project workers identified and analysed tasks and, without any central co-ordination of this process or any guiding methodology about what constituted a task element, the same groups of tasks were analysed and re-analysed *ad infinitum*. Commonly occurring tasks like operating a photocopier, operating a till, checking deliveries and typing a letter were analysed again and again in different workplaces – with each throwing up a different set of sequences, methods and equipment. As this process of mass analysis continued, the language of YTS was also starting to change, and the outcomes of these analyses were variously described as **competence objectives** and **standards**. What was needed was a means by which to reduce this unnecessary variation in the outcomes of the analysis, an essential component of quality systems.

An attempt to standardise this plethora of overlapping and repeating analysis was pioneered by the Standards and Assessment Support Unit of the Manpower Services Commission.[8] Standard Tasks were designed to standardise the curriculum outcomes of YTS and provide a national focus for assessment. They were developed for two occupational areas, retail and office administration, and went on to influence later standard setting in other occupations which were characterised by procedures and routines.[9] But standard tasks floundered. Expressed in so much detail in their attempt to capture every possible variance in work, they were administratively impossible to manage and implement. There were also concerns that the standard tasks and the whole task analysis approach was failing to capture the essential aspects of competence which the core skills were designed to elaborate. Standard tasks could readily describe practical activities, but where were the planning, problem solving and communication skills which were essential components of the YTS model?

By then tasks and task analysis were firmly embedded in YTS development, and a view emerged that occupational competence was the ability to perform a task to a standard. Thus the emerging term 'standard' was firmly associated with task analysis and the definition of occupational standards was imagined as the wholesale task analysis of the occupational area.

OCCUPATIONAL COMPETENCE

Descriptions of occupational competence had been provided by both the Training for Skill Ownership project and by the four YTS Outcomes, both of which had stressed a broad view of competence. This was in contrast to the task-based approaches which were very narrow in focus.

For many years the concept of occupational competence prevailing in the occupations which were the target for YTS was associated with following rigorous and imposed procedures and the application of minimal skills to high levels of speed and accuracy – a narrow view of occupational competence. Indeed, for many industries these were the only requirements: follow the procedure correctly, work fast, work to the specification and ask no questions. This concept of competence was by no means confined to unskilled and semi-skilled manual occupations. In clerical, retail and administrative occupations this approach dominated as well. This view is part of an historical and philosophical tradition which, when examined, can illuminate the problems of developing descriptions of work activity.

The late nineteenth and early twentieth centuries exemplified this tradition in the development of factory systems and the training of the workforce. Work was subdivided into atomised tasks and skills. All human characteristics were removed as far as possible so that the worker was not placed in the disturbing position of having to think, to be creative, solve problems or make decisions. The role of management was to control work processes, aided and abetted by emerging technologies.

This separation between work activity and the control of work activity was a clear break with tradition. Skilled manual work, up to the nineteenth century, was seen as a broadly based role, involving the planning and co-ordination of activity as well as the activity itself. This model is implicit in the notion of apprenticeship and the guild system. It was the emergence of large numbers of semi- or unskilled workers, together with advances in industrial equipment and machinery, which led to the view that, for the sake of efficiency, the management and organisational aspects of the work role could be separated from the purely manual activities. Planning and co-ordination of work was to be placed in the hands of overlookers, overseers and superintendents – the managers. The work which remained was proceduralised – stripped of all the planning and co-ordination which might interfere with productive efficiency.

The literature and culture of the early twentieth century abounds with visions of this approach. Fritz Lang's film masterpiece, *Metropolis*, shows the worker as part machine and machines becoming the same as people. Aldous Huxley's futuristic novel *Brave New World* depicts programmed humans graded into classes, with the lower classes being little more than unthinking brutes who can work on routine manual jobs. The term 'robot' was coined to describe the man-machine that the modern production systems seemed to be trying to create.

This thinking infused and dominated our approach to industrial training. Workers needed little more than basic training in routine skills to perform routine tasks. Artisans, who inconveniently had to think, were offered a few more skills and a wider range of tasks. Social skills like planning, problem solving and communication were a danger and could reduce productivity. Team working was discouraged as being dangerously unproductive. Production was based on lines, with each individual strictly segregated; production control and flow was handled by conveyors, supervisors and other labourers.

Each operation was further and further subdivided to the extent that in some industries an entire job could be described as a manual operation with a total cycle time measured in seconds. A whole profession, work measurement and work study, arose to co-ordinate and control this system. Another profession, skill instruction, supported it. In this environment the only important training input was routine manual skills. The only measured outcomes were speed and quality. The only reward system was piece rates. The role of VET was to support this system: to train in routines, procedures and good work disciplines.

As we discussed in the first two chapters, our economy is now markedly different from the factory systems developed in the nineteenth and twentieth centuries. Mass and continuous production is in decline as product differentiation increases. There are fewer and fewer markets for cheap, mass-produced goods. Technology, combined with increased consumer expectations, has forced improvements in quality standards and product complexity to the extent that people need to think in order to work. Increased wealth has changed the pattern of demand. Mass production systems – where they still exist – are exported to developing economies where there is still a market. The very car factories where Fredrick Taylor and Henry Ford forged their inhuman systems are now controlled by robotics; technicians monitor production and operatives meet in quality circles to develop innovative approaches to quality improvement.

Nevertheless skills and tasks were the stuff of training well into the 1980s, and the needs and objectives of YTS could do little to dent this firmly established tradition. Combined with theoretical teaching and limited practice in an educational institution, skills training underpinned much of our VET system. Yet in every generation there were sceptics and critics – from the radical Fabians who set up the Workers' Education Association, Ruskin College and the Mechanics Institutes at the turn of the twentieth century to the equally committed educationalists of the 1960s and 1970s who set up and supported the addition of liberal studies, general studies and social and life skills to the otherwise narrow vocational training programmes undertaken in further education (FE) colleges.

The concerns throughout this period were twofold. One was political and the other practical. First, it was argued that the role of education and training should not be limited to preparing young people and retraining adults for limited occupational roles and jobs – and this view was entirely consistent with the YTS aims. The term 'factory fodder' was a favourite jibe, and this concern linked the Fabians with the further education practitioners. The concern, fundamentally, was with the dignity of people and a declaration of the rights of all individuals to have access to quality education and training, not just the job-specific training which met the immediate needs of an employer.

Second, the changes in the economy and social expectations suggested a broader view of occupational competence. The modern worker of the 1960s and 1970s was no longer merely machine fodder. Already employers were starting to complain about a lack of what was usually called 'common sense' and a lack of willingness to take responsibility. Skills like planning, communications, problem solving and decision making started to emerge as key learning needs. There was a fundamental change in what people were beginning to see as occupational competence. A limited collection of tasks and skills was no longer enough. This, in part, was one of the concerns which culminated in the radical proposals for reform of the system contained in NTI.

The UK system, dominated for centuries by élitism and the clear separation between theory and practice, found the wrong solution to this emerging problem by separating the new skills from the traditional manual skills. The practice of on-job learning combined with workshop training was little changed from the 1950s – training for specific and often outdated skills, or those specific skills which met the employer's immediate needs. What was needed, it was argued, was an addition to the vocational curriculum to compensate for the limited opportunities offered by the workplace and skills-based training, or 'narrow vocationalism' as it became known.

The solution varied, but the broad concept was the same. Additional social and personal skills were to be learned in an off-job environment, usually a FE college. The additional knowledge and skills were to provide a compensation for the emiseration of the workplace and the narrowness of skills training: they had to be 'bolted on' to the occupational training programme. The changing requirements for occupational competence, therefore, did not fundamentally change the definition or conception of occupational competence; it was simply recognised that more was required. Occupational competence became the traditional tasks and skills plus 'something else'.

The search for the elusive 'something else' was a key topic for educational research for a decade. Originally emerging as liberal studies – a simplistic addition to the off-the-job training input – then general studies – equally simplistic but with more topics – this approach quickly lost credibility with employers and trainees alike. The search was on for additional skills to bolt on to the occupational programme. Table 3.3 lists the additional skill categories which came and went during the 20-year period between the 1970s and the 1990s. In each category there are numerous variants. In the core skills category, for example, there are over 40 documented core skill lists, one of which is the YTS core skills, following the tradition of defining occupational competence as tasks plus 'something else'.

The main purpose of all these categories was to bridge the ever-widening gap between task- and skills-based occupational training and the emerging and increasingly urgent need for a vocational education and training system based on a new model of occupational competence. In each case, however, the presumption was the same. If only this particular aspect were added to the narrow vocational curriculum then we would produce people with the necessary additional planning, problem-solving, communication, numerical and social skills, and with the appropriate attitudes, values, disposition and willingness to work effectively.

But still the concept of occupational competence remained more-or-less intact. The increasing lists of new skills were seen as useful, but the end result was that

---

- Social skills
- Social and life skills
- Core skills
- Generic skills
- Transferable skills
- Core competences
- Soft skills
- Process skills
- Common learning objectives
- Common learning outcomes
- Enterprise characteristics
- Personal effectiveness
- Personal competences
- Generic standards

Table 3.3 Additional skills, used to supplement occupational skills

most of the workforce was trained in procedures and imposed processes, and were expected to perform limited skills and tasks in controlled and authoritarian learning environments. And YTS, despite its radical nature and its new agenda, could do little to change this view fundamentally. The YTS core skills, despite their empirical nature, were still widely seen as an addition to the VET curriculum which was to be bolted on to narrow occupational training rather than fully integrated within a work-based learning model. Training providers offered core skills courses where communications and planning skills were taught like any other topic. The Standard Tasks contained a list of the core skills thought to be embedded in them, but this was tucked away in a small corner and they could be easily ignored.

The issue of the nature of occupational competence is not solely the contrast between narrow and broad views of the work role. In the debate surrounding YTS and the emerging VET system this tended to be the focus for attention, but that was largely because the roles under consideration were those entered by young people at 16 years of age with, at most, secondary education and first-level educational qualifications (in the 1980s these were O levels, and later GCSE qualifications). Other models of occupational competence were to have an influence on the YTS debate. These were to have a more fundamental impact as attention turned to the broader standards programme which aimed to identify standards for all occupations and at all levels.

COMPETENCE FOR ALL

Models of occupational competence vary. They are derived in different ways, from different perspectives and for different kinds of occupations. Two broad groupings can be distinguished: those which are based on **inputs** – what people need to be like or to acquire – and those which are **hierarchical** – differentiating different models of competence depending on the type and level of work that is being described.

Input models of occupational competence

There are two main input models of occupational competence.

1. **Educational input models** attempt to define what people need to learn, possess and develop in terms of skills, attributes and knowledge and understanding. They view competence as the combined total of the inputs of learning programmes. Educational models are present in all the hierarchical models. This is the root of the educational curriculum, criticised by NTI as inadequate for the development of the competent workforce and a model which YTS was trying to reform.
2. **Psychological models** concentrate on what people need to be like – what psychological characteristics they need to possess for different jobs. These models have a strong influence on some of the hierarchical models. In YTS

they were represented by the search for indices of personal effectiveness which were described in terms of desirable work characteristics, such as dependability and responsibility.

Hierarchical models of occupational competence

Hierarchical models of occupational competence are based on the assumption that different methods and approaches are needed to analyse and describe different types of work, rather than one general model which is sufficiently flexible to describe all work roles. This view is underpinned by a tradition of social élitism, the same tradition that discriminates between education and training and tends to value academic achievement rather then practical capability. There are also clear associations with social class. Three broad models are apparent:

1. manual and service occupations;
2. managerial occupations;
3. professional occupations.

Manual and service occupations are the type to which task and skills analyses are applied, although they are also described in terms of educational input models. The model of competence, however, is defined by the activities performed – activities which are defined by the division of labour. Significantly, the people who work in these occupations tend to have their occupational activities defined by others, usually those from managerial occupations. Even when people in such occupational areas achieve extremely high levels of responsibility and criticality there is still a sense in which they may appear undervalued. The complaint about the relative status of engineers and other technical occupations in the UK in comparison with other cultures is an example of this.

It is in the areas of factory work, bureaucratic administration and routine services, however, that task and skills analyses have been most developed and have fixed the model of occupational competence as the performance of routine, procedural tasks.

Managerial models are usually based on a combination of activity descriptions plus the identification of critical personal characteristics (a psychological model). These characteristics are usually active and positive – qualities such as drive, leadership and strategic orientation are carefully described and indexed. Contrast this with psychological descriptions applied to manual and service workers where, if used at all, there is a concentration on manual capability such as dexterity and qualities – such as responsibility, following instructions and respect for authority, which usually emphasise passivity and compliance.

An interesting variant of the standards approach, which has caused considerable confusion in the standards programme, is the current vogue for identifying 'competencies' for managers in which lists of these desirable characteristics are identified and indexed.

The model of competence is clear: some limited activity description, but in the main competence comprises the personal qualities and attributes of the individual.

Professional occupations are technical in nature but are usually extremely resistant to the notion that they should be subject to an analysis of activities. More often, professional models of competence emphasise the nature of ethical practice, the rarity and complexity of the knowledge base and the nature of relationships with clients. Some personal characteristic models are also adopted, with qualities like creativity, client confidentiality and professional probity appearing to be highly valued. Competence is equated with the knowledge base plus the proper use of the knowledge within an ethical framework.

An outcome model of occupational competence

An outcome-driven curriculum model requires a model of competence which is also based on outcomes. Various attempts were made in the 1980s to define competence in outcome terms. Here are some of them.

In 1983 the *Scottish Education Department* (SED)[10] proposed a new type of VET provision clustered around the aims of:

(i) developing knowledge and understanding of oneself, of one's community and of the environment. It was specified that due to the increasing pace of change in society, this should foster self-confidence and reliance, autonomy, the exercise of independent responsibility, and the understanding of how to gain access to information. It should also foster understanding of, and the social skills connected with, co-operation and awareness of the wider community.

(ii) developing skills. These were described as intellectual, practical and physical, interpersonal, social and vocational skills.

(iii) developing attributes, values and motives which prompt people to act in particular ways or make particular decisions. It was noted that these were not easy to identify and were often associated as much with how something was done rather than the resulting product.

This specification of aims led SED to state in a later document[11] that there were three basic types of learning outcomes (described as competences) which were those that assessed:

1. knowledge and its use (ie not mere recall);
2. skills (performed to a stated level of competence);
3. behaviours, which may reflect certain attitudes to given tasks, such as working safely or hygienically.

This is clearly, in the terms of our previous descriptions, an educational input model, defining what people needed to learn.

The *Further Education Unit* reflected the same educational stance as SED in describing competence as 'the possession and development of sufficient skills, knowledge and appropriate attitudes and experience for successful performance in life roles'.[12]

As we have already noted, *The Manpower Services Commission,* responsible for the design and implementation of YTS, had offered an implicit definition of occupational competence in the outcomes of YTS. This was an outcome approach, although the category 'personal effectiveness' was an attempt to integrate a psychological model as well. Despite the outward appearances, however, the four outcomes still described what trainees should learn, not the nature of competence.

A later and more detailed definition of occupational competence was produced by the Standards and Assessment Support Unit in 1986:

> the ability to perform activities in the jobs within an occupation, to the standards expected in employment. The concept also embodies the ability to transfer skills and knowledge to new situations within the occupational area and beyond to related occupations. Such flexibility often involves a higher level of mastery of skills and understanding than is common among even experienced employees. Competence also includes many aspects of personal effectiveness in that it requires the application of skills and knowledge in organisational contexts, with workmates, supervisors, customers, while coping with real life pressures.[13]

This is a description which is clearly referenced back to the aims of NTI, and it is the first, apart from Training for Skill Ownership, which tries to tie down what occupational competence is. But the description still appears to include a mix of models: work expectations, input measures (knowledge and skills) and psychological attributes.[14]

The 1986 Review of Vocational Qualifications (RVQ) (Manpower Services Commission and Department of Education and Science, 1986), which led to the formation of the National Council for Vocational Qualifications, discussed the nature of a **'statement of competence'** and the content of new vocational qualifications, later to be known as National Vocational Qualifications (NVQs). But RVQ did not tackle the issue of the nature of competence. RVQ made the assumption that there was a common understanding about the concept, and when a view of competence is specified it seems narrower than the concept proposed for YTS:

> Many existing vocational qualifications do not adequately assess or indicate competence. Mostly there is either an assessment of knowledge relating to occupational skills and understanding (assessment commonly reflects performance in a written exam) or performance in stated skills is assessed. Neither form of assessment in our view necessarily indicates an occupational competence, by which we mean **the ability to perform satisfactorily in an occupation or range of occupational tasks** [our emphasis].[15]

Notice that the RVQ seems to have reverted to the task-based approach in describing competence. In later parts of the document the RVQ authors seem to confuse an educational input model and the notion of task descriptions:

> A vocational qualification as a statement of competence should incorporate the assessment of skills to specified standards, relevant knowledge and understanding, and the ability to use skills and apply knowledge and understanding in the performance of relevant tasks.

and

> The concept of competence must reflect these three aspects of performance – ie

competence is about performance (in a variety of modes) to standards specified (by industry) in relevant tasks. It is not merely about performance in artificially created situations (either of decontextualised skills or knowledge) but the application of these – that is the bringing together of elements to perform effectively (in real life situations).[16]

Having appeared to back a rather narrow and task-based view of competence, RVQ appears to contradict itself in its vision for NVQs:[17]

vocational qualifications should reflect competence and be a means of ensuring a more competent workforce, better fitted than now to meet the challenge and the changing demands of employment ... with standards ... not based on a narrow interpretation of occupational competence.[18]

Such was the confusion in the 1980s – reeling between educational aims and objectives, psychological concepts and descriptions of existing tasks. There was clearly room for a description of occupational competence, firmly based on outcomes, which could resolve these confusions.

NOTES

1. Manpower Services Commission, *The New Training Initiative*.
2. At an early stage in the development of this outcome, two versions were proposed. The first is the one quoted here. The second dropped the ambiguous and potentially narrowing term 'a job and/or' to leave outcome 1 as 'competence in a range of occupational skills'. By an unusual oversight, both descriptions survived and the alternatives appeared in different MSC documents up until 1988.
3. Hayes, *et al.*, *Training for Skill Ownership*.
4. For the influence which this has had on the structure of functional maps and the development of occupational standards, see Chapters 6 and 9 of this book.
5. Levy, *The Core Skills project and Work Based Learning*.
6. A number of projects related to developing accreditation of work-based learning followed on from the work-based learning project and included: in England, Caterbase, the Clothing and Allied Products ITB Project, the Institute of Meat Project – all of which were evaluated by PRD Ltd in their report Boning, Blanching and Back-tacking; In Scotland, The 16+ in YTS Project based in Fife and the two Accreditation of Work-Based Learning Projects and Competency Testing project at SCOTVEC; and in Wales, the AWBL project based at the Welsh Joint Education Council (WJEC).
7. Prescott, 'Competence analysis flow chart'.
8. The Standards and Assessment Support Unit (SASU) was a technical section of the MSC Youth Development Branch, set up by Gilbert Jessup. The Unit was instrumental in the formation of the Technical Advisory Group (TAG) which produced the first methodological guidance for the standards programme. It was superseded by the Standards Methodology Unit and then the Learning Methods Branch.
9. The standard task approach was applied in the Clothing and Allied Products ITB (CAPITB) Project, the Caterbase Project and the Institute of Meat Project.
10. Scottish Education Department, *16s – 18s in Scotland: An Action Plan*.
11. Scottish Education Department, *16s – 18s in Scotland: Guidelines on Curriculum and Assessment*.
12. Further Education Unit, *Towards a Competence-Based System*.
13. Manpower Services Commission, *SASU Note 16*; (mimeo).
14. Gilbert Jessup was the prime mover in SASU. A mix of models can still be seen in his more recent work, *Outcomes: NVQs and the Emerging Model of Education and Training*. As in the following quote: 'By specifying learning objectives, in the form of outcome standards, independent of any course, programme or mode of learning, it becomes possible to create a framework of such standards, which can be adopted by any course or programme. The standards provide the unifying concept for all learning. A framework of standards provides the reference grid within which different forms of learning can be related'.

15. Manpower Services Commission and the Department of Education and Science, *Review of Vocational Qualifications*, London: HMSO.
16. Ibid.
17. It is interesting to note that the current model of competence offered by the NCVQ is also rather muddled in concept:

    The NVQ statement of competence derives from an analysis of functions within the area of competence to which it relates. It must reflect:

    1 competence relating to task management, health and safety and the ability to deal with unexpected events, organisational environments and relationships with other people;
    2 the ability to transfer the competence from place to place and context to context;
    3 the ability to respond positively to foreseeable changes in technology, working methods, markets and employment patterns and practices;
    4 the skill, knowledge and understanding which is required for effective performance in employment.

    National Council for Vocational Qualifications, *NVQ Criteria and Guidance*.
18. Manpower Services Commission and the Department of Education and Science, *Review of Vocational Qualifications*.

4   The Job Competence Model

THE JOB COMPETENCE MODEL

To advance beyond a description of competence which merely reflected existing practice a new model of occupational competence was needed which clearly expressed the broad view of competence implied by the NTI and YTS. It eventually appeared in 1985 in the form of the Job Competence Model, and was developed by David Mathews and Bob Mansfield whilst they were working with the ESF Core Skills Project. The Job Competence Model is different from previous notions of competence because it is based on a description of the outcomes which the individual needs to achieve rather than the skills and knowledge which they need to have, the attributes they should possess or the tasks which they should be able to perform.

Before looking at the Job Competence Model in detail, it is important to be clear about its characteristics, which can be summarised as:

- a focus on the concept of **work roles** in contrast to tasks or personal attributes;
- recognition that work roles are formed by **social expectations**, the outcomes which individuals are expected to achieve;
- work role expectations emerge and change through a process of **negotiation** between different groups who are able to use their influence to define those expectations: as the balance of power and influence changes, so do role expectations;
- all work roles have common characteristics – described in the Job Competence Model as **components** – although the components vary in predominance between different roles. This means that the model is not concerned with who usually fills the roles – man or woman, professional or non-professional – or where the roles are traditionally located in the social structure.

The Job Competence Model is consequently holistic, designed to cover all work-role expectations and relationships, emphasising the interrelationship between the different components.

The Job Competence Model has its roots in the social sciences – sociology and economics – in contrast to many other models of competence which usually derive from a psychological perspective. In the model, occupational competence is defined in terms of work roles which are socially defined and negotiated. Roles are based on the notion that the expectations which define them are beyond the immediate influence of the individual who performs the role at any one time. There are different groups of roles: family roles such as parent, son, daughter, sister and brother; community roles such as neighbour, taxpayer, voter and citizen; and in the workplace a range of occupational or work roles such as bank clerk, doctor, builder, accountant. Each of these roles is defined by social expectations. For example, the expectations of the role of doctor include diagnosis, methods of alleviation or cure, confidentiality, and respect for patients' beliefs and rights. The individual doctor is required to meet these expectations but will have very little opportunity to define them, although he or she may participate in changing and renegotiating role expectations over time.

Drawing from this social science perspective on the nature of work, work roles can be seen as a combination of the sets of expectations held by different groups – between economically active individuals and key social groups within society – modified by the variable power relationships between them.

The Job Competence Model uses the flexible concept of dynamic work roles by suggesting four underlying components, present in all work roles but in different proportions and with different emphases. The actual proportion of each component in any one work role is a combination of factors to do with the nature of the occupation, plus social expectations which may limit or expand the full expression of the work role. Such an approach allows constructs like common sense, responsibility, communication skills and problem solving to be operationalised meaningfully and in context.

The Job Competence Model states, quite simply, that work roles have four[1] interrelated components, all of which are present in all work activity. The components are described as:

1. **Technical expectations** – achieving the expectations of the work role which characterise the occupation (eg producing manufactured items, processing information, promoting health, treating illness).
2. **Managing contingencies** – recognising and resolving potential and actual breakdowns in processes and procedures (this may include coping with emergencies).
3. **Managing different work activities** – achieving balance and co-ordinating a number of different and potentially conflicting activities to lead to the successful conclusion of aims and goals.
4. **Managing the interface with the work environment** – achieving the expectations which arise from natural constraints, the quality measures which are applied, the nature of work organisation and the nature of working relationships. This component was originally referred to as the 'role/job environment' component.

Each of these components is described in more detail below.

TECHNICAL EXPECTATIONS

Competence in the technical aspects of work roles is often related to the achievement of tangible outcomes such as a typed letter, a milled block of steel, a totalled column of figures, a completed audit, a hairstyle, a working drawing, a land survey, an appendectomy. The outcomes, however, may also be intangible, such as a client who is less distressed, a recommendation which has been made or a well-delivered lesson. The technical expectations are those which clearly distinguish one occupation from another. In the past, it was the tangible, technical expectations of the work role which were the focus for, and the largest component of, vocational education and training and the part which task analysis was best able to elaborate. In the Job Competence Model, the technical expectations are important but are not *the* most important; they are one component of a much larger picture.

MANAGING CONTINGENCIES

Contingency management is one of the expectations which emerges from our changing concept of occupational competence related to expectations that all the workforce should be adaptable and flexible. It can be identified as one of the key aspects in multiskilling and delayering within organisations. There is an increasing demand for individuals who can meet the technical expectations of the work role and who can manage to return systems to full operation when things go wrong, or at least summon expert help and provide a clear explanation of the problem.

Contingency management involves planning, problem solving, decision making, choosing alternatives, evaluating results and knowing when it is necessary to summon expert help. The latter is a tricky balance. Whilst we do not expect people to stop and wait when something simple goes wrong, we do not want them to delve into their malfunctioning computer and start taking it apart, causing further and potentially expensive or dangerous problems. The balance is to be able to return a system to normal as quickly as is possible without creating further difficulties.

Notice, though, that this way of describing work roles provides a clearer context for the application of generalised process skills like planning and problem solving. In this component of the model, planning is used *in order to* anticipate and allocate resources to manage likely contingencies. Problem solving is used *in order to* diagnose faults if they occur and return systems to an operational state. Highlighting the statement 'in order to' demonstrates that general skills have more explanatory value when linked to a clear purpose. The outcome statements:

- anticipate and allocate resources to manage likely contingencies;
- diagnose faults;
- return systems to an operational state

are statements which are more useful for structuring learning programmes than are generalised terms such as planning skills.

It is possible to find some occupational roles which have a high proportion of contingency management as the roles in themselves are concerned with the management of variance rather than the achievement of specific technical outcomes. In these cases the dividing line between contingency management expectations and the technical expectations of work roles become blurred as the two are closely intertwined. Such roles would include the emergency services as well as much professional advisory work.

The production systems of the nineteenth and twentieth centuries tended to separate the management of contingencies into specific jobs such as those of supervisor, manager or specialist adviser. If a contingency arose the operative was usually expected to stop work and wait for technical help. This approach – stop and wait – survived for many years as a rigid procedure to be followed at all times. In clothing factories operatives stopped and waited if the needle snapped because only mechanics were allowed to change the needle (a task which all operatives were capable of achieving). On production lines the operative stopped and waited if any breakdown occurred until a maintenance engineer was available. The rest of the line stopped as well. Even the maintenance engineers stopped and waited if an electrician was needed to isolate a power supply. Office walls still carry facetious posters which describe what to do if something goes wrong. The advice usually involves hiding the mistake, blaming it on someone else or leaving the scene promptly before someone pins it on you.

The expectation, to cope in situations of breakdown and contingency, was one of the first to signal a change in our expectations of the competent workforce. As systems became more complex, more contingencies arose. The first response was to add more and more procedures, rules and regulations in order to catch contingencies, but this resulted in unmanageable rule-books and created greater confusion. It was eventually realised that people had to manage the inevitable breakdowns in increasingly complex systems for themselves.

MANAGING DIFFERENT WORK ACTIVITIES

Competent workers are expected to achieve many different, but linked, outcomes. And it is the achievement of the optimum balance between these different outcomes which is often seen as the key difference between average performance and occupational competence. Most patterns of work organisation do not expect individuals to move in a steady sequence from one activity to another, or to finish one thing before starting another, or to go to their manager to be allocated a further task when one is finished. Individuals usually have to achieve many outcomes concurrently, managing the interface between the variety of demands which are placed on them.

This small insight – achieving concurrent outcomes – came to the authors of the Job Competence Model whilst watching a skilled administrator in an office. She started photocopying a large batch of documents which she set up on the machine. As soon as she was happy that everything was working properly, she started filing some documents. Then the phone rang. She went to answer the phone and took a message, which she noted down. As she put the phone down the copier stopped. She went to check it, refilled the paper tray and went back to the note. Having checked it she decided to pass it on immediately and phoned the intended recipient – aware that she was disturbing a meeting but judging the message to be sufficiently urgent. She went back to the filing, checking the photocopier *en route* to remove finished documents from the tray and to monitor progress. All this happened within five minutes. If her job had been described using a task analysis, we would have been faced with an apparently simple list of tasks:

- operate a photocopier;
- file documents;
- answer and take messages from a telephone;
- pass messages to recipients.

But this list gets nowhere near the nature of competence which the administrator was displaying. She was managing to achieve a number of aspects of her work at once. She was constantly judging between options, deciding priorities, monitoring progress, estimating the time it takes to do something – all of which hold the different aspects of work together to achieve the overall demands of her work role. This essential component of occupational competence is aptly named **task management**. In many work roles we believe that task management is perceived as being more important than the technical expectations, in the sense that employers take the technical skills for granted and see competence as the ability to apply the technical skills flexibly to meet the changing demands of the work environment.

Some work roles could not be conceived without considerable levels of task management ability. The work roles in our own business are a good example. Normally our directors and consultancy staff are working on a number of different projects which may be completely unrelated. Some of our clients are surprised at this because they may be working on just one project for their organisation, and they imagine that we work in the same way. We don't! As an example of the importance of task management to our roles, here is a brief description of 'A morning in the life of Lindsay Mitchell'.

Lindsay is writing a steering group report for one project when she is interrupted by a series of telephone calls relating to two or three other projects. She saves the report on the computer, deals with the phone calls, assuring the clients that their own interests are being taken care of and making notes of the various matters raised to be dealt with later. Just as she starts back on the report a colleague seeks help on how to analyse some particularly complex responses to a questionnaire. She recalls that an earlier project dealt with similar issues and she had included information on the analyses in an appendix, so she refers the colleague to this as a starting-point and arranges to meet with them the following morning to confirm their progress. She goes back to the report. The phone rings ...

Task management increases in importance as people are expected to take more responsibility. The manufacturing groups and production teams which now characterise production systems are also their own task managers. They set priorities against production targets, arrange the workplace, decide on the most efficient methods of working, monitor their own work, provide assistance to others when bottlenecks occur, manage safety practices, complete production records, input information into control and monitoring systems, decide on job allocation and rotation. All this is task management. This is quite different from traditional production systems where:

- such practices would be positively avoided;
- systems would be in place to control these processes;
- it would be considered non-productive down-time (for which the individual worker would receive a lower payment rate).

In learning environments teachers are now expected not only to pass on their own knowledge and skills to others but also to enable learners to manage their learning process effectively. They must balance the needs of learners within the group who have different learning needs and different starting-points, manage the learning process through the effective use of initial, formative and summative assessment, complete learning and assessment records and contribute information to overall management systems, which are likely to include resource use.

Such demands for task management can be found in most occupations at every level. Since we no longer have long, repetitive production runs, people must adapt and change continuously. We have neither the resources nor the tolerance of inefficiency to let specialists alter production lines whenever there is a new model change, to bring in the training department whenever a new skill or process is needed or to call on work and method study whenever efficiency is in question. We have not the time to let skilled people inspect the work in progress of other skilled people, or to let managers compile records by walking up the lines keeping tally. People must manage their own activities in situations of incremental change – they must be flexible and adaptable – which is what task management, in operational terms, is mainly about.

Task management, like contingency management, has traditionally been seen as increasing in importance in higher-level work roles, mainly because that is how work was organised. Management and supervision were often concerned with task managing on behalf of others by exerting controls over people and processes. Now they are devolved, leaving smaller and flatter hierarchies. Consequently the nature of managing others has also changed, with less emphasis on control and direction and an increasing stress on facilitation and enabling skills. But such skills will only be effective if managers believe that individuals are able, willing and competent to manage their own work for themselves.

MANAGING THE INTERFACE WITH THE WORK ENVIRONMENT

The Job Competence Model does not stop at the technical expectations of work roles, however well integrated by the management of tasks and contingencies. Work roles exist within complex environments which themselves affect work-role expectations.

Work environments, or work contexts, can be characterised at two extremes: one could argue that the requirements for competence are the same everywhere and that context makes no difference to expectations about what should be achieved. This view underlies some of the approaches to common or core skills: it is assumed that context will not alter either the application of the fundamental skill or the outcomes to be achieved. The other extreme is to argue that any change of environment, however small, will change the application of the skill and hence the outcomes to be achieved. The result of this view is the 'doctrine of uniqueness' which argues that each occupational context is so unique that it is impossible and fruitless to draw any comparisons or lessons between one context and another. This radical reductionism would turn an already-specific task statement like 'operate a photocopier' into a myriad of subtly different tasks – 'operate a Cannon X13 monochrome photocopier', 'operate a Cannon X235 Colour photocopier with collation facilities', *ad infinitum*. It would also lead us to question why we have any vocational education and training, or even any education, if competence is solely related to the specific environment!

Both these extremes must be firmly rejected. The occupational environment varies, and thereby changes the context of application, but the patterns of variation are recognisable and can be described with some precision. These distinct patterns form a bridge between the two extreme views and allow us to show that so-called 'common skills' are deployed differently in different contexts which can be grouped around common outcomes.

But first we need to make some critical distinctions concerning what is meant by the term 'environment' and distinguish between those aspects which are set by the constraints of the natural environment and those which are the result of social and political processes.

The natural environment is relatively fixed: coal mining and nuclear power production, for example, are potentially hazardous occupations because of the location of coal and the hazardous nature of nuclear fuel. Very little can be done to change these contexts – they are a natural consequence of the occupation itself.

The social and political environment, on the other hand, is adaptable because it is based on values, commitments and power relationships which may change over time. For example, the degree of supervision and control applied to subordinates can be largely determined by the values and assumptions made about people's capabilities rather than any natural reasoning. Even the term 'subordinate' is a cultural description of relationships; and is fast disappearing in many organisations. The freedom to make decisions and the organisation of work are also cultural and political decisions. There is no natural constraint or law to support the scientific management principles of Taylor.

Consequently, in discussing the effect that the environment has upon the application of work roles, we need to keep this distinction in mind, because when we come to identify standards for work roles we need to recognise that many of the role patterns we see around us are based on social, cultural and political decisions which are themselves subject to change.

The four important patterns of variation within the nature of the work environment can be classified broadly as the nature of:

1. *Natural constraints* – where the work takes place and the intrinsic characteristics of any materials and equipment which are used.
2. *The quality measures which are applied* – the quality of work which is expected closely linked to why the work is taking place.
3. *The nature of work organisation* – how the work is organised.
4. *The nature of work relationships* – clients and colleagues: who is involved and the nature of the relationships.

Each of these patterns subdivides further to reveal characteristics of the work environment which have a significant impact on work-role expectations. The purpose of this approach is not to provide a discrete classification into which any one work role can be neatly slotted. Rather it is to help identify significant patterns in work environments, show the impact of these on work roles and the corresponding changes in expectations of occupational competence.

THE NATURE OF NATURAL CONSTRAINTS

There are two aspects of natural constraints which impact on the work role:

1. the location in which the work takes place, such as outdoor working, undersea working, dirt, exposure to weather, cramped conditions;
2. the intrinsic characteristics of the materials and equipment which are used, such as their fragility, value and bulk.

These two types of natural constraints may be either intrinsically hazardous or non-hazardous and will create four distinct patterns which will affect work expectations, as shown in Figure 4.1.

	CHARACTERISTICS OF MATERIALS AND EQUIPMENT	
	Hazardous	**Non-hazardous**
LOCATION **Hazardous**	Pattern 1	Pattern 3
Non-hazardous	Pattern 2	Pattern 4

Fig. 4.1 Hazardous locations, materials and equipment

PATTERN 1: HAZARDOUS MATERIALS AND EQUIPMENT IN A NATURALLY HAZARDOUS LOCATION

Coal mining, underwater welding and steel production are examples of occupations where the materials, equipment and location are all in themselves naturally hazardous. In these environments, health and safety requirements are critical and it can be disastrous to life and property if they are ignored or not fully met. Effective health and safety is maintained by highly structured rules and procedures within which the individual has little or no freedom to make decisions themselves. The essential expectations involve following complex rules and practices combined with being able to monitor hazards, report potential hazards accurately, and to follow emergency procedures exactly. The focus of health and safety is both to contain the natural hazards and to reduce risks as much as is possible.

PATTERN 2: HAZARDOUS MATERIALS AND EQUIPMENT IN A NON-HAZARDOUS LOCATION

In these environments, the materials and equipment are hazardous but the environment is not. Most industrial environments, where there are specific rules about guards on machines, wearing goggles when using grinding machines, age restrictions on the use of certain machines, plus general guidelines on safe personal behaviour, are of this type. In these environments a key aspect of competence is to be able to identify when to shift from the everyday care which we need to take to avoid creating hazards and accidents and the instances where safety becomes critical because of the presence of some natural hazard. Such skills are critical in hospitals where there are overall requirements to do with cross-infection and cleanliness, and specific requirements concerned with sterility, contagion and hazardous drugs. The focus of health and safety in these environments is to contain the risk inherent in the materials and equipment with which people are working.

PATTERN 3: NON-HAZARDOUS MATERIALS AND EQUIPMENT IN A HAZARDOUS LOCATION

Environments which consist of naturally hazardous locations but non-hazardous materials and equipment tend to have procedures to reduce the risk of the environment on those who work in it. Such occupations include construction, sea-fishing and window-cleaning, none of which involve hazardous materials but all of which take place in locations which present dangers in themselves. As the environments in themselves cannot be contained – we do not yet know how to calm a raging sea! – procedures are designed to reduce the risk to those who work there.

PATTERN 4: NEITHER HAZARDOUS MATERIALS AND EQUIPMENT NOR A HAZARDOUS LOCATION

These are environments with few natural hazards and where the materials and equipment used are not in themselves hazardous. There are some potentially hazardous items but no more than we would expect to find in the average home. Here risks to health and safety are more likely to occur due to individuals creating hazards than from the nature of the environment itself. For example, filing cabinets are not inherently dangerous, but if you open a full top drawer when all the other drawers are empty, the cabinet may tip over. A chest of drawers at home would do the same. Electric cables are not hazardous unless they are carelessly trailed across access points, in which case someone may trip over them. In these situations individuals are expected to behave in a manner which minimises hazards and avoids creating risks rather than simply to follow complex rule-books. Monitoring the environment for risk is important, but of more importance is acting safely within your own sphere of action.

These four patterns make different demands in terms of both the response to the existence of hazards and the skills necessary to maintain safety standards within each environment. In practice, most work roles consist of a mixture of the patterns identified. The patterns are a result of natural factors – you cannot wish away the hazards involved in nuclear fuel, hot metals, dangerous drugs or contagious diseases. But responses to them and the effectiveness of methods and procedures are partly a result of social and cultural influences related to the value in which those employed in the occupation are held. Values affect the concern for individual welfare, the development of health and safety legislation and training, and the provision of welfare benefits for industrial injury and disease, all of which are cultural, historical and changeable. The natural and cultural environments have interacted to produce the current practices and expectations. A good example of this was the Bohpal accident, where an American company was shown to be using practices in its Indian factory which would not have been tolerated in the West. The history of industrial relations and industrial development is littered with examples of changing values affecting health and safety practice.

THE NATURE OF QUALITY MEASURES

The second aspect of the work environment to impact on work roles and modify work role expectations is essentially a consequence of the purpose of the occupation – the nature of the quality measures. The nature of measurement which is applied in different occupations relates to its concepts of quality. Broadly, there are two ways of assessing quality in the outcomes achieved, the first relating to a focus on products and the latter relating to a focus on services.

1. In environments where tangible products are produced judgements focus on the **object** which is produced. The judgements therefore tend to be seen as objective and external to the person who is making them because there are an independent product and (usually) precise measuring instruments. In production systems, quality processes and inspection points are set up to trap errors before they do further damage. An error trap is a point at which an error or potential error may be noticed by the individual or others before it becomes irretrievable or critical.
2. In interactive and service environments there are no products as such and judgements focus on the **subject** – the person who is undertaking the activity. Consequently judgements tend to be seen as subjective, as they are attached to the process rather than the product. In such occupations quality measures are attached to the process of service delivery or interaction and the optimisation of client needs. Such occupations generally do not have the error traps which are found in production environments. In service provision, the outcome is achieved at the point of service delivery – a plate of food dropped in a customer's lap or a slip of the scissors leaving an asymmetric fringe cannot be 'trapped' – and the error is both critical and, apart from apologies and compensation, irretrievable.

The differences between product and service environments can take on cultural and social significance leading to misunderstanding and downright suspicion. Engineers and manufacturers may distrust any form of assessment which is less rigorous than precise measurement and which does not provide hard, objective evidence. On the other hand, people in service occupations may dismiss the concept of the measurement of competence as mechanistic or partial. Their concern is with what is often called 'holistic assessment' where the whole process of interaction is included. In truth, both parties are seeking measures of quality, but it is the nature of the measurement which differs.

We also find that sectors make claims about quality measures which are more to do with the work culture than the nature of the measures themselves. For example, product standards in mechanical engineering are usually expressed as measurements of the dimensional accuracy of metal-based products and components. Other quality measures, often treated as subordinate, describe appearance and finish, but with nothing like the same degree of precision. This way of describing product standards – dimensional accuracy – is so prevalent that it can be elevated in importance and can be perceived as the most important measurement for any manufactured item.

By contrast, product standards in clothing manufacture tend to focus on appearance and finish as these are more critical, whilst dimensional accuracy, although important, is able to fluctuate over a wider range of tolerance because it is not so critical and is easier to rectify. This can lead to the argument that product standards in engineering are more rigorous than those in clothing manufacture, whereas they are in fact just different, this difference reflecting the nature of the materials and the purpose for which the product is being manufactured.

This lack of understanding – that quality measures may be expressed differently for different products and services – can cause confusion even within industries or sectors. In the manufacture of aircraft engines the requirements for dimensional accuracy are extremely rigorous because the consequences of inaccuracy, and consequent failure, can be catastrophic. To achieve this high level of precision more time is allowed to manufacture the products and components which are, consequently, much more expensive than equivalent items manufactured for uses which are less critical.

Aircraft engineers, therefore, learn to manufacture products extremely accurately, but they take longer than a colleague working in a less-critical sector of manufacture. In less-critical sectors, the time allowed is much less but the tolerances allowed are more generous. An ill-fitting suit may not do much for the individual's self-confidence or appearance but it is unlikely to have catastrophic outcomes. Thus, in each environment the two key factors of time allowed and tolerance allowed are optimised against the criticality and value of the product.

These differences also apply to working methods. Aircraft engines may be assembled in dust-free environments, where great care is taken to avoid any possible contamination to critical components. Components are carefully handled, cleaned and carefully assembled – all of which takes time.

If individuals transfer from one sector of manufacturing to another, we might expect aircraft engineers to find it quite difficult to adapt to manufacturing operations where there is a less rigorous requirement for product accuracy. This is because the quality measure of dimensional accuracy may have achieved such a pre-eminent position in the individuals' approach to work that, although they possess the basic engineering skills, they need to adjust to the different nature of the quality measures to be seen as competent in other arenas within engineering.

This has an impact on our understanding of the concepts of flexibility, adaptability and transfer. It is not enough to identify basic skills which we presume will transfer to different work roles within and between occupational sectors or enable individuals to adapt quickly to new work requirements. What we have demonstrated is that the 'Managing the interface with the work environment' component of the Job Competence Model is as much a topic for the vocational curriculum as the technical expectations. If this component is not part of the learning process and people are simply expected to adapt to new forms of quality measures as their work roles change, we might end up with some extremely well-made lawnmowers, but some rather inadequate aeroplanes.

THE NATURE OF WORK ORGANISATION

So far we have looked at environmental factors which are fundamentally natural in origin: the nature of the work environment and, second, the nature of the quality measures employed. In both instances cultural considerations may have an effect on practice. The third aspect of the work environment is related to the first two, but is more heavily weighted to cultural and social decisions regarding how work should be organised and the degrees of freedom within which people are able to make decisions and take responsibility for their own actions.

In some environments there will be naturally imposed constraints on freedom of action. Environments which are a combination of hazardous locations and hazardous materials and equipment (referred to above) are such an example. Here, the degrees of freedom which are allowed to individuals will be constrained by the methods and procedures which have been developed to constrain and reduce the risks to themselves and others. Similarly, in environments where individual decision making may have a direct effect on the health and wellbeing of others, such as acute wards in hospitals or passenger aeroplanes, there will be procedures designed to control who can make decisions, when and in what circumstances. More often, however, freedom to act is a function of culture. Job design and work organisation patterns are usually based on values concerned with individual responsibility, capability and potential contribution.

The broad patterns of work organisation are quite distinct:

- keeping closely to set guidelines and procedures;
- making decisions between limited, usually predetermined, options;
- developing criteria and using one's own judgement to decide within broad parameters.

Such patterns may be typical of certain occupations. For example, creative or design-oriented occupations tend towards the open model whereas large-scale assembly plants and bureaucracies tend towards the closed. These different degrees of freedom may also exist within one role, often reflecting the balance between natural and cultural constraints. For example, an architect:

- keeps closely to procedures when dealing with building regulations;
- offers limited options to clients in instances where the design problem has limited solutions, such as in the size of doors;
- develops broad criteria to describe and use creative judgements to visualise the general appearance of a building.

Consequently there are a range of work environments where individual responsibility can be severely constrained, or positively encouraged, and these degrees of freedom will have an impact on the nature of work expectations. So, for example, concepts like initiative, common sense and responsibility, and common skills like decision making, problem solving and personal effectiveness, will have quite different meanings in different settings. Being personally effective in some environments will mean following the rules, concentrating only on your own work and doing what you are told; in others it will mean making decisions, taking responsibility, generating ideas and co-operating with others.

THE NATURE OF WORKING RELATIONSHIPS

The fourth and final aspect of the work environment which affects the model of competence concerns the nature of working relationships. Working relationships are partly a result of the natural environment but are heavily influenced by culture. In retail sales, for example, the customer is a natural part of the environment, as he or she is an essential part of the process, but the way in which customers are treated is a result of cultural influences. Work-role expectations are partly formed by who individuals interact with in their work roles and the basis of these interactions, and partly by the nature of the interactions which take place.

There are two important groups which form the basis of interaction within working relationships: service users and colleagues. Within these two categories there are subcategories relating to the degrees of dependence and power which are brought to each of the relationships. The first group, service users, is usually **external** to the organisation, although organisations are increasingly seeing their operations and functions as a series of 'internal markets' with functional specialists providing internal customers with services such as training, design, purchasing and logistics. Our definition would also include these groups. Such groups are involved with three broad patterns of relationships.

PATTERN 1: SERVICES WHICH ACT FOR INDIVIDUALS AND GROUPS

Such services enable individuals and groups to do, or do for them, what they are unable to do for themselves. In these services the service provider has expertise (knowledge and skills) such as legal advice, accountancy services, health care and design services which the service user wishes or needs to access. The service user may pay for the services or there may be some form of state support. Here the service providers have greater power in the sense that they have expertise which the service user cannot access easily or directly. These forms of relationship are often subject to external controls such as professional codes of conduct.

PATTERN 2: SERVICES WHICH ACT ON INDIVIDUALS AND GROUPS

Such services require individuals and groups to do certain things, since the service user is under a degree of compulsion to use the service whether they wish to do so or not. Such services will include children under the age of 16 in schools, offenders placed under the jurisdiction of probation officers, individuals confined to prison on remand or on sentence, individuals in psychiatric hospitals 'sectioned' under the Mental Health Act and all of us who come under the control of the Inland Revenue for tax purposes. Within these relationships one would expect to see degrees of tension between the aims of the service provider and the interest of the service users who are constrained. Expectations will include the need for workers to be able to diffuse or manage conflicting tensions. Within these contexts there are also likely to be clear codes of practice as to the rights of the service user and the responsibilities of the service provider to them.

PATTERN 3: SERVICES WHERE INDIVIDUALS ACT WITH OTHERS

Such services are characterised by users who choose to interact with them, such as the entertainment industries, the travel industry and sales interactions which enable customers to access products or services. The nature of the sales relationship will relate to factors such as whether the customer has an identified need, their purchasing power and degree of choice, and the pressure to buy which is placed on them.

These three broad patterns of relationship between service users and service providers which characterise certain work environments will themselves contain different role expectations. For example, sales skills which are assumed by many to be common to most, if not all, selling contexts may be modified by different relationships within the sales environment. The key relationships which distinguish sales environments are shown in Table 4.1.

Relationships with other people in the work environment may include one's employers, managers, those working at the same level in the organisation's hierarchy, those for whom one has responsibility and those in other functionally separate work roles. Here, too, we have identified three broad patterns.

Cold selling

In cold selling relationships the salesperson has to establish contact with customers who have exhibited no intent to buy and who have not identified a need for the product or service. Examples would be cold calling by telephone, either structured (selecting categories of the most likely customers) or unstructured (selecting at random), face-to-face cold calling, propositioning (such as sales people in the exit doors of supermarkets handing out leaflets or demonstrators in stores). These kinds of sales often relate to products and services where there is little interest in gaining customer commitment over time, as these are usually high-value, one-off products and customers are not likely to make more than one purchase.

Persuading customers to choose your option

Some customers may have already made a decision to buy (or have at least indicated a willingness to consider buying), but they have not identified the particular product or service which they want. Customers may be shopping around and comparing prices and other factors, or just observing goods on sale and waiting for a particular item to appeal to them. In these sales transactions the salesperson will need to be able to describe features, advantages and benefits and to develop skills of closing the sale. This interaction may also involve the skills of initiating transactions. In professional occupations this process may be the first stage of a client relationship, the stage at which the client is identifying and choosing suppliers of professional services. In such instances the initiation of a transaction may involve highly complex skills and capabilities like presenting proposals, preparing and submitting tenders and making competitive presentations.

Associated product selling

Where the customer has already purchased a product or service, or made a clear commitment to purchase, the role of the salesperson is to suggest associated products which enhance or complement the item or service. The prime example (which has reached the level of a joke) is the shoe salesperson who suggests shoe polish, waterproofing sprays, laces, etc. Other examples are car sales staff who suggest enhancements, accessories and related car purchasing schemes, travel sales staff who recommend holiday insurance and computer sales staff advising on software, printers, storage devices and maintenance contracts. Increasingly associated sales provide essential services without which the product cannot be used and which offer greater profit margins than the actual product, which can be heavily discounted to attract the customer. Examples are mobile phones, where the main profit is in selling air time, and computer game consoles, where the main profit is in the sale of the software.

Advising customers to optimise choice and benefits

Some sales relationships are initiated by the customer who has a general need, which they clearly wish to be met, but they also need advice on which product or service best meets their needs. This involves the salesperson helping the customer identify their needs and then helping them optimise their choice – which is often a balance between the customer's stated needs and the most profitable option for the organisation or individual. Financial services are a good example of this type. This pattern is also typical of professional practice where the professional is offering advice and options and helping the client choose the alternative which gives the optimum benefit.

Taking orders for specific products

Many sales people simply take orders. There may be limited products which customers simply choose and take to ordering points, or customers may have a perfectly clear idea of exactly what they want ('I'd like that camera in the window please'). This may also apply to professional practice – surveyors are simply instructed to arrange a house survey. This role will also involve giving advice and complex reporting, but the initiation of the sale is still an order from the customer.

Table 4.1: The sales relationship and the sales environment

PATTERN 1: INTERDEPENDENT TEAM WORK

The most common and increasingly important working relationship is inter-dependent team work where the actions of one individual directly impact on those of another and where the individuals working within the team have a common purpose. Such teams may be more or less closely interconnected. For example, in health care, the dental team of dentist and dental nurse usually requires closely co-ordinated working, with the dentist unable to proceed before the materials and equipment have been prepared; this is the same for surgical teams in hospitals where the actions of one member are closely dependent on those of another. Other teams are working towards the same outcomes but their individual actions may occur at different times or they make take on roles which can be more clearly separated. Primary health care teams consisting of general practitioners, practice nurses, practice managers, receptionists and other health-care workers will have as their overall aim the promotion and maintenance of the health and well-being of the population which they serve. This will be achieved by each member of the team undertaking quite separate activities but passing on relevant information and seeking advice and support from others in the team. Interdependent team work is becoming more common as people are expected to be multiskilled and work in multidisciplinary project teams made up of members from different areas of work working together for the same purpose. Such teams usually take on important task management responsibilities in addition to their technical roles.

Interdependent work teams may occur within or across organisational boundaries. With the recent changes in health and social care in the UK there are increasing demands for 'a seamless service of care' with teams being formed from individuals employed by the NHS, social service and independent agencies work- ing towards common goals such as the care of individuals with mental health needs. In construction projects, development teams may be drawn from a number of organisations, each supplying its own individual area of expertise, such as architects, surveyors and engineers. Since these teams may be drawn from dif- ferent organisations, this increases the need for effective communication and will include expectations related to negotiating with others, offering and asking for assistance, finding out the needs of colleagues and co-operating in the scheduling of work.

PATTERN 2: WORKING IN PROXIMITY BUT WHERE THE ROLES ARE NOT INTERDEPENDENT

There are some environments in which individuals work in proximity to each other but their roles are not interdependent. The main expectations are for individuals to get on with each other rather than the additional expectations related to interdependent team working. Examples include individuals in open-plan offices who share the same office space but who focus on different work activities and sales teams who each have their own personal portfolio of customers.

What this analysis suggests is that team environments vary from, at one extreme, close involvement to achieve a common purpose to working in proximity at the other. The term 'team-working skills' is often used to relate to both but needs clearer definition to clarify the real expectations.

PATTERN 3: LITTLE DIRECT CONTACT BETWEEN INDIVIDUALS

Other work environments may be typified as having little direct contact between individuals. Such roles would include much agricultural work, mobile sales representatives, long-distance lorry drivers and some auditing work. While many of these roles may be characterised as having high technical expectations of individuals, interpersonal relationship demands are few although there may be requirements to obtain one's own work. There will also be expectations relating to working effectively, honestly and without supervision.

In practice, particular roles will consist of a mixture of these different types of relationships. Agricultural workers may spend much of the year working on their own but at harvest time may be expected to work in interdependent teams with severe time pressures related to harvesting the product when it is at its optimum condition during fine weather periods. Architects will need to work effectively with clients to advise, inform and persuade, work with different disciplinary specialists in project teams, maintain effective relationships with colleagues in the office and take responsibility for their own work when working at home or on urgently needed plans. GPs will spend much of their time working directly with patients, assessing needs and planning and monitoring treatment. However, they also need to communicate with other health and social care practitioners to ensure that patients receive the best treatment possible, encourage and persuade patients to take effective health care measures for themselves and negotiate with colleagues about the organisation and management of the practice and provision of effective services.

The other aspect of work relationships which needs to be considered is the nature of the interactions which take place. Two broad patterns of approach can be identified which form the two ends of a spectrum. The first pattern can be termed an enabling and empowering approach, and the second a controlling approach. These two approaches may characterise interactions with service users and also interactions with others with whom one works in the organisation.[2]

APPROACH 1: THE ENABLING AND EMPOWERING APPROACH

The enabling and empowering approach is characterised by expectations that individuals will seek options from, and offer choices to, the people with whom they work. The values which underpin this approach are based on the view that all individuals have the capability to be self-managing and self-motivated and should be empowered to control their own lives. Within organisations, this style of management is characterised by encouraging and enabling individuals to take responsibility for their own work and its quality, empowering them to make suggestions for improvement and giving them opportunities to challenge practice constructively in order to improve products and services. The enabling and empowering form of management is strongly associated with the principles of total quality management. In relation to service users, the enabling and empowering approach would see service users as individuals and groups with their own unique abilities, needs and wishes. Work-role expectations would include empowering service users to participate fully in the design and delivery of services, encouraging individuals to make their own informed decisions about choices and enabling individuals to develop their own skills and knowledge.

APPROACH 2: THE CONTROLLING APPROACH

The controlling approach to interaction is in direct contrast to the enabling and empowering approach. The values on which this approach are based can be characterised by views that individuals generally need to be controlled as they do not have the knowledge, skills or motivation to act responsibly on their own. The controlling view of management would see a manager's role as to oversee and police the work of their subordinates through rigid procedures, continual inspection and the use of threats or inducements. Requirements for some groups of the workforce to clock on and clock off whilst others work without such controls portray values about those who can be trusted and those who cannot. Schools which require all children to be out of the school buildings during breaks emphasise the fact that the children cannot be trusted to act responsibly inside.

In service occupations the controlling view sees service provision as fitting in with the needs of the service organisation and its employees rather than the needs of those whom the service is there to serve. *In extremis*, service users may be seen as an inconvenience to be controlled, leading to the ironic complaint 'this school/ hospital/shop would run much more smoothly if it weren't for the pupils/ patients/customers'. More seriously, in this kind of environment service users are often starved of information and schedules are arranged to meet the administrative needs of the organisation.

In practice, most organisations fall somewhere between the extremes of these two models. We should also recognise that many service providers are consciously attempting to move themselves from a controlling to a more enabling approach.

JOB COMPETENCE MODEL – A SUMMARY

The Job Competence Model provides an approach to describing occupational competence by identifying four key components in work roles which reflect the complexity of work. These are summarised in

Occupational competence means being able to meet the technical requirements specific to the occupation, manage and control breakdowns and variance, co-ordinate different activities to meet overall objectives, and adapt and modify to meet the requirements of different environments. This is a shift from a concentration on operations and activities to a concern with function, purpose and the description of the subtleties of the complete work role.

Managing different work activities
(Task Management)
achieving balance and coordinating a number of activities

Managing contingency
(Contingency Management)
recognising and resolving potential and actual breakdowns in processes and procedures

Work Activities
(a number of Technical Expectations)

technical expectation	technical expectation	technical expectation	technical expectation

interaction between outcomes and processes (technical expectations, contingency and task management) and the context of work (organisational and cultural environment)

Managing the Interface with the Work Environment
the organisational and cultural environment in which work takes place

NATURAL CONSTRAINTS	QUALITY MEASURES	WORK ORGANISATION	WORKING RELATIONSHIPS
Location Intrinsic characteristics of materials and equipment	Quality focused on the 'object' (usually tangible products) Quality focused on the 'subject' (actions of the person)	Keeping closely to set guidelines and procedures Making decisions between limited options Developing criteria and using judgements to decide within broad parameters	Service users: acting **for**; acting **on**; acting **with** Colleagues: interdependent work team; contact with others but not interdependent; little direct contact with others Nature of interaction: enabling and empowering; controlling

Fig. 4.2 The Job Competence Model

The Job Competence Model proposes a considerable expansion to the concept of occupational competence. In the past, occupational competence has often been expressed as the ability to apply skills and perform tasks to standards. To this has been added – not integrated, just added – a number of additional constructs designed to compensate for the narrowness of many jobs and which also attempts to align occupational competence with the real needs of the economy, variously described as adaptability, flexibility and willingness to change and take additional responsibility.

Having briefly described the different models of competence which exist and explained the Job Competence Model in detail, we explore in the next chapter the links between competence and standards.

NOTES

1. In Mansfield and Mathews, *The Job Competence Model*, the authors proposed that there were three interrelated components of occupational competence which could be described as:

   - task skills;
   - task management skills, which are used when there are a number of tasks to do, where additional activities or responsibilities are required, or where problems and difficulties occur;
   - role/job environment skills, which relate to managing the work context.

   This original definition has since been refined, principally by Mansfield, to suggest that the task management category has in fact two components – task management and contingency management. See particularly, Mansfield and Mathews, *The Components of Job Competence*; Mansfield, 'Competence – two views'; Mansfield, 'Competence and standards'.

2. Examples of such approaches may be found in a range of literature. For example, in relation to the health and social care sector: Smale and Tuson, *Empowerment, assessment, care management and the skilled worker*; Labonte, 'Health promotion and empowerment: reflections on professional practice'. In relation to management: Moss Kanter, *When Giants Learn to Dance*; Harvey and Brown, *An Experiential Approach to Organisation Development*; Kilmann, *Beyond the Quick Fix*.

5 Competence and standards

The Job Competence Model gradually emerged in response to a series of problems which arose as the NTI vision, realised through the YTS objectives, threw up contradictions and tensions between the rapid changes in the nature of work and the traditional tools of training design. Although the concept of outcomes had been introduced as a potential replacement for the language of tasks and skills, the detail of how this might be done was still elusive.

YTS providers and designers needed help in planning work-based learning, off-job training and the assessment systems to generate evidence for the YTS Certificate. The processes involved were set out in the YTS design criteria and involved:

- Setting up work placements for trainees with local employers. The trainees could be employed by the placement provider, but more often were not employed. Arranging different placements was designed to encourage transferability; originally three placements within the one year scheme were required.
- Alternatively, employing the trainee in a single organisation but allowing placements in different departments.
- Planning a structured programme of learning and assessment within the work placement.
- Linking learning in the work placement with off-job training which could take place in an educational establishment or a training centre. This could be linked to a formal vocational qualification where an appropriate one existed.
- Accumulating the assessment information and producing a certificate of achievement.

YTS was faced with a serious problem. Employers were accustomed to vocational training systems and vocational qualifications which were usually based on attendance at a college course and assessed by a mixture of skills tests and traditional qualifications. In these systems, three important things were standardised. Trainees followed a standardised curriculum, collected evidence of competence or engaged in tests and examination under standardised conditions, and were assessed using standardised assessment criteria and marking systems. This gave enormous face credibility to the traditional systems – even though, in practice, employers were often unaware of the precise nature of the curriculum content away from the workplace. Indeed, the criticism of the relevance of the vocational curriculum was one important reason for the original NTI review. Yet many employers believed in traditional vocational qualifications. This apparent irony was noted in the final report of the Certification Project,[1] a project set up to provide regional certification in YTS.

> The picture of ... traditional vocational qualifications ... is one of formal and strict control over the assessment process. It is this control which gives status to ... [vocational] ... qualifications. The key factor is *standardisation*, or the application of uniformity over each stage of the learning and assessment process. Most employers have no idea of the actual content of a GCE O Level mathematics syllabus – indeed many employers have no clear idea of the content of vocational qualifications which they value highly. It can be contended that credibility in these instances derives from that fact that content, conditions and processes are standardised in such a uniform way that the 'user' of the qualification (the employer) is able to feel confident that a standard content has been tested in a standard way to standard criteria. The precise nature of the content, conditions and processes appears to be less important than this general perception of standardisation and subsequent belief in it.

The problem with work-based learning and accreditation is that it offers considerable variance in all the factors which appear to offer credibility to traditional examination and skill-testing systems. Workplaces are variable, so what is learned and how it is learned will vary, the conditions under which evidence of achievement is collected are variable and the assessment process is variable. What was needed was a standardised curriculum based on the activities of the work environment with a standardised method of work-based assessment. Without this, learning could not be systematically planned and achievement would not be recognised.

We need to understand that this process of standardisation is not designed simply to generate a more standardised and reliable system of learning and assessment for its own sake. What was at stake was the issue of validity. To retain the validity offered by both workplace learning and assessment, it was necessary for one of the variables to be standardised so that learners and assessors had a 'benchmark' against which to plan learning and judge performance. This notion of a benchmark is important and underlines the search for a quality system.

The reduction of unnecessary variation is a key factor in total quality management systems and is pursued to improve quality assurance processes. Without an integrated approach to product and service design it is quite possible to design different products, components and services to meet needs as they arise, and to end up with a number of different products or services which achieve the same function but which create additional quality assurance problems because of the diversity of specifications and activities required to produce them. This can be resolved by an integrated approach to design where components are designed to maximise the achievement of the core function. Note that this is not an averaging process where functional compromises have to be made, but one which maximises functionality and general applicability.

For example, a car manufacturer may discover that many different types of door handle have been designed for different models of car developed over a number of years. This means that the manufacturing system will have different designs which have to be updated, different supply specifications, different manufacturing specifications and different inspection and quality assurance checks. This unnecessary variation generates quality assurance problems – quite simply, there are more things which can go wrong. An integrated design approach is to have at best one, but at least the minimum number of door handle designs as can be accommodated for the different models of car. Allowable variations may include different designs for different grade or model style, but within one grouping there would be, ideally, a single design.

This elimination of variance helps contribute to quality assurance. The integrated design would be achieved by concentrating on functionality – what are the essential characteristics of a car door handle – and how can this be generalised to fit existing body shells with minimum disruption and to look right on all appropriate models.

This is not to argue for standardisation for its own sake. Eliminating variance and concentrating on functionality reduces quality assurance variations but also allows the designers to concentrate on the parts of the car which will vary and offer the diversity of different models and grades within a model range.

This process is a principle of total quality management and can be used as an analogy to show why it is desirable to have a single set of specifications for work role expectations within an occupational sector. But standardisation has its limits – bounded by functionality.

Let us take a different example. A product manufacturer observes that many different types of screw fastener are used for a variety of products and decides to eliminate variation by specifying a single screw fastener. This is a dangerous thing to do because the screw fasteners in different products, although apparently similar, may be designed to perform many different functions. The fasteners may support different components with different weights, may be subject to different levels of vibration, tension and stress, or may be hidden or visible to the user. Each of these functional differences needs to be taken into account when fasteners are specified before, within each functional grouping, the minimum number of types can be specified.

What this suggests is that **commonality** – or elimination of variance – only works within functional boundaries. Apparent similarity needs to be tested against functional similarity. Thus, the car-door handle needs to be specified functionally as: 'a mechanism which will enable the user to open and shut a car door manufactured from metal panels and components, horizontally, securely and safely and will enable the door to be locked against potential intruders. The handle mechanism should be secure enough to maintain its function when the car is travelling at its maximum speed and additional safety features should enable adult users to adjust rear doors to be incapable of opening from the inside'. This is a functional specification. This kind of specification separates a car-door handle from a door handle in a house and separates a car-door handle from the locking mechanism of a car boot. To try to extend the common specification to cover all door handles or all fastening mechanisms on a car would clearly be fruitless because important differences in function would be obscured. This was described in the Certification Project[2] – how to optimise the need for standardisation with the flexibility inherent in the range of experiences and achievement within the learning programme.

The Certification Project developed common analyses for each occupational sector, aligned to the outcome statements in the OTF Work Learning Guides. This gave a standardised and consistent format for both learning design and assessment. This was the start of the development process which produced functional analysis and gave a clearer focus to the description of occupational standards.

Some comments from organisations which were using the original analyses[3] designed for processing occupations (which at the time were referred to as modules) demonstrate both support for the approach and the concern that the task analyses being used were not able to keep up with current technologies, nor identify the non-task aspects of competence:

> It [the module] describes every operation within the factory ... *within the last five years we have changed our process activities from hand operations to sophisticated micro processor led systems. Our operators are now required to interpret VDU information, care for high cost equipment, attend and participate in regular consultative meetings. Today's operator requires a high level of knowledge, developed communication and monitoring skills* ... this ... will certainly give us ideas for extending our YTS programme. (Frozen Food Plant – Training Manager)

> Operators need to *understand implications relating to build-up of back pressure in flow systems in terms of materials costs/loss and cost implications if readings are not taken regularly on products prior to baking. Factory jobs are not what they used to be. We now expect our personnel to have an increased responsibility for noticing and reporting problems* as our Supervisor ratio has gone from 1:12 to 1:60 ... The model seems to indicate a basis for training of the young people which would relate much more to the work we do. (Bakery Chain – Training Officer)

It was in response to the sorts of issues expressed above, by the employer partners in the scheme, that the Job Competence Model gradually started to change. The issue of contingency was the first to be seriously addressed. The researchers in the Certification Project started to identify irregularities – those aspects of tasks which were not part of the routine and which could be unpredictable. A report from the project consultant describes this stage of development:

> For example, a trainee might be in a placement where they are involved in photocopying. The task analysis can capture the 'basic skills' (those necessary to fulfil the ... learning ... objective), but cannot easily express general levels of responsibility – except by creating different task analyses. So if a trainee is responsible for replacing consumables and printing medium, including ordering new supplies, a different analysis would be needed to cope with this additional element. The effect is to generate a different analysis for each variation within workplaces.

Other significant variations occur when trainees act outside of normal operating procedures, or take on responsibilities which are accepted [by the employer] as being 'higher level' skills and competences. In the photocopying example, employers would immediately discriminate between trainees who can replace toner medium when the appropriate light showed on the operating panel, and those who are able to anticipate future needs by ordering supplies in advance from the supplier.

The first solution [to this problem] was to extract all the non routine elements from the bank of analyses and group them below the task analysis – they were labelled 'irregularities' or 'contingencies'.[4]

Table 5.1 shows an example of one of these analyses. A number of important points can be drawn from this example:

Occupational Training Family 1: Information Processing
Module: Reproducing copies of documents and information
Is the trainee able to:

Performance objectives (all to be achieved together)

(a) Reproduce copies which are square on the paper, free from unwanted marks or smudges, to schedule and of the correct size/type/quality of paper, density and quantity
(b) Follow company procedures for security and confidentiality
(c) Keep the working area visibly clean and tidy

Additional objectives (can be achieved individually)

(d) Start up equipment, according to the manufacturers instructions
(e) Deliver copies and originals to the next stage in the process to the correct person/location(s), to schedule
(f) Provide written records in copy record book accurately, legibly, completely and to schedule
(g) Restock equipment with correct type/quantity of paper, correct type/quantity of ink/printing medium (as appropriate) and to schedule
(h) Clean, use and maintain the equipment according to the manufacturer's instructions
(i) Shut down the equipment according to the manufacturer's instructions

Dealing with irregularities (can be achieved individually)

(j) Reproduce copies to user's requirements without a formal specification
(k) Maintain supplies of consumables for current and future needs
(l) Diagnose faults within the operators responsibilities
(m) Seek technical assistance promptly for faults which are outside the operator's responsibility

---

Table 5.1 An example of a Learning and Assessment Model

- The title of the analysis (called a 'module') is an outcome statement taken from the Occupational Training Family Work Learning Guide, in this case OTF 1 Processing Documents and Information.
- The criteria are stated as learning objectives written as task instructions, although the phraseology anticipates the **evaluative phrase** used for performance criteria in occupational standards.
- There is a distinction between 'performance objectives' and 'additional objectives' which were an indication of level in the original scheme.

- The section 'dealing with irregularities' contains components of both task management (Maintain supplies of consumables for current and future needs) and contingency management (Diagnose faults within the operator's responsibilities).

The report continues:

A particular problem was that some contingencies recurred constantly – for example in retail analyses contingencies dealing with effective customer relationships appeared in almost every analysis, and health and safety also featured in most of the tasks as well. This led to the first attempt to distinguish what were called 'general work skills' which seemed to be characteristic of particular occupations rather than contingencies deriving from specific tasks. [*This was a critical observation – contingency arises in the context of the technical expectations – managing the work environment is common across an occupation.*]

The issues raised at YHAFHE [the Yorkshire and Humberside Association for Further and Higher Education] paralleled the development of the occupational competence model. [*The original title of the Job Competence Model. It was changed to the Job Competence Model because of the YTS emphasis on 'competence in a job'.*] To fully reflect the complexity of job competence, the YHAFHE project wished to treat the contingency elements and general work skills seriously – at the same time it was becoming apparent that the task and core analysis being used were themselves falling short of the notion of occupational competence.

What the occupational competence model offered was the ability to put these rather vague ideas into a tighter conceptual framework – contingencies were redefined as 'task management skills' and the general work skills as 'role/job environment skills' ... they were ... incorporated ... into a framework referred to as 'Learning and Assessment Model'. [*In subsequent developments of the Job Competence Model, contingency was separated from task management to become 'contingency management'.*][5]

Other comments about the nature of this new model are significant:

The YHAFHE team developed the idea of a functional analysis[6] (the Learning and Assessment Model) ... in which ... the elements are displayed using the 'core analysis' technique which identifies and references the YTS core skill which is being employed.

The significance of this model is that it takes serious note of the task management element, and is currently being implemented. The methodology is economic in that only eighteen analyses are required to accommodate the range of clerical and administrative functions (early versions of task analyses which accounted for variations in practice could run into the hundreds).[7]

The Learning and Assessment Model (LAM) was the forerunner of an occupational standard. As contingency management had been associated with the application of the task skills, contingencies in the form of breakdowns in procedure were incorporated into the list of performance objectives, not separated as in the example analysis shown above.

Three different types of LAM eventually emerged which expressed the different components of the Job Competence Model. This development was anticipated in the final report of the Certification Project:

There is a need to explore methods of summarising the task management skills and to include the role and environment management skills within the model, probably by providing superordinate LAMs which will identify those task management skills that are used to integrate a number of tasks within a role, and those skills which are specific to the environment. There could also be ... a short series of LAMs, universal in application and independent of functional areas ... covering such themes as role and environment management, relationships at work and health and safety.[8]

The presentation of the performance objectives was changed by splitting the activity description from the evaluative phrases. The actions, called 'occupational skills' were described using the 'core skill keyword', and 'performance criteria', phrased in the passive tense, were placed next to each occupational skill. These were Occupational LAMs, specific to the technical skills of each occupation.

The role/job environment skills were separated and listed beneath the occupational skills, and because they tended to be common to each LAM they were eventually grouped together as Common LAMs. The co-ordinating task management components were separately stated in Task Management LAMs – which had an overarching function – providing a context in which the occupational LAMs were achieved.

Table 5.2 shows examples of LAMs developed for the materials processing sector in 1986 (the first two are occupational) showing contingencies embedded in the performance criteria and also demonstrating that some role environment skills are common. The second covers aspects of task management:

This tracking of the process of development shows that the Job Competence Model was being developed and used to provide answers to a particular problem in youth training: standardising learning and assessment processes. This process of standardisation could have led to a highly proceduralised view of competence, as indeed was the case in early developments. The Job Competence Model was developed in response to concerns about this process of proceduralisation and was seen as a model which could help retain the essential concept of occupational breadth and consequently a broad view of competence which was an explicit aim of the original NTI.

The Job Competence Model also provided clearer and more operational descriptions of the capabilities which employers valued but for which they had no precise language. The new demands of the changing economy were described in such vague terms that few could agree on their meaning, causing considerable confusion when attempts were made to address them seriously in training pro-grammes and assessment systems. Constructs like common sense, flexibility, communication skills and personal effectiveness were not, and are not, standard-ised terms with a common meaning. The Job Competence Model was an attempt to focus on the outcomes which people recognised when common sense was applied and the different circumstances and outcomes which resulted from the application of communication skills, and the whole model provided a metaphor for concepts like flexible and adaptable.

This is not to suggest that the Job Competence Model had an immediate or even lasting impact on VET. It was, eventually, adopted by both the Department

1.1. Receive and check bulk supplies of raw materials

Occupational skill	Performance criteria
CHECK delivery documentation against company order	Deliveries match orders Discrepancies are noticed and reported
ASSIST delivery personnel by identifying an unloading area	Loads are deposited in an approved location
OPERATE automatic transfer equipment	Manufacturer's procedures for the attachment, operation and detachment of automatic transfer/unloading equipment are followed
CHECK the quality and quantity of delivered goods	The correct quantity/weight is recorded The delivered quantity conforms to the order Discrepancies in quantity are noticed, recorded and reported Goods below quality specifications are noticed and reported
PROVIDE WRITTEN RECORDS of goods delivered	Records are complete, accurate and legible Records are passed to the next stage in the documentary system to schedule

Role Environment Skills	Performance criteria
MAINTAIN effective working relationships with delivery personnel	Appropriate language and behaviour are used Instructions and explanations are clear and accurate Appropriate assistance is offered
MONITOR the safety of the workplace	Hazards are identified and rectified or reported The working area is visibly free from hazards
CARRY OUT health and safety PROCEDURES	Routine health and safety checks and procedures are followed Health and safety procedures relating to hazardous materials and equipment are followed Safe working practices are adopted Loads are manually lifted and transported using an approved and safe method

1.2. Store and monitor raw/processed materials

Occupational skills	Performance criteria
LIFT and TRANSPORT goods manually	An approved/safe method is used
LIFT and TRANSPORT goods using electro-mechanical equipment/aids	Manufacturers procedures for starting up and operating equipment are followed Loads do not exceed safe load limits Safe working practices are adopted

Table 5.2 Occupational and task management Learning and Assessment Models

STORE GOODS by INTERPRETING codes and written descriptions	Goods are stored in the correct location Company procedures for stock rotation, date coding are followed Goods are stored in a manner which optimises available space
MONITOR the quality and condition of goods	Defective/damaged goods are noticed, stored and reported Routine/scheduled checks are carried out to schedule
PROVIDE WRITTEN RECORDS as required	Records are complete, accurate and legible
Role Environment Skills	**Performance Criteria**
MONITOR the safety of the workplace	Hazards are identified and rectified or reported The working area is visibly free from hazards
CARRY OUT health and safety PROCEDURES	Routine health and safety checks and procedures are followed Health and safety procedures relating to hazardous materials and equipment are followed Safe working practices are adopted

Task management: Monitor processing operations

Occupational skills	**Performance criteria**
MONITOR the availability of stocks and materials	Sufficient stock/material is available to ensure continuity of output
MONITOR the processing operation/NOTICE that things have gone wrong and that action is required	Output conforms to the specification Outputs below specification are noticed and rejected Machinery faults or malfunctions are noticed and reported before irretrievable damage has occurred Corrective action is taken within the operator's responsibility
DIAGNOSE and correct faults	Routine faults are diagnosed correctly Corrective action is taken within the operator's responsibility
EXPLAIN to others about problems that have occurred	Explanations are clear, complete and understandable
PROVIDE WRITTEN RECORDS of activities and faults	Records are complete, accurate and legible
Role environment skills	**Performance Criteria**
MONITOR the safety of the workplace	Hazards are identified and rectified or reported The working area is visibly free from hazards
CARRY OUT health and safety PROCEDURES	Routine health and safety checks and procedures are followed

Table 5.2 Occupational and task management Learning and Assessment Models (continued)

	Health and safety procedures relating to hazardous materials and equipment are followed Safe working practices are adopted
DECIDE on a correct response when accidents or emergencies occur	Action taken optimises down-time and personal safety Emergency procedures are followed

Table 5.2 Occupational and task management Learning and Assessment Models (concluded)

for Education and Employment and NCVQ as an example of how a broad notion of occupational competence could be embodied in both occupational standards and National Vocational Qualifications – but not without considerable debate and controversy. The Job Competence Model represents a point of divergence between two schools of thought which persist to the present day and which are implicit in the design of both occupational standards and qualifications.

We must always remember the context of YTS. The process which culminated in the standards programme and National Vocational Qualifications, for all levels of responsibility and sectors in the economy, originated in an initiative designed to provide training and accreditation for young people who, on the whole, had not succeeded at school and who tended to enter very limited occupational roles. The concept of occupational competence in manual trades and routine service and administrative occupations is dominated by a routine task view. Competence means being able to carry out a limited number of routine tasks and requires minimal manual and cognitive skills. In some occupations this atomisation of occupational competence is taken to an extreme – a legacy of the scientific management traditions of Fredrick Taylor. This view is usually associated with the requirement for compliance with management control systems and the slavish following of procedures.

If this is the concept of competence, then the descriptions of work activity which emerge will also be atomistic and task based, requiring little more than the following of structured routines.

A problem arises when this concept is applied to what are called 'higher-level roles'. Clearly the routine task approach does not apply, so such occupational groups demand that a different system of analysis and description is required. As we suggested in a previous section, such groups usually suggest that different analysis systems are needed for different types of occupational role.

But the problem is not that the task description is appropriate for 'lower' skill levels and hence needs to be replaced with alternative analysis systems at higher levels. The real problem is that in our advanced economy a task-based description is inadequate for all occupational roles. That was the central message of the Job Competence Model: that the view of competence proposed by the model is applicable to **all** occupations and **all** levels.

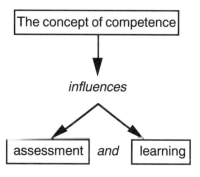

Fig. 5.1 The relationship between competence, assessment and learning

This insight, that our concept of occupational competence will directly influence the way in which working practice is described and the ways in which learning and accreditation will be modelled, can be expressed as a simple diagram (Figure 5.1).

If the view of competence is narrow and task based, learning will be designed in the same way and assessment will follow suit. Take industrial sewing as an example. Most of the clothing industry in the 1970s employed sewing machinists to perform extremely limited operations – usually a single seam type on one machine. Competence meant being able to do one very limited task very quickly and to high standards of accuracy. Very little else was required. Problems in scheduling work, machine breakdowns and quality control were in the hands of supervisors, mechanics and inspectors. Production lines were highly organised to pass part-finished garments from one operative to another so that each could perform their minute contribution. Payment was by piece-rate. Training was basic and limited to machine control and the performance of the single operation – anything more was regarded as a waste of resources. Machinists lacked flexibility – speed could only be assured and built up on long production runs – and the introduction of new styles caused severe disruption and usually required training in another minuscule job.

This concept of competence was justified in a number of ways. In the main, efficiency arguments were advanced. The method enabled garments to be produced quickly and to high standards in mass-production environments. But there were other, less subtle, reasons advanced. It was commonly held that since most sewing operatives were women they were not capable of carrying out routine maintenance and adjustment of sewing machines since women were not thought to be mechanically minded. Small routine tasks were better for women than more extensive and complex activities because women were mainly interested in 'pin-money' and had no commitment to career advancement or job satisfaction, their main focus being the home and children. They would also prefer a routine job which could be done without too much thought because this would allow them to chat with other women and work at the same time. Social values, therefore, provided a rationale for the concept of competence.

These views combined into a concept of occupational competence which was extremely limited and was also thought to be immutable. With some variations it was common in most other manufacturing sectors. Small wonder then that when standards were produced for sewing machinists they consisted of minute tasks concentrating on the sewing of a single seam.

By contrast, you do not have to travel too far to see a quite different concept of competence for the same occupational group. In Holland and Germany operatives in clothing factories are not described as 'machinists' but as 'garment workers' or 'garment assemblers'. In Holland and Germany in the 1970s clothing industry workers were expected to be able to contribute to the manufacture of whole garments, to adapt quickly to different jobs as production needs fluctuated and changed and as different styles of garment came into the factory. They were also expected to contribute to the management of the work process, to monitor the quality of their own products and maintain their own equipment and machinery. They were not paid on individual piece-rates but on a generous basic wage plus a team bonus. This was based on a broad view of competence – one more akin to that proposed by the Job Competence Model. Not surprisingly their training was complex and of much longer duration, and covered all machining skills combined with the other components of the Job Competence Model: the management of breakdowns (contingency management), the planning and scheduling of work (task management) and the skills of co-operation in work teams (managing the interface with the work environment).

This approach is rather more sympathetic in its assumptions about people's capability, but it was not just for this reason that German and Dutch companies adopted this broad concept of competence. Rather, it was because the clothing industries of both countries had rejected mass-production systems where the object is to produce cheap garments as quickly as possible. These industries had recognised that a more important market was for fast response, fashionable garments which offered the customer greater diversity – and manufacturing for this market required the ability to move jobs, change styles and contribute to production systems and processes. This fast-response market meant that it was impossible to set up complex production lines with the associated control systems, only to take down and rebuild the line when the style changed a week later.

By contrast the British industry was still dominated by mass-marketing approaches. One factory we visited in the early 1980s had been producing the same style and colour of shirt for a leading chain store for 17 years; this required little in the way of flexibility!

However, in other parts of Europe a market strategy which required flexible, adaptable workers influenced the expectations of competence. The training system was aligned to this new model. This is not to suggest that markets determine the view of competence. Markets can be discovered, developed and nurtured, and clear choices can be made to work in different market segments.

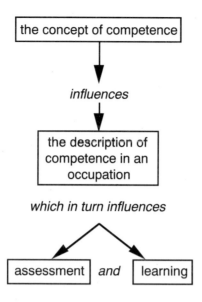

Fig. 5.2 Competence, assessment, learning and the description of competence

But it does show that a need for flexibility and adaptability to meet those new market requirements requires a redefinition of what we understand by occupational competence. And the trends are clear, as we pointed out in Chapter 2: markets of the type chosen by German and Dutch clothing industries are the markets of the future.

We have, then, a broad and a narrow view of competence. The narrow view is a survivor from traditional market activity where the object was to produce and distribute cheap goods quickly. The broad view is consistent with the economic changes which we have already described. But the narrow view lingers, largely because the justification for it has become embodied in beliefs about people, their capabilities and the relative status of different jobs. At worst, it is authoritarian and profoundly anti-democratic – and it is for that reason also that we firmly reject it.

But the idea that the view of competence (which varied between two distinct models) affected the structure of vocational education and training was to have an important impact. What is missing from Figure 5.1 is that between the concept of competence and the assessment and learning processes is the clear **description** of competence within the occupational context. That was what the ESF Core Project had been attempting to provide, in the form of the LAM, and what other people in YTS also provided, in the form of task analyses. The elaborated model is shown in Figure 5.2.

As attention turned towards the identification of occupational standards across whole industries and the National Council for Vocational Qualifications shifted into gear, this simple model gained important explanatory power. The focus also changed. In YTS we had been concerned with deriving assessment and learning

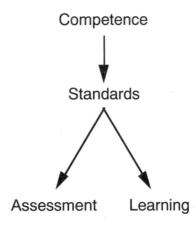

Fig. 5.3 Competence, standards, assessment and learning

materials in the absence of qualifications. The description of competence in an occupation, which in the Certification Project became the Learning and Assessment Model, was derived from assumptions about what people needed to learn and how they would be assessed. In the world of NCVQ, occupational sectors would be asked to identify occupational standards, from which learning and assessment systems would be defined, and the assessment systems would be used to demonstrate competence in the occupational standards which were also used to form qualifications.

The model changed to incorporate the new occupational standards shown in Figure 5.3. This demonstrated how the components of the VET system operated and we used it for many years to introduce the fundamental change which turned

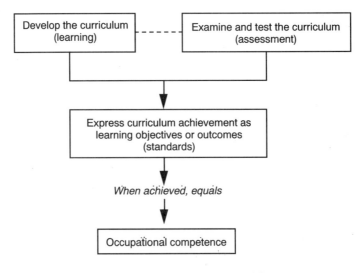

Fig. 5.4 The educational input model

the curriculum concept on its head. Previous systems had defined learning content, set up an assessment process and, from this, developed standards – the concept of learning outcomes. The learning outcomes, taken together, constituted occupational competence. This input-led model is shown in Figure 5.4.

The Competence, Standards, Assessment and Learning Model (which we called the CSAL Model) reverses this approach. It proposes that we need to start with a clear concept of occupational competence which is appropriate to the challenges of a modern economy. Using this concept to guide and structure the development process, we develop descriptions of what is expected in work roles, both now and in the future. These are occupational standards. From the standards we can derive the curriculum – what the individual needs to learn to achieve the standard – and the assessment system – how the individual will demonstrate that they have achieved the standard.

Thus, standards, learning and assessment are **separated**. This is critical, and is the key to the current VET system. It allows the separation of accreditation of competence from learning programmes. People are no longer obliged to attend a compulsory course to gain access to assessment because assessment is separated. The standards can be assessed independently from a learning programme.

Learning programmes, in this model, **support** the achievement of occupational standards. Attendance on the programme is not the standard in itself. This is widely misunderstood and has led to the claim that NVQs reject any formal learning process. This is not the case. Rather, NVQs are designed to be independent of the learning process, so many different learning processes can be used: learning in a structured work environment, open learning, formal learning. What is important is that formal learning programmes are not the only access route to assessment as was the case with traditional vocational education and training.

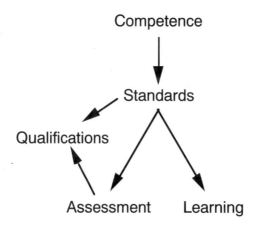

Fig. 5.5 Competence, standards, assessment, learning and qualifications

The final part of the CSAL Model explains the role of qualifications in this system (Figure 5.5). Qualifications (specifically, NVQs) are **selections** from a set of occupational standards which are subjected to a process of formal assessment. Learning is now completely separated from the qualification model, enabling previously acquired competence to be presented as evidence for assessment purposes. Interestingly, qualifications are also separated from standards, which opens the possibility that standards can have a life and independent purpose apart from their use in providing the structure for qualifications.

This series of diagrams and explanations of the emergence of the VET system underline the importance of starting with a clear and future-focused description of occupational competence, one which, we argue, is provided by the Job Competence Model. Without this we are faced with two options, both based on task descriptions. In the first we can simply try to apply task analysis to all occupations. This doesn't work, for all the reasons we have expressed, so we are forced to the second option, which is to propose that different roles require different methods of description and analysis.

But the question remains: how do we get from the Job Competence Model, which describes occupational competence, to the detailed occupational standards? The answer is provided by the method, initially developed in the Certification Project and since refined to provide an alternative to the task analysis of occupations: functional analysis.

Functional analysis and the detailed description of occupational standards is covered in Chapters 6–11. Before moving on to what is primarily a technical manual on functional analysis and standards design we need to establish that the focus of the Job Competence Model and its origins in concerns over the nature of work in a changing economy are also reflected in our concept of occupational standards.

To do this, we intend to concentrate on the notion of **quality**. The whole purpose of the developments in VET since 1981 has been to **improve the quality** of the workforce – to improve our industries so that they can compete in complex international markets, now and in the future. In the development of systems which are designed to deliver worthy aims it is often too easy to forget the original intention, and such has been the case in critical milestones in the development of the VET system. The whole debate over the appropriateness of task analysis often missed the simple point that a system of description based on an analysis of **existing** activity would have little to offer in designing a structure which was intended to provide for **future** capability. Many of the current concerns about NVQs are to do with the fact that NVQs are often designed to be in excess of existing needs, despite the fact that they are precisely intended to do just that, and to improve, not merely consolidate, existing practice. A discussion of the concept of quality helps put this issue into perspective.

Consider the quality specifications used in industry, which describe in ideal terms what a product or service should be like. The specification is the most important part of quality achievement and the quality assurance process. The specification is not the product or service itself, nor the means of making the product or delivering the service, nor the means of measuring and assessing quality. The specification, or standard, is an independent description of what the product or service should be like – a benchmark against which all actual products and services are compared. Without a precise standard we cannot even start to consider quality. Quality exists only where there is an independent description against which each particular product or instance of service delivery can be judged.

Quality, in the sense in which we use it here, refers to **function** – fitness for purpose, not to grade – the intrinsic value of a product. This distinction is highlighted by Tom Peters,[9] and we can do worse than use his examples. A Rolls-Royce motor car is an example of quality expressed in terms of grade. It has high-grade, high-value components, bristling with luxurious accessories, and is manufactured using methods which guarantee extraordinary reliability. This grade of quality is reflected in a very high price. However, a Rolls-Royce is not particularly functional if you need to drive across a moor, in winter, with a couple of pregnant sheep in the back. A Land Rover is.

Land Rovers, that is Land Rovers before they were replaced by the smooth panelled versions of today, appeared to be made from girders held together with strong and durable bolts and rivets – which showed. They were, however, functional and fit for purpose if you were a moorland farmer. They were not the vehicle to drive if you wanted to make an impression when arriving for a Royal gala. This is the distinction between function and grade – and quality in this discussion is about function – a specification which meets the criterion of **fit for purpose**. Perhaps the clearest way to distinguish function and grade is another of Peters's examples – the leaking gold tap. High on grade, it fails utterly in terms of function.

Quality standards and specifications have other important characteristics which are essential to our approach in developing occupational standards. Specifications for products and services often have the following characteristics:

- They are developed against a vision of an improved product or service and use parts of existing specifications only where they are examples of best practice.
- They often anticipate requirements, thereby generating demand and meeting anticipated rather than existing needs. For example, developments like NICAM stereo appeared on video recorders before there were many TV receivers capable of recording or reproducing NICAM. Catalytic converters appeared on cars before there were international regulations requiring such devices.
- Concepts like beauty and elegance are not in themselves part of the quality standard – they are built-in to the design.

An occupational standard is the same as a product or service standard, but applied to the performance required of people. It also shares the same broad characteristics. Occupational standards describe in ideal terms what should happen in employment for a given occupational area. Occupational standards are not the performance itself (specific activities or tasks), nor the means of achieving competence (knowledge and skills learned through a learning programme) nor the means of measuring quality (assessment). They are **benchmarks** – descriptions of the expectations of employment against which the actual performance of individuals will be compared and assessed. In other words, we use occupational standards to judge the quality of the workforce, for without standards we have no concept of quality.

Occupational standards also share the same additional characteristics of product and service standards:

- They are developed against a vision of improved performance and use parts of existing specifications only where they are examples of best practice.
- They should be able to anticipate occupational requirements, not merely reflect current activities and expectations.
- Concepts which attempt to describe fundamental characteristics of human behaviour, like leadership and creativity, form part of the standard; they are not separately defined and stated.

So, occupational standards are analogous to quality specifications in our manufacturing and service sectors – except, of course, that they describe the outcomes of human action. The principles, though, are the same. So are the limitations. Remember, a standard is the description of the outcome, what should happen. It is not:

- a description of what a specific person is expected to do – which would be specified in a qualification;
- evidence of what a person can do and how well they can do it – which would be the assessment process embedded within a qualification;
- a description of what a person needs to learn – the learning outcomes, learning strategies and evaluation processes which are part of the curriculum.

This does not mean that standards will not influence all these things. They will, as we showed in the previous discussion, but they are separate.

This characterisation of a standard rules out task analysis. It must be developed against a vision of improved performance, extracting only the best practice from existing work activity. The vision is not objective. Standards are statements about what work **should be like**, not what it is like now. The vision is negotiated in the development process and is informed by the components of the Job Competence Model which suggests that work roles **are** composed of all four interrelated components despite how the roles may be organised in current practice.

An occupational standard also requires that we are able to **anticipate** occupational practice, which must be based on a negotiated process involving facts, extrapolations and opinion, not objective observation. Many of the themes we described in the first two chapters can be used to help people in occupations focus on the key changes which are happening now and which can be extrapolated into anticipated future practice.

Finally, standards are not attempts to describe the totality of human existence and experience. They have a limited purpose which is to describe the expectations of employment – the outcomes. Standards are descriptions of what people are expected to **achieve**, not what they are **like**. Personal competence models or any descriptions of personal characteristics are not standards.

This typification of standards – that they are negotiated – fits easily with our previous discussions of work roles and their negotiated nature. But this also raises a potential problem. The process of development implied by our description of standards is potentially highly democratic, a theme which we noted in Chapter 1. But it is democratic only if all the stakeholders who have a legitimate interest in the description of work roles have a part to play in the development process. This is not always the case, and we have to say that many of the Lead Bodies who are responsible for setting standards within occupations have been dominated by particular interest groups which can lead to a distorted version of the standards. The dominant interest is usually employers, which may be consistent with national policy but which may not be the best way to manage a process of empowerment, openness, improved access and democratisation.

Despite this reservation, the link between the broad concept of competence expressed by the Job Competence Model combined with this **strategic view of standards** linked to best practice and future capability offers, we believe, the most effective way of designing and delivering VET systems. The link between competence and standards – functional analysis – and the technical detailing of standards form the next chapter.

NOTES

1. Mansfield, B. and Horton, P. *Work Based Assessment*. The project was an ESF Core Skills 'satellite' based at the Regional Examining Board for Yorkshire and Humberside (YHAFHE).
2. Ibid.
3. Taken from internal YHAFHE project reports, *c.* 1985.
4. Mansfield, 'Design, Learning and Accreditation'. The article was part of a project report to the ESF Project Technical Working Group, which was redrafted and presented to the first SASU Conference.
5. Ibid.
6. The first published reference to functional analysis.
7. Mansfield, 'Design, Learning and Accreditation'.
8. Ibid.
9. Peters, *Thriving on Chaos*.

Part 3
THE KEY METHODOLOGIES

6 Functional analysis – rationale and origins

STANDARDS AND OUTCOMES

Occupational standards describe what should happen – the outcomes which people in particular work roles are expected to achieve. Despite the apparent simplicity of this statement, three of the terms used are of particular importance and require explanation to avoid confusion:

1. **'Outcomes'** are the results of activity. They are not the activity itself, which would be the focus of task or job analysis. They are not just the production of tangible products either – an outcome can be a physical product but it can equally well be a decision or an interaction. For convenience we often distinguish between outcomes which are **products** (tangible: an artefact or document, for example) and those which are **processes** (non-tangible: a decision, a diagnosis or an oral presentation, for example).
2. **'Work roles'** are the occupational functions which have to be achieved within the occupational sector. Work roles are not necessarily expressed or structured in the same ways in which jobs are described. A work role is holistic – it combines all the components of the Job Competence Model.
3. The term **'Expected to achieve'** reminds us that standards do not necessarily describe what is currently achieved. Standards are quality specifications which describe what should happen. They are not an average of what exists now. If they were, we would be merely replicating existing practice, and the aim of the new system of standards and National Vocational Qualifications is to **improve** on current practice. Standards, therefore, combine specifications of best current practice with realistic future expectations. For that reason current jobs are only one of the sources of data when developing standards.

The methodology for developing occupational standards is called 'functional analysis'. Functional analysis is recommended both by the Department for Education and Employment, who partially fund Lead Bodies who are responsible for developing occupational standards, and by NCVQ, who expect the standards on which NVQs are based to be derived from a functional analysis.[1]

FUNCTIONAL ANALYSIS – AN OVERVIEW

Most people come across a functional analysis in its finished form, usually presented as a complex diagram showing interlinking boxes containing outcome statements. The diagram is normally called a **functional map** and often appears in the introduction to a set of occupational standards, where it provides an overview of the relationships between the standards and acts as an index. The map represents an entire occupational sector although, when presented as an index to a set of standards or a qualification, only a portion of the complete functional map may be shown, but it is still likely to be labelled as a 'functional map'. A representation of a functional map is shown in Figure 6.1, with all the key components identified.

All the components of the map are described in detail in subsequent sections. This section merely gives an overview of the key components and terms used in the map.

We need to make clear that the descriptions of the components, characteristics and analysis methods described in this chapter are those which we have identified and developed in our work with standard setting organisations. This book contains *our* opinions and views about what functional maps and functional analysis *should* be like. This means that other functional maps which readers may have seen may differ from the models we present._

The different components and characteristics of the functional map are described in brief below.

1. All the statements in a functional map are **outcomes** – they describe the results of activity.
2. The map starts on the left-hand side with a **key purpose** statement which describes the unique nature and characteristics of the sector which differentiates it from all other sectors. As we noted earlier, this is the same terminology used in the Occupational Training Family Work Learning Guides.
3. The key purpose is separated in the **first stage analysis** into a number of main functions which enable the key purpose to be met. By convention, these statements are called **key areas** and are coded, usually with a letter of the alphabet. In Figure 6.1 we have used the letters A to D. There can be as many key areas in the first stage analysis as are necessary to separate all the main functions. We have shown four for illustrative purposes. In practice there may be more or less than this. We use a particular model for arriving at the first stage analysis which is described below.
4. After the first stage analysis, the **second stage analysis** involves the use of two processes to develop the key area statements to greater levels of detail. They are called **disaggregation** and **iteration.** Disaggregation means the logical and structured analysis of an outcome statement into substatements

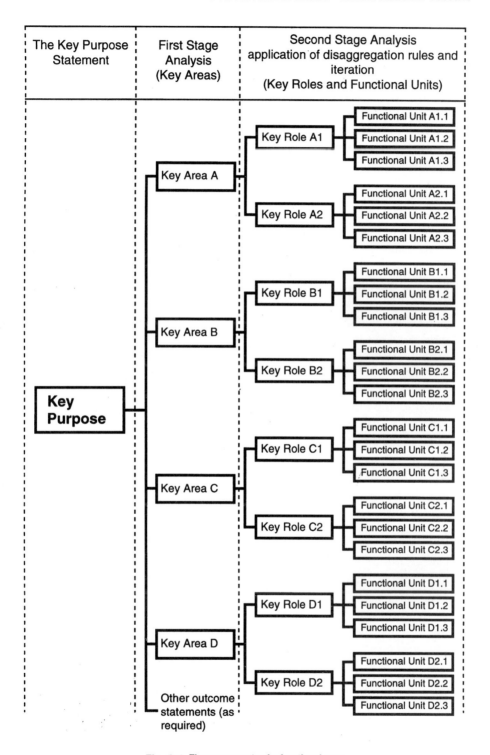

Fig. 6.1 The components of a functional map

by the separation of functions. Iteration refers to the process of constantly checking and rechecking the general coherence and structure of the analysis. Both terms are fully explained in the appropriate section below.

5. The coding system used to separate the statements in the first stage analysis is used consistently throughout the map. The normal convention is to add a numeric notation for the first level of detail in the second stage of analysis, which are called **key** roles. So, key area A is analysed into key roles A1 and A2. Key area B is analysed into key roles B1 and B2.

6. This convention continues as the statements are analysed into greater detail. So, key role A1 is separated into statements A1.1, A1.2 and A1.3 and so on. In this illustration, three substatements are shown. In practice there may be more or less (but no less than two) substatements.

7. Figure 6.1 shows only two analysis stages in the second stage analysis: key roles coded A1, A2, B1, etc, further detailed as statements A1.1, A1.2, A1.3, etc. In practice there may be more stages than this depending on the complexity and scope of the occupational sector.

8. The map is complete when the analysis reaches a level of detail where each statement represents an outcome for which an individual, alone or as part of a team, would be responsible for achieving. In the illustrative map shown above, this level of detail is represented by the statements shown to the right of the map and coded A1.1, A1.2, etc. In the terms used to describe National Vocational Qualifications this level of detail is referred to as a '**unit of competence**'. In the functional map, we refer to this level of detail as a **functional unit**.

9. The connecting lines on the map show the relationship between statements. Thus, functional units B1.1, B1.2 and B1.3 are all substatements of key role B1. Equally, key roles B1 and B2 are substatements of key area B. In a real functional map, key area B will represent a substantial function in an occupational sector. For this function to be delivered, the more detailed functions described by key roles B1 and B2 and their respective functional units, B1.1, B1.2, B1.3, B2.1, B2.2, and B2.3, must be achieved.

10. Despite the appearance of the map, the statements are not placed in any order of priority or importance. Statements in key area A are no more important than statements in key area D. Nor do the order of the statements imply a sequence of activities. The different groups of statements simply represent **different** and **separate** functions.

11. The most detailed statements, functional units, which represent the outcomes which individuals take full responsibility for achieving, are the starting-point for the development of occupational standards. For each of the functional units separate standards are identified using the same process of analysis, and for each standard **performance criteria** and **range indicators** are developed. These terms are fully explained in the appropriate sections below.

FUNCTIONAL ANALYSIS – FEATURES, BENEFITS AND PURPOSE

The process of functional analysis involves the classification of an occupational area by the separation of functions.[2] Functional analysis is used because it has the following features and benefits:

1. It is based on the description of outcomes – the results of activity rather than specific tasks or activities. This means that **how** a particular organisation does something – the procedure or activity – is subordinate to **why** it is done – the purpose. The description of purpose allows apparently different activities to be linked by their common purpose. It also allows a national standard to be set which is independent of specific workplaces.
2. It is negotiated (ie achieved by consultation, clear decision-making processes and consensus) rather than objective (ie based on empirical observation of existing phenomena). Many may see this as a disadvantage because the term 'objective' is often contrasted unfavourably with 'subjective'. But the process of functional analysis quite deliberately identifies and makes explicit underlying values and ethics in occupational sectors and actively seeks opinion on best practice and future trends and developments. It makes no claim to be an objective and fixed view of an occupation.
3. It is holistic – it describes all the essential outcomes within an occupation and the relationships between them. The holistic overview is also facilitated by the conventional structure – the functional map – which provides a diagrammatic model of the links between the outcomes. However, in practice, this attempt to display the relational nature of the map is often interpreted as further evidence of a mechanistic or reductionist approach.
4. It is dynamic – the process of analysis allows changes to be made to the overall framework at any stage and changes in one part of the framework may impact on other areas.
5. It offers different levels of detail for different purposes, At high levels of generality it describes occupational and organisational outcomes in very broad terms. At the most detailed levels it describes the capabilities expected of individuals and teams. By offering both levels of generality and description it is a powerful tool in examining the relationship between organisational requirements and priorities and individual/team contribution.

It is important to note a further feature of functional analysis. Like all analysis systems which attempt to describe the rich nuances of human behaviour, it is limited in scope. It cannot, of itself, describe all facets and aspects of human behaviour. It is fit only for its purpose, which is to describe precisely the outcomes which people are expected to achieve in work environments based on best current practice and anticipated future requirements. This is all that the analysis process is designed for and is capable of doing. The most important single distinction which can be made is that functional analysis and the associated methodology of developing occupational standards describes **what people are expected to do**, not **what they are like**. This distinction is critical and is worth expanding. In describing what people are expected to do, we need to be clear that:

- the analysis does not necessarily describe what people **actually** do, but what they are **expected** to do – what should happen;
- the analysis does not claim to match particular jobs or job titles – these are current descriptions of how people and organisations decide who does what;
- by taking the focus of 'expected to do', the analysis and the standards do not describe what people may need to know, nor what cognitive processes are involved in work performance – the analysis describes only the outcomes, not the means by which the outcomes are achieved (however, the further elaboration of occupational standards involves the identification of underpinning knowledge and understanding, but this is to facilitate the development of learning and assessment processes and is not part of the performance standard);
- functional analysis and occupational standards do not describe peoples' state of mind, nature, beliefs, attitudes or dispositions (what they are like).

In recognising these limitations it is easy to fall into the trap of assuming that functional analysis is limited to describing only tangible and routine outcomes. This is not the case, as will be explained in subsequent sections.

FUNCTIONAL ANALYSIS – MYTHS AND MISUNDERSTANDINGS

Before describing the methodology in detail we need to correct some of the myths and misunderstandings which surround functional analysis. This is because it is probably the most misinterpreted, misunderstood and most haphazardly applied method ever to emerge from the discipline of occupational analysis. Blamed on the one hand for being atomistic, mechanistic and lacking integration[3] it is conversely, and perversely, blamed for being too broad, too holistic, idealistic and impractical.

Yet for all the venom and accusations of sinister intent, functional analysis is a modest method with modest claims. It has respectable antecedents, a sound theoretical base and a clear role to play in the analysis and description of human action although, in fairness to the critics, these aspects are rarely described and made explicit.

Functional analysis suffers as much from its name as from anything else and at least two different groups are concerned and aroused by the term.

The first are sociologists and political theorists who remember theories of functionalism and structural functionalism, a rigid and rather impersonal approach to describing social action and social structure developed by the American sociologist Talcott Parsons[4] in the 1940s and 1950s. This approach was indeed mechanistic, seeing human action as highly determined, labelling socially acceptable and conforming behaviour as 'functional' and unsocial action as 'dysfunctional'. In this theory all the 'functions' of society worked and interacted together like a well-oiled machine, striving for a mystical balance of forces.

In the 1960s functionalism was largely discredited as a theoretical approach to the description and analysis of social action, but memories are long and the similarity of terminology can apparently strike fear and trepidation into the hearts of social scientists. It can also lead to the groundless claim that functional analysis shares the characteristics of functionalism: mechanistic, conforming, resistant to change and deterministic. The most damaging charge is that functional analysis has nothing to say about human values, since people are mere reflexes of the *deus ex machina* of social forces, occupy structured and imposed roles and are even described as 'functions'. If this were all true, the developers and users of functional analysis would probably have been the first to cast the stone!

Second, there are those who react negatively to the term 'function' since it appears to revisit the functional approach to describing organisational structures – functions like sales, research, finance, etc. Since many organisations are now described in terms of key processes, interdependency and devolution, a return to 'functions' seems retrograde, reactionary and out of keeping with more modern and strategic approaches to organisational analysis. Again, the name has set the wrong tone. Functional analysis is not an attempt to return to functional, separated, departmental thinking, although the very appearance of the functional map, with formal statements in boxes, joined up with lines in an apparent flow chart can appear to represent the very essence of rigid, operational thinking.

If these are the demons and nightmares which are unleashed by the terminology there is ample justification for people being concerned. But this is not the case. Functional analysis owes nothing to, and has no connection with these approaches, just as critical path analysis has nothing to do with the identification of the most important public rights of way for ramblers.

But there has been a continuing problem of 'guilt by semantics'. However, the fact that the word 'function' is shared by these different approaches is no more significant than the fact that national socialism and democratic socialism share a common term – it does not mean that the value systems or methods of application are compatible! In retrospect, however, the term 'function' is not the best one to have chosen, given the possibility of association with quite different approaches.

In origin, functional analysis is associated with the hermeneutic and dialectical traditions of social science. For readers not familiar with these terms, they relate to social theories and methodologies which are based on a process of 'interpretive understanding' and, in turn, reject reductionist and behaviourist approaches which attempt to define and analyse social action using empirical methods adopted by the natural sciences.[5]

We have already described the inherent problem of using task analysis for the identification of occupational standards in Chapters 3 and 4, and functional analysis is partly a reaction to task analysis. The reaction is both practical and theoretical. Practically, trying to describe all the tasks in the world is tedious and time consuming. Describing all the tasks in the UK is only slightly less so!

As we suggested in Chapter 3, task analysis has a value base and economic purpose which is antithetical to the development of occupational standards. It was originally designed to contribute to the automation, control and atomisation of work processes, not to account for the richness and complexity of human action. Because of this origin there are a number of important problems in using task analysis as a method for uncovering and elaborating human action in work environments to create occupational standards which exemplify best practice and future requirements.

Task analysis describes **current activities**, what people do now, whereas part of the purpose of developing occupational standards is to anticipate the employment needs of the future. Tasks, when taken together, give us only an average of performance. Standards, by contrast, are intended to describe best practice – what **should** happen. This means that the observation of existing activities is only one base from which to develop standards. Standards also require informed opinion, information about known and emerging trends and decisions about what **ought** to be.

Where task analysis has been used to develop standards the results are extremely detailed task descriptions which are quickly outdated and which require constant revision. Task-based standards emphasise manual or tangible activities – the kind that are fast declining in the modern economy. They also play down (or ignore) the valuable and much-regarded process skills which employers increasingly recognise as being essential requirements in a competitive economy and which are expressed as outcomes in the Job Competence Model. Task analysis gives us a string of beads, with no holistic rationale or structure. Each task is separately identified and added to an accumulating pool of information. This bottom-up accumulation of tasks is then analysed for match and pattern as if some organising framework will arise, phoenix like, from the mass of unstructured information. It doesn't.

Task analysis tends to concentrate on the routine components of the work role, the technical expectations of the Job Competence Model. The method is useful for describing tangible results, known routines and clear procedures within an organisational context. It is less useful where we find considerable variation and uncertainty in work roles in which people spend much of their time organising, planning, diagnosing, interacting with colleagues and customers, and managing work processes (the contingency management, task management and work environment components of the Job Competence Model). These work role components are not tasks with routine and tangible characteristics. The articulation of these non-routine components becomes more important as organisations move away from the control philosophy of scientific management to the quality assurance models which place the competence of people and their contribution at the centre of organisational success.

As industries change from mass production and the finely tuned division of labour – one of the main economic trends we identified in Chapter 2 – people are expected to contribute to decision making, problem solving and process management.

Our values with respect to the human contribution to work have also changed. We no longer believe that the worker has to be rigidly controlled, reduced to an automaton and removed from the management process. This is now seen as both morally degrading and operationally ineffective. It is perhaps for this reason most of all that we should firmly reject task analysis as an appropriate approach for the description of human activity at work.

Functional analysis was developed to overcome problems which task analysis cannot solve. Functional analysis explores the areas of human capability (described by the contingency management, task management and work environment components of the Job Competence Model), which task analysis fails to address. It was designed for the sole purpose of developing descriptions of human capability, which we call occupational standards, by concentrating on the expectations of employment, broken down through a process of structured analysis which eventually produces a level of detail which we describe as an **occupational standard**.

THE ORIGINS OF FUNCTIONAL ANALYSIS

Functional analysis acquired its name almost by accident, and consequently it has become confused with approaches which have a similar name. As a matter of interest, the method was originally called 'work role analysis' but the term was rejected by practitioners on the grounds that it would not be understood!

In this chapter we described how functional analysis was originally developed by a team of researchers working with the ESF Core Skills Project[6] who found that conventional approaches to occupational analysis did not work well when applied to developing standards. The system which they devised looked at occupational functions. In those early days of development, before the start of the standards programme, the terminology was not fixed or well defined and the implications of using particular terms were not properly anticipated.

From these early developments functional analysis gradually gained acceptance as a feasible alternative to task analysis, operating in parallel to the evolving Job Competence Model.

As the Youth Training Scheme became established and new publicly funded schemes came on-line, the idea of an outcome-based curriculum, based on modular or unit accreditation, became an imperative to provide national consistency and coherence. A number of initiatives were introduced by the Manpower Services Commission and its successor, the Department of Employment to provide guidance to the newly emerging Lead Bodies on the development of what were first called 'competences', then 'competence objectives' and finally 'occupational standards'. As these guidance documents were being developed the target became broader than the relatively narrow confines of training schemes aimed at young entrants to work. The target expanded to include standards for all occupations and all occupational levels. This was the start of the **standards programme**. This period also saw the foundation, in 1987, of the National Council for Vocational Qualifications.

These national programmes required a coherent methodology to inform the development of both the new occupational standards and National Vocational Qualifications. This was provided by the Technical Advisory Group (TAG), which was set up in 1987 to produce a series of eight guidance notes, published in 1988 and 1989.[7] We were members of TAG and contributed substantially to the guidance documents, particularly those on functional analysis, standards development and assessment. The guidance notes were subsequently modified and combined into a single document,[8] published in 1991, which became the key source of guidance for the organisations (Lead Bodies, Industry Training Organisations, technical consultants and Awarding Bodies) involved in the development of standards and National Vocational Qualifications.

The TAG Notes and the combined guidance document describe early versions of functional analysis which had become the recommended approach endorsed by the Department for Education and Employment and NCVQ. It is significant, however, that this process of endorsement and recommendation was not automatic: a clear case had to be made for its adoption in the TAG meetings. This is evidenced by the changes in titling which occurred as the TAG Notes were published. In the first Note, the forthcoming TAG 2 was titled 'Deriving elements of competence'. When it was finally published, TAG 2 had the title 'Developing standards by reference to functions'.

Functional analysis dared to speak its own name in a compilation of articles[9] taken from the Department for Education and Employment journal *Competence and Assessment*, published in 1989, which served as a bridge between the fast-outdating individual TAG Notes and the compilation volume of 1991. In an article titled 'Functional Analysis – A Personal Approach', Bob Mansfield outlined the processes and methods which had been developed and tested in practice since the first experimental use of the methodology in 1986.

Since that date little has been published on advances and refinements to the method, giving ample opportunity for misunderstandings and misinterpretations to develop and fester. In the next chapter we hope to demonstrate that functional analysis has now come of age as a valid and robust methodology for occupational analysis.

NOTES

1. See Fennell, *Developing Assessable Standards* and NCVQ and the Employment Department, *NVQ Criteria and Guidance.*

2. David Mathews, in his introduction to the process of standards development in Fennell, *Developing Assessable Standards*, makes the case for a functional approach for identifying the 'outcomes' of activity: 'Functional thinking involves the separation of functional problems from physical ones. It is concerned with activity specified by its ends or outcomes rather than the means by which the outcomes are achieved' (Miller, 'Task taxonomy: science or technology').

3. This view was taken by the Personnel Standards Lead Body. The project director reported: 'the methodology [for NVQs] is overly rigid and "given" ... functional analysis, while possibly appropriate to simple jobs, is not tenable among the professions. It focuses too heavily on elements being performed in isolation, rather than integrated sequences – and it concentrates too much on outputs (*sic*) to the exclusion of necessary work processes' McKiddie, 'Personnel NVQs: Preparing for take-off'.

4. See Parsons, *The structure of social action*, and Parsons, *The social system*.

5. In a conference paper, Jac Christis from the Netherlands Institute for the Quality of Working Life (Nederlands Institut voor Arbeidsomstandigheden) suggested that theories of social action could be broadly categorised against three distinct types: (1) those which claimed to be MIRRORS of the world; (2) those which tell a STORY about the world; (3) those which provide a MAP of the world. These types make different claims and are associated with different philosophical traditions. Mirrors are represented by positivist and empirical approaches – we would associate this with task analysis. Stories are interpretations which are designed to be representational – different stories can coexist and their power is related to how well the story fits with the experience of the reader. This accords with the hermeneutic tradition. We would characterise the Job Competence Model as a story. Maps are an attempt drastically to reduce the infinite complexity of the world to give us usable tools for analysis and decision making. In Jac's words, 'Maps help us find our way – the information they give us must be true, but it is not complete and may not be presented in the same way as the world we see'. It is no accident that we often refer to functional analysis as a functional map.

   The above is summarised from Christis, *Sociotechnics*. This model is further developed in: Christis, *The sociology of work stress and wellbeing*.

6. Mansfield and Horton, *Work Based Assessment*.

7. The eight Guidance Notes are: (1) 'A code of practice and a development model'; (2) 'Developing standards by reference to functions'; (3) 'The definition of competences and performance criteria'; (4) 'The characteristics of units of competence'; (5) 'Assessment of competence'; (6) 'Verification and monitoring of assessment'; (7) 'Project management, standards and NVQ/SVQ development'; (8) 'Consulting on standards: establishing the national applicability of draft standards' (Employment Department).

8. Fennell, *Developing Assessable Standards*.

9. Fennell, *Competence and Assessment*.

7 Functional analysis – the analysis process

The process of functional analysis starts with the identification of a **key purpose** statement which attempts to describe the **unique contribution** which an industry or occupation makes within the economy, together with an indication of the values and commitments which underpin work roles. The key purpose is similar to a mission statement which an organisation uses to set clear objectives and targets for success.

It is worth noting that the key purpose statement is intended to apply to an occupational sector. This is the main focus for functional analysis, and projects which are sponsored by the Department for Education and Employment normally require that the whole occupational sector is subjected to a functional analysis before standards development is started. However, in practice the analysis can take a starting-point which is less comprehensive or encompassing than an occupational sector. In the examples below we have used functional analyses which have different starting points: an occupational sector (construction); a cross-sector occupation (training and development); and a single occupational role (professional trade union officers). What this demonstrates is the flexibility of functional analysis. Although designed as a large-scale analysis tool it can also be useful in the analysis of subsectors in occupations and even individual organisations.

It is often tempting to try to describe everything with the key purpose statement. This is not necessary. What is needed is a starting-point for analysis which is sufficiently detailed to describe the unique contribution. A key purpose statement is also the level at which underpinning values, or balances between potentially conflicting interests, are introduced. Table 7.1 shows key purpose statements from the three sectors described above.

In each of these key purpose statements we see three similar features:

1. They all use the same grammatical structure – active verb(s), which describe **what** happens; an object, which describes **to what** or **to whom** performance is directed; a conditional statement which describes the **context** in which performance takes place. The conditional statement is only added if the context is not apparent from the first two parts of the statement – the active verbs and

Occupation/Sector	Key Purpose Statement
Construction sector (an occupational sector)	Establish, maintain and modify the use of the natural and built environment, balancing the requirements of clients, users and the community
Training and development occupations (a cross-sectoral occupation)	Develop human potential to assist organisations and individuals to achieve their objectives
Professional trade union officers (an occupational role)	Protect, maintain and improve the collective and individual employment conditions, job security, status and social well-being of members as defined through the union's decision-making processes*

*(It is worth noting that although the analysis of professional trade union officers started with a specific role, the key purpose statement has subsequently been applied to the entire trade union sector)

Table 7.1 Key purpose statements

the object. Here is an example which contains all three parts of the grammatical structure:

- active verbs (what happens) – *establish, maintain and modify;*
- object (to what or whom) – *the use of the natural and built environment;*
- condition (the context) – *balancing the requirements of clients, users and the community.*

This format is recommended for all stages of the analysis and is described in detail in Chapter 9 in the section on developing element of competence titles. It is helpful to use this grammatical structure rather than use a more compact shorthand which might make sense to occupational specialists but which might have little meaning to others. In general, each individual statement in the functional analysis should be capable of standing alone and offering immediate sense to a reader.

2. All the key purpose statements contain a balance between factors which could, in practice, be in conflict, thus generating tension and presenting practitioners with complex choices:

- construction balances the requirements of 'clients, users and the community';
- training and development balances the needs and objectives of 'organisations and individuals';
- trade union officers are required to meet both 'collective and individual' needs.

3. They all contain an implicit statement of values which is often no more than a clue to a more elaborate value base which is explicitly stated within the standards or in a separate code of practice:

- in construction the use of the term 'environment' and the recognition of the needs of 'users and the community' suggests a level of social and ecological responsibility;
- in training and development the use of the term 'assist' (rather than 'teach' or 'train') suggests a supportive and facilitative approach;
- trade union officer standards explicitly refer to the value of 'collectivism' even though it is contrasted with individual needs;
- the value of democratic decision making is also evident in the final conditional statement 'as defined through the union's decision-making processes'.

Note that the values do not have to be totally clear and explicit at this very general stage of analysis. It is sufficient to simply signal values which will be elaborated at subsequent stages.

The key purpose statement, like all other parts of the functional map, is subject to comment and change during the development process. Consequently it is often quite acceptable to work with an initial rough draft, accompanied by a commentary which provides a rationale for the statement. During the initial drafting of the key purpose the tendency to overelaborate the statement can be countered by logging specific matters of detail for later consideration.

FIRST STAGE ANALYSIS

Having established a draft key purpose statement it is necessary to consider the ways in which highly generalised roles operate in the sector. This is the first stage analysis which produces the key areas. The fundamental question is 'in order to achieve the key purpose of the occupational sector, what are people expected to be able to do?'.

Based on our work with many occupational sectors we have developed a common pattern of key areas which typify the functions necessary to develop and sustain the sector. The pattern is based on a very simple series of propositions which are themselves based on an interpretation of the components of the Job Competence Model.

- Occupations need a strategic function related to scanning the wider environment for trends in markets, new developments in materials and products and other technical advances, and planning what is to be done.
- Scanning the environment can result in innovatory developments: identifying and putting into operation new ways of doing things and new methods for improving the competence of staff and the development of new products and services.
- Strategic plans are achieved by the planning of operations and the

implementation of operational plans, which is the point at which the technical expectations deliver the key purpose. This is usually the main focus for occupational analysis because it contains most of the tangible activity.

- Operations are co-ordinated in order to achieve the goals set.
- Organisations involved in implementation are managed to achieve the goals of implementation and any additional goals of the organisation.
- The sector can often be typified by a number of underpinning values which link the operations of the sector to **why** things are done – the purpose.

This pattern is translated into a number of key areas, which we will detail in a slightly different order:

1. **Operational, or technical roles** – roles which are relatively unique to the occupation or sector and which ultimately deliver the key purpose. They are the roles associated with the technical expectations of the Job Competence Model. These roles are usually the first consideration in starting the analysis because they are the most familiar to practitioners. In construction, the obvious technical roles are to do with building operations, site clearance and maintenance. At managerial and professional levels in the sector they are to do with planning and designing buildings and structures, setting out sites, procuring materials and plant. In training and development, the technical roles are concerned with the design and delivery of training. For trade union officers the technical roles centre on the representation and organisation of members.

2. **Strategic roles** – roles which set overall direction, provide the plans and set the specifications against which the operational and technical roles take place. Often, these roles are more complex and demanding versions of the technical/operational roles. So, for example, a technical role in training and development might involve identifying the current learning needs of individuals and groups. The associated strategic role might describe the identification of future competence requirements for an organisation. It is important to distinguish between the function of operational planning (arranging resources to achieve a given objective) and strategic planning (deciding what is to be done). In the terms of the Job Competence Model, operational planning is part of the task management component and strategic planning is part of the work environment component. Strategic roles are usually associated with greater responsibility and status in organisations although, increasingly, many organisational stakeholders are involved in contributing to the strategic planning function through consultative processes, feeding back customer and market information and interpreting signals from the environment.

3. **Creative and innovatory roles** – these are the source of new ideas, concepts and developments which are designed to both solve current problems and identify future possibilities. These roles operate at all levels but for some people they define their key expectations – people working in research, design

and product development, for example. However, as we have noted previously, more people are encouraged to participate in developing new products, services and work methods, so for some organisations this role may become merged with operational and technical roles.

4. **Management roles** – these can be of two sorts: those which enable the technical and operational roles to take place (operational management) and those which support the efficient functioning of organisations (organisational management). Some management roles are associated with level of responsibility, ie they are peoples' jobs (like project managers and logistics managers). However, most work roles now require that individuals take increasing responsibility for the management of working processes, team relationships and allocation of work, so these task management aspects will need to be considered as well.

5. **The value base** – this is not a distinct set of roles but a context in which all other roles take place. The value base is an expression of some of the human issues and conflicts that arise in the work environment component of the Job Competence Model. The value base clearly expresses in outcome terms the values which underpin best practice in an occupation. The values may vary quite widely. In accountancy, for example, we would expect to find values to do with client confidentiality, honesty and integrity in dealing with client interests (the interactive part of the work environment component). These values will be common to many professional occupations. In occupations which impact on the land we may find values associated with environmental and ecological responsibility (physical constraints – part of the work environment component). In many service occupations we may find values dealing with the nature of interactions with clients.

Functional analysis makes the values explicit: it expresses the essentially human nature of work activity. The value base is a critical link to the social and human values which underpin all occupations. To argue that an occupation, or any analysis of an occupation, is somehow neutral or objective is futile. Indeed, many of the problems with previous forms of occupational analysis have been caused by the assumption that work roles may be considered as abstractions, divorced from the networks of power and values which make them distinctly human systems. These values change over time and it is the value base which sets a context for the up-to-date expression of good and ethical practice.

The model structure described above allows practitioners to consider all the essential parts of occupations rather than just the technical or operational roles with which they will be the most familiar. In summary, the roles, which are called 'key areas' in the functional map, may be expressed as:

- operational/technical;
- strategic;
- creative/innovatory;

- management (operational and organisational);
- the value base.

This pattern of key areas may be used to start the process of analysis. The pattern may be used explicitly and offered to participants in the development process to trigger discussion and reflection. Alternatively, it may be used by the analyst as a method of auditing the results of the first stage analysis and suggesting further consideration of key areas which appear to be underdeveloped.

The data source for identifying key areas may be literature based (reports, studies, training needs analyses of the sector) or practitioners. If practitioners are used to help in this initial process then they should be people who are able to take a broad overview of an occupational area rather than concentrating on fine detail – detail will come later! Very often there are well-known and commonly understood ways of separating key areas within the sector and these may be used as a starting-point for discussion and exploration.

An example of this broad first stage analysis can be seen in the first draft of the standards developed for the construction sector. The first step was to outline the major functions in construction which are commonly understood and part of the everyday language of the sector. They are:

A   Planning;
B   Designing;
C   Building/maintaining structures;
D   Co-ordinating (construction) operations – project management.

Immediately we can see the functional separation between key areas is starting to emerge:

A   Planning – strategic;
B   Designing – innovatory and operational/technical;
C   Building/maintaining structures – operational/technical;
D   Co-ordinating operations – managerial, operations and organisational.

Note that there is no separate value base. In this instance the values which underpin the sector were signalled in the key purpose statement and embedded in the standards as they were developed. What we also notice is that the first three key areas operate as a sequence: plan, design, build. This is often the case, but it is not a rule of analysis. In other sectors and occupations the logical structure may be quite different.

These four key areas can be expressed in the outcome terminology which is used throughout the analysis:

A   Plan the built environment.
B   Design the built environment.
C   Construct, maintain and adapt the built environment.
D   Co-ordinate and control the development, construction and maintenance of the built environment.

Note that each of the statements will stand alone as a coherent description of the outcome. The single-word descriptions, like 'planning' and 'designing' may make sense to those who know the context and focus of the analysis, but to others they immediately beg questions like 'plan what?'. The grammar of the outcome statements uses more words but it is precise and makes sense.

Now we have the first stage of analysis it is appropriate to add a cautionary note. This separation of functions is not intended to follow the particular ways in which jobs are designed. Any particular activity or job may draw from all four of the separated functions. The separation does not imply exclusivity. The four key areas (and the detailed analysis which may be developed from each) acts rather like a menu in a restaurant. Any one meal will normally involve a selection from each part of the menu; we simply group together each course – starters, main courses, desserts – for convenience and to assist choice.

There is, however, a significant difference between the way in which the functional analysis works and the menu. If we look at the construction example above we will quickly see that if we were to use the functional analysis to describe any job which involves managerial responsibilities then this would always involve a selection from key area D. So, for example, an architect with project management responsibilities will draw from key areas B and D. A planner with management responsibilities will draw from key areas A and D. A site manager will draw from key areas C and D, and so on. This understanding of the mapping process is of critical importance when qualifications are developed from the standards.

The first stage analysis is the starting-point for an entire occupational sector. But functional analysis does not always start with a sector. It is possible to develop analyses for cross-sector occupations, that is, those occupations which are not determined by the key purpose of a single sector. These are usually occupations which provide services to organisations to help them improve and sustain performance. Cross-sector occupations include general management, training and development, human resource management, purchase and supply, information systems development and accountancy. Analyses can also start at the level of a single role or group of roles. In instances where the scope of the functional analysis is less than an entire occupational sector, the first stage analysis can be rather different.

Training and development[1] is an example of a cross-sector occupation. For this occupation the starting-point was to adopt a model commonly used and well-understood by practitioners – the training cycle:

A Identify training needs.
B Plan and design training.
C Deliver training.
D Evaluate the effectiveness of training.

In training and development occupations, these are seen as operational roles. This

111

means that the strategic, managerial, innovatory roles and the value base are missing. To qualify this imbalance a number of decisions were made:

- The strategic roles were expressed in key areas A and B by identifying an organisational as well as an individual/group focus for the identification of training needs and the planning of training.
- General managerial roles were imported from the standards for general management developed by the Management Charter Initiative and allocated to a new key area.
- Innovatory roles were identified and allocated to a new key area.
- The value base was expressed as a code of practice and also embedded in the standards (subsequently, this was changed and the values are now more explicitly stated in the standards).

The new key area E was designed to locate the management standards and to accommodate the contribution practitioners made to advances in training and development. The complete first stage analysis, adopting the outcome format, is:

A Identify training and development needs
B Design training and development strategies and plans
C Provide learning opportunities, resources and support
D Evaluate the effectiveness of training and development
E Support training and development advances and practice

Finally, we can examine the process adopted for a single work role: professional trade union officers.[2] Here, a literature research and discussions with practitioners uncovered four key areas which were well understood and commonly recognised:

- Recruitment of members.
- Organisation of members.
- Representation of members.
- Negotiation on behalf of members.

It was further recognised that these four responsibilities tended to group into two areas, the first to do with recruiting and organising members, a constant process which has an organisational maintenance function, the second to do with specific interventions and activities as required – representation and negotiation. All the key areas are operational or technical.

To these operational roles were added two other broad areas which were not based on specific activities:

- Management of resources.
- Representing and promoting the values and interests of the union and the wider movement.

Having taken all this into account, the first stage analysis emerged as:

A Contribute to the maintenance and improvement of the organisation and membership level of the union

B Support and enable members to advance their individual and collective interests

C Contribute to the effective management of union resources and the provision of member services

D Promote, support and represent the values and interests of the movement

If we examine this first stage analysis against the five key areas of our suggested model for first stage analysis, we see that key areas A and B are the operational roles with the addition of an innovatory role ('improvement of ...' in key area A). Key area C is the managerial role and key area D contains the value base. There is no separate strategic key area at this level of analysis. This is because the analysis concentrates on one work role. Professional officers do not have a strategic planning role – that is the responsibility of senior officers. In an analysis of the entire sector the strategic key area would appear. However, the professional officer does have a role in feeding back important information to senior officers to inform strategic decision making, and this is embedded in the standards.

Note that the term 'contribute to' appears in this analysis. This is also a result of the analysis starting with a single work role. The professional officer does not take full responsibility for either organisation, recruitment or management of resources, so the term 'contribute' is used to indicate the partial responsibility. Again, in an analysis of the whole sector, the term 'contribute' would not appear at the first stage analysis level.

SUMMARY

1. In developing the first stage of analysis it may be useful to adopt a common format for the key areas:

- operational/technical;
- strategic;
- creative/innovatory;
- management (operational and organisational);
- the value base.

This model is intended to be only a starting-point for discussion and consideration.

2. It is not always necessary for each key area to be explicit in the first stage analysis. In particular, cross-sector occupations and those concentrating on

one work role may not apply this format. If all the key areas do not appear at this level, a number of decisions need to be made to account for the key areas at some stage in the subsequent analysis. This may include:

- noting important points for later consideration;
- deciding to embed a particular key area within the standards;
- combining some of the key areas.

3. Individual jobs do not fit neatly into one key area. In general, the management and value base key areas act as a foundation for all the other key areas. When qualifications are developed it is usual to select standards from the operational key area and to include standards from the management and value base key areas.

4. Although strategic and innovatory roles tend to be associated with higher levels of responsibility and seniority, it is important to recognise that they are increasingly important at all levels in an occupation or organisation. Such a contribution to strategic and innovatory functions may take the form of:

- contributing to the improvement of systems and processes;
- feeding back information and advice on practice to inform decision making.

5. The starting point for analysis should be descriptions which make sense in the sector and which are widely recognised.

6. The general purpose of the analysis is to separate key areas which produce different outcomes, so each main category should be discrete. Overlaps at this stage will create problems at subsequent analysis stages.

SECOND STAGE ANALYSIS – DISAGGREGATION AND ITERATION

The second stage of the methodology involves the use of the two methods of functional analysis:

- the application of **disaggregation rules**;
- the process of **iteration**.

The use of these methods will generate subsequent levels of analysis which will stop when the statements reach a level of detail which approximate to the outcomes which an individual is expected to achieve. However, before exploring disaggregation and iteration it is worth reminding ourselves about the purpose and characteristics of analysis and classification. A functional analysis is a classification of an occupational sector, therefore the classification must follow the rules of all classifications. It must be (as far as is possible and practicable):

- complete (all occupational roles must be contained within it);

- comprised of categories in the form of outcome statements which are mutually exclusive – each statement must be functionally different from other statements to avoid duplication and confusion;
- credible and fit for purpose – it must be credible with the sector as a representation of what happens in the sector. This does not mean that the language needs to be simplistic, but it must make sense to practitioners.

It is by the application and use of disaggregation rules and the process of iteration that we are able to maintain a logical and structured analysis which conforms to these requirements.

DISAGGREGATION RULES

Despite the awesome title, disaggregation rules are quite straightforward. The process involves exploring different ways in which a key area from the first stage analysis may be further elaborated. The key areas are extremely generalised, so the same question is applied as to the key purpose: 'in order to achieve (the outcome described by the key area), what are people expected to be able to do?'. The answer to the question will generally follow one of a number of patterns, which are the disaggregation rules. In general, the rules follow one of a number of patterns:

- a linear or sequential process (eg plan, design, build);
- a cyclical process (eg develop, implement, evaluate);
- separation of different processes or methods (eg identify information sources, evaluate information sources);
- separation of different products or outcomes (eg test mechanical components, test electrical components).

In addition there are hybrid rules where the above patterns are combined or where additional statements are added to accommodate contingency or task management components. So, for example, a group of statements may list a sequence of technical activities such as:

- set up x equipment;
- produce y products;
- finish y products;

together with the statement:

- monitor and control the production process (which might, in turn, comprise more detailed statements to do with maintaining supplies of raw materials, monitoring the operation of equipment, recalibration, fault recognition and diagnosis).

The first three statements in this hypothetical example are a **sequence** of specific operations, but the final statement has an overarching function which involves controlling and integrating the whole sequence of operations. In fact, the last statement is not a discrete activity like the first three. It is a process which is activated when things go wrong (contingency) and to integrate different activities to achieve overall objectives (task management). This is very similar to the structure of the Learning and Assessment Model described in Chapter 5.

There is no absolute logic for determining how the disaggregation rules operate in different occupations. There may be a number of different ways of disaggregating a statement. What is important is to identify the one which will make most sense to practitioners as a representation of the ways in which work roles are grouped within their occupation. To illustrate the fact that different rules may be appropriate for different purposes and occupations we can use an analogy. If we wish to classify trees we could use a number of different disaggregation rules. If we classify trees by the density of wood which they produce the classification would be:

Trees $\left\{ \begin{array}{l} \text{hardwood} \\ \text{softwood} \end{array} \right.$

Disaggregation rule: density of wood.

If, on the other hand, we classified by whether trees lose their leaves in winter, the classification would be:

Trees $\left\{ \begin{array}{l} \text{deciduous} \\ \text{coniferous} \end{array} \right.$

Disaggregation rule: whether leaves drop in winter.

The significance of this example is that both classifications are entirely acceptable and logical – neither is right or wrong. However, each classification is useful for particular purposes. A cabinetmaker is interested in knowing whether wood is hard or soft because this affects the working qualities of the timber. A gardener is not particularly interested in this information. On the other hand, the gardener choosing a small avenue of trees to line a garden path may want to know whether the leaves fall in winter because they will have the task of clearing them up. By contrast, cabinetmakers are unlikely to be interested in this feature – unless they happen to grow their own supplies of timber.

Here are some examples and analyses of disaggregation rules taken from a number of functional analyses. In each example the rule used for the disaggregation is illustrated and analysed. This is followed by an illustration of an alternative rule of disaggregation which might have been used where this is possible. The alternative rule makes logical sense, but is clearly not the most appropriate within the occupational context.

Example A. Assess resource procurement and technical constraints on the development process[3]

This has been classified into the following sub-statements:

A1	Assess resource procurement constraints on the development process
A2	Assess resource utilisation constraints on the development process
A3	Assess technical and physical constraints on the development process

The substatements in this example, taken from the construction industry, describe different kinds of constraints which apply to the procurement process: resource procurement, resource utilisation, technical and physical. They have been disaggregated in this way because different **methods** are used for the three different types of assessment.

An alternative disaggregation could be to separate the stages in the analysis process. For example:

A1	Identify and summarise information required to assess constraints on the development process
A2	Analyse and synthesise resource procurement, resource utilisation, technical and physical constraints on the development process
A3	Assess, evaluate and recommend methods and techniques to minimise constraints on the development process

This is a **linear, or sequential, process**: identify and summarise information; analyse and synthesise constraints; assess, evaluate and recommend methods. It is entirely logical but is not appropriate to the context. In this case, the different methods of analysis would be grouped together within each substatement and would require further disaggregation to make any sense of the work roles in the sector. What this could lead to is another level of analysis as each method is then separated from each substatement, as follows:

A1	Identify and summarise information required to assess constraints on the development process

could be further disaggregated to:

A1.1	Identify and summarise information required to assess resource procurement constraints on the development process
A1.2	Identify and summarise information required to assess resource utilisation constraints on the development process
A1.3	Identify and summarise information required to assess technical and physical constraints on the development process

> A2   Analyse and synthesise resource procurement, resource utilization, technical and physical constraints on the development process

could be further disaggregated to:

> A2.1   Analyse and synthesise resource procurement constraints on the development process
>
> A2.2   Analyse and synthesise resource utilisation constraints on the development process
>
> A2.3   Analyse and synthesise technical and physical constraints on the development process

> A3   Assess, evaluate and recommend methods and techniques to minimise constraints on the development process

could be further disaggregated to:

> A3.1   Assess, evaluate and recommend methods and techniques to minimise resource procurement constraints on the development process
>
> A3.2   Assess, evaluate and recommend methods and techniques to minimise resource utilisation constraints on the development process
>
> A3.3   Assess, evaluate and recommend methods and techniques to minimise technical and physical constraints on the development process

This extended analysis process and the disaggregation rules used to produce it are still entirely logical, but the resulting analysis makes no sense in occupational terms. The three significant groups of methods and techniques used to assess the different types of constraints have become completely separated into artificial groupings which suggest that there are work roles which involve identifying and summarising information on all three types of constraint, separated from other work roles which concentrate in analysing and synthesising the constraints arising from each type, which are in turn separated from roles involving the processes of assessment, evaluation and recommendation.

In reality, work roles involve the combined processes of identification of significant information, analysis and assessment of each type of constraint. Particular work roles may combine the assessment of all three types, but the **sequential process** is activated separately for each type. Consequently, the first disaggregation – separating each **method** of assessment – is the more appropriate in the occupational context.

Example B. Dry and reel paper and board by machine process[4]

This has been classified into the following substatements:

B1	Set up, operate and maintain dry end process
B2	Dry and reel formed paper and board
B3	Monitor, adjust and control variables to meet production targets and product specifications

The substatements in this example, taken from the paper and board industry, are identical to the hypothetical example shown earlier. This is a **hybrid** disaggregation. The first two substatements are stages in a sequential process ('Set up, operate and maintain dry end process' … then … 'Dry and reel formed paper and board'). The third is a task management component which co-ordinates the specific activities to meet overall objectives ('to meet production targets and product specifications').

An alternative disaggregation would be to separate the different **products** identified in the first statement – paper and board – to produce the following disaggregation:

B1	Set up, operate and maintain dry end process for paper manufacture
B2	Dry and reel formed paper
B3	Monitor, adjust and control variables to meet production targets and product specifications for paper manufacture

and a parallel disaggregation:

B4	Set up, operate and maintain dry end process for board manufacture
B5	Dry and reel formed board
B6	Monitor, adjust and control variables to meet production targets and product specifications for board manufacture

Again, this is entirely logical but it artificially separates paper and board manufacture which are combined in the equipment used and the work roles and processes adopted in the industry.

Example C. Design and develop power train assemblies[5]

This has been classified into the following substatements:

> C1 Design, test and develop new power train components and subassemblies
>
> C2 Develop and improve existing power train components and subassemblies
>
> C3 Contribute to the integration of systems and subsystems within the overall design

The substatements in this example, taken from standards for vehicle engineering, power train design, is also a hybrid disaggregation. The first two statements describe **different products** ('new power train components' and 'existing power train components') and **different outcomes** ('design, test and develop' and 'develop and improve'). In addition, there is a task management statement which integrates the systems into the overall design of the vehicle.

This combination of technical statements with a task management statement is quite common and reflects the widespread use of the Job Competence Model in the development of functional analysis and presentation of occupational standards.

This disaggregation could follow a **sequential** or **cyclical** process as follows:

> C1 Design new power train components and subassemblies
> C2 Test new and existing power train components and subassemblies
> C3 Develop new and existing power train components and subassemblies
> C4 Improve new and existing power train components and subassemblies
> C5 Contribute to the integration of systems and subsystems within the overall design

The logic of the alternative disaggregation is flimsy because 'existing' power trains have to be excluded from statement C1 because they have already been designed. The disaggregation lacks occupational logic because it fails to separate the different outcomes and products. The testing methods for new and existing products are different, as are the development and improvement processes.

Example D. Contribute to the management of aggressive and abusive behaviour[6]

This has been classified into the following substatements:

> D1 Contribute to the promotion of non-aggressive and non-abusive behaviour
>
> D2 Contribute to the management of episodes of aggressive or abusive behaviour by clients

The substatements in this example, taken from the care sector standards, separates two different **outcomes** which combine with different **methods and processes**. The first substatement describes general promotion of non-aggressive and non-abusive behaviour (the outcome) which occurs throughout working activity by the application of processes of observation and taking opportunities to promote. The second is **episodic** – it occurs only in response to 'episodes of aggressive or abusive behaviour' and the outcome is to manage the episode using methods and processes different from those used in the promotion of non-aggressive and non-abusive behaviour.

It would be possible to suggest the following **sequence** of substatements:

D1	Identify and monitor instances of aggressive and abusive behaviour
D2	Contribute to the management of episodes of aggressive or abusive behaviour by clients
D3	Contribute to the promotion of non-aggressive and non-abusive behaviour

This is another hybrid with a two-stage sequence: 'identify and monitor' followed by 'contribute to the management of'. The third statement acts as a task management function. However, this does not describe the operation of work roles in the sector because the process of identification of instances of aggressive and abusive behaviour is an integral part of the other two statements. Identifying the instance triggers the responses of either managing the episode or taking the opportunity to promote non-aggressive and non-abusive behaviour. Identification, of itself, is not a separate role.

Example E. Plan, control and record audit work[7]

This has been classified into the following substatements:

E1	Obtain background data for the purpose of audit planning
E2	Plan and allocate resources to meet audit objectives
E3	Design audit programmes and working schedules for the recording and storage of evidence
E4	Determine and record the organisation's accounting system and its manner of operation
E5	Monitor and maintain the recording and storage of evidence against audit requirements

The substatements in this example, taken from standards for auditors is a **linear sequence** of outcomes, each of which has to be completed before the next can start. In this example there is no other logical pattern which could be used.

In all but one of the examples above there are alternative ways of applying the disaggregation rules, but one pattern makes most sense in terms of the occupational roles which are described. This is a useful lesson for those developing a functional analysis because it emphasises the importance of involving both occupational specialists and people with expertise in the functional analysis process.

A functional analysis specialist may identify a disaggregation rule which is logical and coherent but which fails validly to represent roles in the occupation. By contrast, occupational specialists may come up with a haphazard list of activities for which the specialist in functional analysis may be able to suggest a more logical and coherent structure which will facilitate the overall coherence of the analysis.

It is often useful to try out different disaggregation rules where it appears that a number of different analyses are possible and to track the analysis down to another stage of detail to observe the subsequent effect of the rule. This is what happened in Example A. It is at the next stage of the analysis that problems occur requiring a revision to the structure. Although this may use more resources, it is preferable to sticking with a preferred or apparently obvious rule which may create difficulties at subsequent analysis stages.

This process of experimentation and modification of stages in the analysis is referred to as **iteration** and is described in the next section.

Summary

1. In general, disaggregation rules take the following patterns:

   - a linear or sequential process (eg, plan, design, build);
   - a cyclical process (eg, develop, implement, evaluate);
   - separation of different processes or methods (eg, identify information sources, evaluate information sources);
   - separation of different products or outcomes (eg, test mechanical components, test electrical components).

2. In addition to these patterns, there are hybrid rules where the patterns may be combined or where a task management statement is added to integrate the activities described in the other statements.

3. Disaggregation rules have no absolute logic – they make sense in the context of the occupation. Different rules will be appropriate to different work roles in different occupational sectors and a particular statement may be capable of analysis in a number of different ways. In developing a functional analysis it may be useful to try different rules and follow the analysis through to see which rule gives the most realistic and credible representation of occupational roles.

ITERATION

The identification of disaggregation rules involves a series of discrete decisions. The process of iteration (dictionary definition: 'to perform again, repeat') is integral to the development of the disaggregation rules and occurs throughout the functional analysis.

Often, different groups are given responsibilities for the development of different parts of the general classification. This makes good practical sense, particularly where the analysis involves an entire occupational sector consisting of different occupational groups and specialisms. However, this can lead to overlaps, duplication and other inconsistencies as the separate groups expand their spheres of interest and inadvertently start to operate in adjacent or common areas of concern. These inconsistencies can also occur within a single development group if attention is focused on one area of the classification without regard for the effect on the whole.

Iteration offers the opportunity to retrace the analysis process and adjust the whole framework to maintain discrete statements, to give a more logical or acceptable structure and to regroup functions which have become separated by the analysis process.

Iteration requires that the developing analysis framework is seen as a draft, which can be modified and amended at any stage. In general, a significant change in any statement may have an impact on other statements in the same grouping or on the title of the grouping. If the title changes this may in turn impact on other titles, and so on.

Changes to titles and groupings are affected by the three different, but interlinked, factors that form the standards evaluation framework described in Chapter 14. They are: technical issues, political issues and implementation/ practical issues.

Technical issues are to do with the overall logic and coherence of the analysis – whether the classification and disaggregation rules used are logical and consistent and whether the analysis is concentrating on the separation of functions. The application of this factor avoids the generation of lists of activities which relate to existing job descriptions and activity sequences. Technical issues also include the process of auditing the analysis as it develops to apply the components of the Job Competence Model. Task management statements may be added to groups of activities and work environment components may be used to group together important process skills like interactions with colleagues and clients.

Political issues are to do with what is likely to be acceptable and credible within the occupational sector. This can result in the analysis framework being deliberately distorted to place certain statements in positions of prominence or to retain descriptions which are so familiar in the occupational sector that the analysis would lack credibility if they were changed, even though they are not strictly in accord with the analysis process. By contrast, changes can also be made to signal anticipated future requirements which are not currently widespread.

Implementation/practical issues are to do with the next stages in standards development – the design of qualifications and assessment systems. Statements in the analysis may be functionally similar, and consequently grouped together, but the resulting grouping may be so entirely different from current practice that it might have the consequence of denying access to potential candidates when qualifications are developed.

Given that there are three different issues to take into account, the iteration process often involves complex consultation and decision-making processes, particularly where different issues conflict. For example, the political aim of signalling important future requirements may conflict with the practical implications of restricting access to candidates in employment where such changes have not taken place and consequently reduce credibility. The consideration of these issues is best illustrated by a practical case study.

DISAGGREGATION AND ITERATION – A CASE STUDY

In the first draft of the analysis for professional trade union officers, the title of key area B was expressed as:

B	Represent and advance the interests of members

The most obvious disaggregation rule is the distinction between 'representation' and 'advancing' (which includes negotiation). These are different **outcomes**, so the first separation was:

B1	Represent the interests of members
B2	Negotiate terms and conditions with employers

However, it was generally felt that the distinction between individual and collective interests (mentioned in the key purpose statement) should be retained as this often involved different methods and processes. Consequently, B1 was further developed to give:

B1	Represent the collective interests of members
B2	Represent the interests of individual members
B3	Negotiate terms and conditions with employers

This is a hybrid disaggregation – different outcomes (representation/negotiation) combined with different processes (representing individual/representing collective interests). The rules used are **technical** in character – designed to maintain coherence.

However, as the analysis progressed to further levels of detail, it quickly became apparent that the processes involved in B1 and B2 were functionally identical and any actual differences could be accommodated in the detail of the standards which would emerge from the analysis. Furthermore, it was recognised that the competent officer is expected to achieve both outcomes.

The consultation process suggested another significant factor. As stated, the outcomes imply that the officer **takes responsibility** for representation and negotiation. In fact, the expectation (and growing trend) is for the officer to provide the necessary support to **enable** representatives and members to look after their own interests. This is part of the change from control to empowerment models of organisation which we described in Chapter 2.

B1 and B2 were recombined with different wording to emphasise the supportive role, as follows:

> B1   Support the representation of members' interests

In technical terms, the difference between 'representing' and 'supporting representation' is not immediately apparent. But the use of the term 'supporting' gives clear signals about the changing role and the support of the Lead Body for that change. Consequently, the modification is a **political** factor, but it will also have a **technical** impact because it will affect the way in which the performance criteria are phrased.

The structure of B2 was endorsed during the consultation, but the wording changed to emphasise improvements in terms and conditions because the original title appeared to imply a once-and-for-all negotiation. A strategic component was also added to B2 to emphasise the development of a collective bargaining agenda – in effect, a plan of action designed to maximise the success of negotiations. B2 was altered to:

> B2   Negotiate and improve terms and conditions to meet an agreed collective bargaining agenda

However, the detailed changes to B2 suggested a series of modifications to the title of B to emphasise the supportive role and to state the expectation that both individual and collective interests were to be represented (since this was now lost by the recombination of B1 and B2). To reflect this, the title of key area B was changed to:

> B   Support and enable members to advance their individual and collective interests

Finally, participants in the consultation process expressed a preference for the order of B1 and B2 to be reversed. Although it was fully accepted that B1 and B2 did not imply a sequence, since the analysis of this area was based on separation of different outcomes, it was felt that the change in sequence would offer greater acceptance and credibility because gaining recognition for the union was contained in B2 and this logically preceded representation because representation is not possible unless the union is recognised for such purposes. This is another example of a **political** factor. The final version of this analysis is:

B Support and enable members to advance their individual and collective interests

B1 Negotiate and improve terms and conditions to meet an agreed collective bargaining agenda

B2 Support the representation of members' interests

This case study illustrates how the different change factors – technical, political and practical – combine to produce an analysis which achieves a clear and logical separation of functions, which is credible within the occupational sector and which takes into account important changes in work roles.

Iteration – Summary

1. Iteration is integral to the development of the disaggregation rules and occurs throughout the analysis.
2. Iteration involves retracing the analysis process and adjusting the whole framework to maintain discrete statements, to give a more logical or acceptable structure and to regroup functions which have become separated by the analysis process.
3. A change in any statement may have an impact on other statements in the same grouping or on the title of the grouping.
4. Changes made to the framework may be made for technical, political or practical reasons – which usually have to be balanced through consultation with practitioners and occupational specialists.

NOTES

1. All the examples of training and development standards are taken from the first version of the training and development standards, The Training and Development Lead Body, *Standards for Training and Development*. These standards have been revised but the revised version was not available in time to be included in this book.
2. Trades Union Congress, *National Standards for Full Time Trade Union Officials*.
3. Taken from The Construction Industry Standing Conference, *Occupational Standards for Technical, Managerial and Professional Roles*.
4. Taken from the National Vocational Qualification *Dry and reel paper and board by machine process*.
5. This standard was developed in-house by a vehicle manufacturer, not a Lead Body.
6. Taken from standards developed by the Care Sector Consortium and incorporated into a number of National Vocational Qualifications. NCVQ ID: U1014053.
7. Taken from The Chartered Association of Certified Accountants, *Standards for auditors*.

8 Functional analysis – the final stages

FURTHER STAGES OF ANALYSIS

The combined process of disaggregation and iteration continues until a level of detail is reached which describes an outcome which an **individual** might be expected to achieve. When developing standards, we call this level of detail a **functional unit** to distinguish it from a **unit of competence** in a National Vocational Qualification. Although the terms are different, the scope is intended to be the same.

It is important to keep standards and NVQs separate. NVQs are one of the ways in which occupational standards may be used, but there are many other uses of standards. It is crucial that users of standards and qualifications understand the differences. Standards are national specifications for performance, they describe what should happen in employment but they may be used and modified by organisations to meet their specific needs. Qualifications describe what an individual can do. They are also national, but they are not available for adaptation by organisations. Once agreed and accredited, the units of competence are fixed and combined with an assessment specification which cannot be altered.

A candidate assessed against an NVQ unit of competence has attained a credit towards a nationally recognised qualification. A person assessed locally by their own organisation against a modified functional unit from a set of standards has not achieved a credit towards a qualification.

This level of detail is not easy to define with absolute precision. Since the scope of the functional unit and the unit of competence is intended to be the same, we will look for guidance in the documents which define the scope of a unit of competence.

In the original Technical Advisory Group Guidance Note No. 4,[1] a unit of competence is defined as:

> the smallest unit worthy of separate accreditation. It should be a self-standing group of elements of competence, which would be recognised as having high value in employment.

> Units of competence should have high value in employment ... encourage individuals to progress ... [and] .... enable transfer.

The NCVQ *Criteria and Guidance* document[2] states

> Units should, as far as possible, be complete statements of the competence required, including any requirements relating to health and safety, organising work, solving problems and dealing with people. Units should not deal solely with separate tasks or knowledge. They signify a rounded achievement worthy of public accreditation.

Perhaps the best way to illustrate the scope of a functional unit is with an example showing why more general or more detailed statements would not conform to the level of detail required by a functional unit.

Example. Construction – Contract Management

The standards developed by the Construction Industry Standing Conference contain a number of functional units grouped together under a single title which describes the function of securing contracts for the supply of goods, materials and services. The full title of the statement (coded D11 in the original document) is:

D11	Secure contracts for supply of works, goods, materials and consultancy services

At the next level of detail, this statement consists of five functional units:

D111	Prepare and agree the development of a procurement programme
D112	Negotiate strategic sourcing partnerships
D113	Prepare and process estimate, bid and tender enquiries
D114	Prepare and submit estimates, bids and tenders
D115	Prepare and agree contracts

Each functional unit, in turn, has been further analysed into individual occupational standards or elements of competence. The titles of the elements of competence in each functional unit are (see boxed text on opposite page):

D111   Prepare and agree the development of a procurement programme
- D111.1   Plan and document a procurement programme
- D111.2   Specify the work content and duration of a contract

D112   Negotiate strategic sourcing partnerships
- D112.1   Evaluate the benefits and risks of partnership/strategic sourcing
- D112.2   Agree and implement alignment of systems with suppliers
- D112.3   Monitor and control arrangements for strategic sourcing

D113   Prepare and process estimate, bid and tender enquiries
- D113.1   Evaluate and select potential tenderers
- D113.2   Obtain estimates, bids and tenders
- D113.3   Assess and select successful estimates, bids and tenders and negotiate changes

D114   Prepare and submit estimates, bids and tenders
- D114.1   Evaluate estimate, bid and tender enquiry documentation
- D114.2   Assess the resource requirements and costs within an estimate, bid and tender
- D114.3   Finalise and submit an estimate, bid and tender application

D115   Prepare and agree contracts
- D115.1   Prepare and modify forms of contract
- D115.2   Negotiate and conclude a contract for the supply of works, goods, materials and consultancy services
- D115.3   Negotiate and conclude a contract for financial services

In developing this structure CISC had a number of choices to make about what constituted a functional unit. There are at least two possibilities.

The first is that the more general outcome, D11, could have been taken to be a functional unit, with the functional units, D111–D115, treated as elements of competence. This was not thought to be practical because the overall function of 'Securing contracts for supply of works, goods, materials and consultancy services' is usually the function of an entire department in an organisation. This broad outcome, and the five substatements derived from it, are considerably **in excess** of the sort of outcome which an individual might be expected to achieve.

In addition, the five functions grouped within D11 represent quite different roles. The preparation of procurement programmes (D111) is a complete work role in its own right which might be undertaken by many different job holders. The negotiation of strategic partnerships (D112) is also a separate work role which may be continuous and may be quite separate from the preparation of procurement programmes and the linked processes of preparing bids, submitting tenders and preparing and agreeing contracts.

The next two statements, prepare and process estimate, bid and tender enquiries (D113) and prepare and submit estimates, bids and tenders (D114) are two sides of the same coin. In practice, organisations seeking suppliers require competence in the first outcome and supplier organisations require competence in the latter. Consequently work roles in the industry tend to concentrate on one or the other – the two outcomes rarely occur together in the same work roles.

The final statement, prepare and agree contracts (D115), could be coherently grouped with any one of the previous statements.

The fact that statements do not conform to current work roles is not always a basis for decision making. There are instances where anticipated changes in working patterns might suggest a different structure, but in this case no such changes were anticipated.

Setting a functional unit at the level of statement D11, is impractical, therefore, for these reasons. When judged against the criteria available it is clear that:

- It is considerably in excess of the requirements of an individual in typical work roles in the sector.
- The grouping is not coherent in terms of existing or anticipated future work roles. Functionally, the series of statements make sense for the sector as a whole – all these outcomes need to be achieved for supplies to be secured – but this involves different kinds of outcomes achieved by different job holders in different work roles and in different organisations.
- The structure would not facilitate progression. Candidates who wished to present evidence from their workplace as a primary source of evidence would be required to work for a number of different organisations in a variety of different work roles before sufficient evidence of competence could be collected.

The second option available for CISC would be to recognise each element of competence as a functional unit and then further disaggregate to reach the level of occupational standards/elements of competence. Taking the first set of statements, currently grouped under unit D111, as an example, this would mean two separate functional units:

Functional unit 1   Plan and document a procurement programme
Functional unit 2   Specify the work content and duration of a contract

These would be further subdivided into occupational standards. Our first problem would be to suggest a disaggregation rule which would make sense in the sector. For the first statement we might distinguish between the planning of the programme and the documentation of the programme (different outcomes), giving two elements of competence:

Functional unit 1	Plan and document a procurement programme
Element 1.1	Plan a procurement programme
Element 1.2	Document a procurement programme

This analysis makes no sense because the process of planning results in documentation and the production of documentation has to be preceded by planning. The two outcomes are integral and to further distinguish between them has no logic in the sector.

The second functional unit, specify the work content and duration of a contract, is almost impossible to analyse further. There would no case for distinguishing between the 'work content' and 'duration' of a contract since both are an integral part of the whole specification and separating out the stages involved would simply result in a series of small tasks. The end of the analysis point has been reached, so the two statements are occupational standards or elements of competence, which means that the most appropriate level at which to set the functional unit is the statement that groups them together:

D111	Prepare and agree the development of a procurement programme

This statement does conform to the outline criteria:

- It represents what an individual might be expected to achieve.
- The grouping of the standards (the elements of competence) is coherent – the documentation of the programme and the production of a specification of work content and duration are part of the same work role.
- The grouping is of value in employment – people are employed to 'Prepare and agree the development of a procurement programme' rather than being employed merely to 'Plan and document a procurement programme'.

This process of tracking potential functional units down to the next level of detail is a crucial stage in the iteration process. When the analysis reaches the point where the next level of detail starts to generate potential occupational standards/elements of competence, it may be useful to track back up the level of detail in the framework to confirm that the next level up is not too broad and generalised. This process of checking and re-checking allows valid decisions to be made about what should constitute a functional unit.

The discussion of functional units in the context of a functional map always refers to potential units of competence in a National Vocational Qualification. Units of competence are the building-blocks of National Vocational Qualifications. This stage in the analysis process generates the starting-point for the development of the occupational standards which will eventually be used to construct NVQs. This means that the standards may be combined in different ways to form units of competence when qualifications are designed. Although the functional unit is at a level of detail which conforms to the description of a unit of competence, there is no guarantee that the functional unit will appear in the same format with the same content in any subsequent NVQ.

The relationship between the functional units in a functional map and subsequent units of competence in an NVQ is illustrated in Figure 8.1. In this representation the functional map is deliberately simplified by having only three levels of analysis from the key purpose statement and only two outcome statements disaggregated from the key purpose (in practice there can be many more). The first thing to note is that a functional map is much more comprehensive than a qualification. This is often misunderstood and practitioners can become very concerned if they believe that the functional map also represents a qualification. This underlines the importance of separating standards and qualifications. A functional map and its constituent standards represents **all** the roles in an occupational sector; a qualification is a **selection** from the standards. Many different qualifications may be developed from a single functional map.

Figure 8.1 shows three ways in which functional units in a functional map might be structured when qualifications are designed. The functional map, which has 12 functional units, is on the left and the qualification, which has seven units of competence, is on the right. The structures also differ in that the functional map has a number of levels of analysis, whereas the qualification only has one – the overall qualification title and the units of competence.

In the examples labelled 1 in the figure, the functional unit in the functional map is simply translated in its entirety into a unit of competence in the qualification. This is quite common. If the map is an accurate identification of work roles in the sector we should expect many of the functional units to translate in this way.

The examples labelled 2 represents an instance where two functional units from the functional map have been combined to produce one unit of competence in the qualification. This may represent a combination of **all** the elements of competence from the two functional units or a rearrangement of **some** of the constituent elements of competence. This might be done to reflect existing work roles and to facilitate better access for candidates.

The example labelled 3 shows a functional unit which has been split to form two units of competence. This might happen in cases where a functional unit in the functional map is extremely demanding and could result in candidates taking a considerable period of time to complete the unit of competence – which could be demotivating.

These examples serve to emphasise that the scope of a functional unit is never clear cut and defies an absolute definition. What we can be sure about is that:

- it represents what an **individual** might be expected to achieve, rather than the achievement goal of an entire department or organisation;
- when the functional unit is subsequently developed to the next stage of analysis the grouping of the standards is coherent and recognisable as part of the same work role;

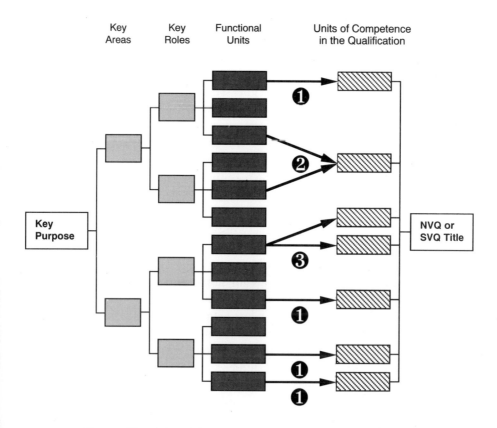

Fig. 8.1 The relationship between functional units and units of competence

- the outcome described by the functional unit is of value in employment – which means that if a potential candidate for employment were to say 'I can do … [functional unit title]', this would have immediate meaning to, and be perceived as relevant by, an employer.

FUTURE CAPABILITY

Functional analysis is designed to identify competence requirements for the future as well as best current practice. An important consideration throughout the functional analysis process is the identification of future trends to guide both the development of the functional map and the subsequent standards setting exercise. The requirement for standards to be future focused needs to be more than rhetoric. There must be practical means available to identify the significant trends which are likely to impact on future work roles.

This intent can be treated with a certain suspicion and cynicism, appearing to be

133

little more than *ad hoc* crystal-ball gazing. It also raises the criticism that previous attempts to predict the nature and structure of jobs and skills for the future have often been confounded by unanticipated changes which can result in wasted training provision.

Statistical extrapolations have often gone badly wrong in the past. Assumptions about how many technicians, engineers, bricklayers or accountants might be needed in the future have been used to structure training and educational provision, only to find that markets have changed and the predicted need does not arise.

This method of prediction is not the pattern adopted in functional analysis. We are not really interested in specific jobs or specific skills – these do change over time in quite unpredictable ways so we believe that there is little point in trying to predict them with any hope of accuracy. But changes in work roles, consequent upon changes in technologies, social values, economies and markets, are capable of anticipation if not precise prediction.

As we suggested in Chapter 1, identifying the main features of social and economic change which are likely to impact on work roles is relatively straightforward. The information is all around us and our ability to extrapolate from what has happened in the past serves us well when we contemplate the future. But the question remains 'how is it done?'. The answer is to make the prediction of the requirements for future capability part of the consultative process which underpins functional analysis. The factholders – practitioners who are engaged in the occupation – are the most valuable source of information for identifying the important factors which are changing now and are likely to continue to influence work roles.

Groups involved in the consultative process can be invited to consider changes in three categories:

1. Changes which have a history, that is they have been impacting on the occupation for some years and the influence of them is likely to continue – for example, the impact of computers in office systems.
2. Changes which are only starting to emerge, but which are likely to have future impact – for example, the emergence of electronic communications systems like the Internet.
3. Changes which have not yet emerged, but which can be anticipated with some certainty – for example, programmed legislation due for future implementation.

To help focus practitioners it is often useful to encourage them to reflect on changes in the occupation which have occurred over the past five years and to identify key benchmarks. This is done by selecting a particular aspect of change and identifying what its characteristics were five years ago and what its characteristics are now, to enable participants to identify the scope and pace of change in key areas. This benchmarking can then be used to extrapolate into the future along the lines of 'if this is the nature and pace of change in the last five years, what could we anticipate happening for this aspect over the next five years?'.

We gave an example of this approach in Chapter 1 where we traced the development of our own computer systems. In five years we have seen exponential increases in memory capacity, storage capacity, display systems (screens, monitors, etc.) and improvements in printing technology, all combined with a dramatic reduction in cost.

Most people with an involvement in computer systems could take this information and make some useful extrapolations which would assist in anticipating the kinds of work roles which might emerge in the future – characteristics which should be addressed in occupational standards. To take our own systems as an example, here are some extrapolations for the future:

- Communications technology will improve and costs will reduce to the extent that all our staff will be able to have portable computers (we have four already) equipped with modems (electronic devices which enable computer systems to connect through telephone lines) which will enable us to access our central files from anywhere in the world through a telephone line.
- The modem systems will replace paper-based fax systems so all staff will be able to send and receive fax messages from any location.
- Portable telephone technology will link to the modem communications systems so we will be able to communicate literally from any location; we will not need to attach to a fixed phone line, just to plug into the portable phone.
- Portable computers will ride the same curve of increased power and reduced cost as desk-based machines. This could mean that fixed desk computers become obsolete – each person will have their own computer with full communication facilities.
- The same pattern will apply to telephones – each person will have a phone with their own phone number. Fixed telephones will no longer be necessary.
- Printing technology will improve and colour printers and copiers will decrease in cost. This will dramatically improve the quality of our presentational materials.
- The keyboard may become obsolete as voice-operated systems are developed.
- Documents will become interactive. Reports will be distributed on CD ROM and may include sound, movie clips and opportunities for users to select indexes and portions of the document to read in more detail.
- Access to library and information facilities through the Internet may make our existing library and archives obsolete.

These are just some of the anticipated changes which could impact on our work practices over the next five years. Many of them are already possible – but at enormous cost, which is likely to diminish if the pattern of the last five years with respect to computer technology is sustained.

These kinds of extrapolations are important for considering the future shape of work roles. If reports may not be written documents in the future, should standards for occupations where written reports are commonly used include the generation of 'multimedia' publications in range statements, even if this would require simulations for assessment? If keyboards become obsolete, describing the transcription of documents will focus less on the manual capabilities of keyboard operation and more on the ability to draft, check and modify information. If portable phones become personal phones for a significant proportion of the population, telephone reception will change from the routing of transmissions to the management of communication systems. If information workers can work from any location, what will team work be like if the team is scattered over a wide geographical area? These considerations may seem rather futuristic, but many of the assumptions we would have made five or ten years ago might have seemed equally impractical at the time.

But it is not just the impact of technology which needs to be taken into account when we are considering future work roles. The aspects which may impact on future work roles will include:

- technological development (this can be a vast category and includes computer systems and new materials);
- social and political changes;
- market and economic changes;
- legislation and codes of practice;
- patterns of work organisation.

When invited to anticipate future developments, practitioners may concentrate on any of these areas, depending on their particular interests. Not all the changes may need to be reflected in the functional analysis and the occupational standards but some will provide crucial signals which will guide the development of qualifications and future education and training provision.

For example, the consultation on the standards for professional trade union officers identified a number of significant developments which are shown in Table 8.1.

A number of these changes were selected for inclusion in the standards. The likely impact of European legislation and the increased liaison with European trade unions is reflected in a number of range statements. References to legislation include European legislation and directives and the standard describing policy promotion is titled 'represent the union within local, national and *international* organisations'. [The authors' emphasis.]

The change in role from a representative to an empowering relationship between full-time officers and voluntary representatives is reflected in the language used to describe the representative and organisational roles with terms like 'support', 'assist', 'advise' being used to emphasise this emerging role.

Other emerging trends were addressed by the ways in which the standards

Emerging Trends

As part of the workshop activity, participants were asked to identify important trends which suggested critical outcomes for the future. The key points raised were:

- There will be fewer members and fewer trade unions. Unions will need to amalgamate to retain influence, they may also need to share resources in areas like research and education
- Unions will have to operate within an increasingly hostile political and economic environment, anticipating additional legislation designed to further reduce trade union influence. In particular, the anticipated 'checking off' legislation and changes in the collection of the political levy could drastically affect membership and subscription income
- There will be a larger number of decentralised bargaining units with the associated fragmentation of collective bargaining, reduction of membership and reduction in influence. New topics for collective bargaining will need to be identified to retain membership commitment
- There will be an increasing reliance on workplace representatives and the importance of developing robust structures as professional officers attempt to make the best use of their time and resources (this is a key theme throughout the standards)
- There will be an increasing move to a more facilitative and enabling role for the professional officer (this change in role is represented throughout the standards)
- Increasing 'professionalism' of the professional officer to match the increasing professionalism of management
- Impact of Europe:

  - more complex European legislation and directives, some of which may have clear benefits for trade unions and their members
  - the spread of European social values which tend to be more positive towards trade unions
  - more international links between unions and amalgamations across Europe
  - an increase in 'social partnership' concepts and expectations from European based employers

- An increase in a community focus to replace the traditional communication device of branch meetings and to present trade unions as responsible co-operating bodies
- New technologies will tend to make more and better information available. Technology will also impact on local administration and organisation
- An increase in providing tangible services to members as traditional values of collectivism and union membership decline and unions need to develop new ways to attract and retain members
- An increase in 'individualism' encouraged by:

  - performance related pay systems
  - individual contracts
  - self and contract employment

- More complex UK legislation
- An increase in the 'Human Resource Management' (HRM) approach to personnel management and industrial relations requiring new roles and perspectives from professional officers. The HRM approach will tend to replace negotiation with consultation direct to the workforce
- Questions about accountability and responsibility, particularly in unions where professional officers are elected, moves towards a professional career structure for professional officers, with professional officers being better educated and appointed rather than elected
- A change in balance between specialist and generalist roles. Roles such as recruitment may become so time consuming that they are taken over by regional specialists, and tribunal representation may become so 'legalistic' and complex that local specialists are necessary, whereas centralised and specialist negotiations may be devolved to local offices and individual professional officers

Source: TUC, *National Standards for full time trade union officials*

Table 8.1 Emerging trends identified during the trade union standards consultation

were grouped into qualifications. Outcomes concerned with recruitment and personal advocacy were separated into different qualifications to reflect the trend towards more specialised officers and two qualifications were carefully designed to encourage clear progression routes for officers to reflect the increasing professionalism of the role.

In these ways emerging trends can be addressed within occupational standards and NVQs and provide a practical way of expressing the need for future capability.

Other Lead Bodies have made similar attempts to identify emerging trends and to incorporate them into standards and qualifications. For example:

- The Construction Industry Standing Conference identify strategic resourcing and supplier development as an important trend which was incorporated into the standards.
- The Training and Development Lead Body recognised the increasing importance of evaluation by requiring that the first set of qualifications developed from the standards all included evaluation of training.
- The Care Sector Consortium deliberately developed standards in advance of practice to reflect changes to support roles as a result of changes in the education and training of nurses.

It is important to note that many of these emerging trends are not commonly practised in the occupational sector. This is quite proper – the role of standards is to lead practice, not follow it. But it does raise a potential problem when such requirements are incorporated into NVQs which, on the whole, are based on the assumption that much of the evidence for an NVQ will be gathered in the workplace. If Lead Bodies deliberately include outcomes which are likely to have future impact but which are not common in current practice then they need to make parallel arrangements to provide the education, training and assessment opportunities which will be required to develop and assess potential future capability.

FUNCTIONAL MAPS – REPRESENTATION OR REALITY?

The product of the process of functional analysis is a functional map. The functional map is a broad representation of an occupational sector and is the outcome of a decision-making process. It starts with the definition of the key purpose – the unique contribution which the occupational sector makes within the economy. The key purpose also defines the scope of the subsequent map. From this very broad statement a number of substatements are generated, by a process of analysis, which represent outcomes which must be achieved to account fully for the key purpose. This process of elaboration and classification continues, usually to one or two more levels of detail, to give the characteristic tree diagram which separates the functions but links them together to show that all of them are essential if the key purpose is to be achieved.

The use of the term 'map' is not accidental. A functional map has many of the characteristics and limitations of a conventional physical map with which we are all familiar. Imagine a large-scale road map or an Ordinance Survey map of the Leeds area. If we examined the map in the belief that the features represented on it were real, then we would infer that the M1 and M62 are blue, they are each nearly half a mile wide and the words 'West Yorkshire' are painted in mile-long black letters on the landscape to the north of Leeds! Despite the views of some southerners on the strangeness of the north of England, this is not the case. The map is a **representation** of the real world – it does not claim to be an exact copy.

A physical map will separate features which, if we flew over the area in an aeroplane, would appear to be the same thing. For example, if you fly into Leeds/Bradford airport from the south or west, the landing approach takes you across Bradford and then the north of Leeds. All that you can see from the aircraft is one large built-up conurbation – there is no discernable distinction or point of separation between the two cities. Yet the physical map identifies Bradford as a separate city from Leeds and even shows where the boundaries lie. It also describes districts, like Pudsey, Pool and Yeadon, which cannot be inferred in any way from the physical observation of the reality from the aircraft window. This imbalance between reality and representation does not usually bother us at all. We are quite accustomed to it and we accept that a physical map is simply a representation which has limited but useful purposes.

Physical maps are unreal, but useful tools for a number of purposes. Usually, a physical map reproduces locations and features which already exist but sometimes a map identifies features which have existed in the past ('site of disused railway') or are likely to exist in the future ('proposed route of new road').

Different kinds of map can be produced for different purposes, each emphasising different kinds of information at the expense of features which, in other circumstances, would be a critical omission, or by showing proportions or scales which are quite unrealistic. Town plans designed for visitors may disproportionately highlight tourist features but omit hospitals and schools. Maps showing the location of national parks will ignore airports and large towns. Specialist maps will represent features such as climatic regions and population distribution by quite deliberate distorting real physical proportions.

Route maps and plans devised by motoring organisations show routes as straight lines when they actually feature numerous junctions with many changes of direction. Routes are usually shown vertically, top to bottom of the page, which in map-making conventions indicates north/south, whereas their real orientation may be quite different. Location maps sent out by hotels and many other organisations show their building three times the size of the town hall. None of these distortions of reality bother us because they have a purpose and we can interpret them.

A functional map is similar in many respects to a physical map. It does not claim to be an exact copy of the real world of jobs and activities. It is a **representation** of functions which exist and those which may exist in the future. It may also refer to functions which have existed in the past. A functional map is highly generalised

– like, for example, an outline map of the UK – it does not show detail. Functional maps group functions according to rules of classification, therefore real current jobs and activities will be scattered about the map in the same way as cities and rivers are scattered around a geographical map.

Functional maps have a very limited purpose:

- to identify key functions at a number of levels of detail (analysis);
- to show ways in which key functions relate to one another (synthesis).

The overall purpose of the map is to provide a starting-point for occupational standards to be developed – to provide a framework to which detail may be added.

In this sense the functional maps, once again, are analogous to physical maps. A functional map may give no more detail than a country map showing county boundaries, ie two levels of detail, the outline of the country (the key purpose in a functional map) and, within it, the outline of the counties, which also shows the physical relationship between the counties (the key areas or first level of detail in a functional map). Often a functional map will go to a second level of detail, in the same way as a physical map might show the location of major cities or county towns.

This means that the functional map will not show things which people may think are very important, like jobs (particularly their own job), underpinning skills, or knowledge. The map will describe functions in very general terms, so detailed roles, functions and standards have to be inferred from the broad statements. Often a functional map will be accompanied by a commentary which describes what each function contains so that people are aware that the detail has not been ignored; it simply has not been identified – yet.

A functional map, therefore, is limited in its scope and application. It is an extremely generalised picture of broad functions and relationships, no more. Expecting the functional map to show more detail is to fail to understand its purpose. Your job, occupational area, profession or discipline is unlikely to be highlighted in such a general picture, just as your street, favourite restaurant or local pub will not appear on an Ordinance Survey map.

An outline map of the UK showing the main towns will be of no use if you are trying to find your suburb, house or street. It is simply too generalised to show such detail. There are town maps which show detail, street by street, at the expense of failing to show the relationship between towns. Such maps have different purposes – a street map is useless if I am trying to find my way from Leeds to Bristol. Equally, national road maps are of little use if I am trying to find a particular street.

A functional map is, quite deliberately, a very generalised and sometimes distorted representation of an occupational area. Detail is added at later stages of development as precise standards are identified, but the map remains as a complete picture of the occupation to show how the various functions relate to one another and how the analysis was derived. As standards develop it becomes impossible to show the whole picture, so, conventionally, the overall functional map is retained as a reference or index to show how the whole structure fits together. Each main area is then elaborated, often as a separate document, into the constituent standards: the units, elements, performance criteria and range indicators. The analogy between a national road map (the functional map) and town plans (the standards) is very close.

This is the strength of the functional map and is the reason why it needs to be retained as a development tool. Without this representation of the analysis process the dynamic development and application of the standards will be haphazard.

As the occupational standards are developed, the whole structure may then be broken up and rearranged for different purposes. Standards may be selected to form qualifications, they may be grouped to relate to particular jobs or roles, just as physical maps are broken up and rearranged for particular purposes to show particular towns, areas of cities, routes of roads, rivers, National Trust properties, routes of national trails, the location of your office.

This also explains why standards are of little interest to the casual reader. Just as we do not retire to bed to read a street map, we are not likely to gain any literary insights from a functional map or a set of occupational standards. Like a book of physical maps, functional maps and standards are works of reference.

The map, then, is a starting-point from which the subsequent standards will be developed. For each of the functional units, which correspond to a unit of competence, we change the development process to identify occupational standards.

THE RAGGED MAP

In our description of functional analysis and the development of the functional map we have shown idealised models of functional maps which represent only one or two levels of detail. The examples of the full functional maps from which our examples in this chapter have been taken are shown in Appendix 1. These are more detailed and usually show more analysis steps, but they do share one key feature: the right hand, the functional units, are all at the same analysis level. This does not always happen – and when it doesn't, we have the phenomenon of the ragged map. Figure 8.2 shows an example of a ragged map.

A ragged map is usually the result of concurrent but separate development, with different groups having responsibility for part of the map, but there is limited overall co-ordination. Groups can analyse to different levels of detail, which can be corrected by agreed common criteria for the scope of a functional unit. If this has been done, and the map is still ragged, attention needs to turn to the iteration process.

The key purpose and the functional units are the most important part of the

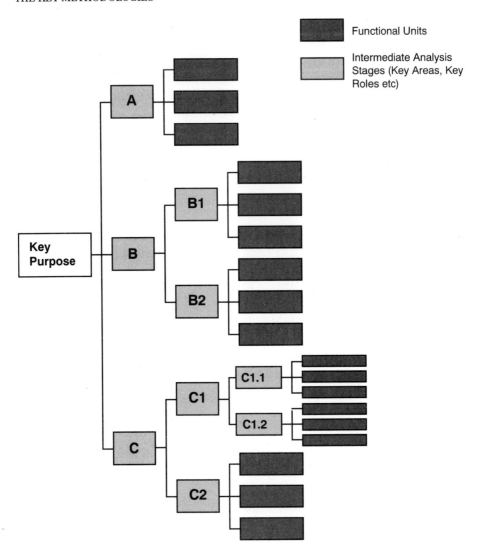

Functional Units

Intermediate Analysis Stages (Key Areas, Key Roles etc)

Fig. 8.2 A ragged functional map

map. The intermediate levels of analysis are there to connect the functional units logically, so that the groups of functional units are separated in terms of different functions but clearly linked to the key purpose. This means that intermediate descriptions can be sacrificed and adapted to make the map as a whole more coherent.

It is possible to do nothing and simply live with the slightly out-of-balance appearance. This may cause problems in the future, however, as different parts of the map are further developed and the relationships between different areas of the map take on increased significance. A more constructive approach is to review the whole map and develop iteration processes and disaggregation rules which give the map greater coherence.

In the example map shown in Figure 8.2 three areas would need careful consideration and review. These are indicated in Figure 8.3.

At point 1, the developers would need to consider whether A is actually a substatement of B or whether B could be rephrased to accommodate A. This will push statements A and the functional units to the right and level out the map. However, it might be necessary to completely revise the structure of A, B, B1 and B2.

At point 2, C1.1 and C1.2 would need to be examined to determine whether they

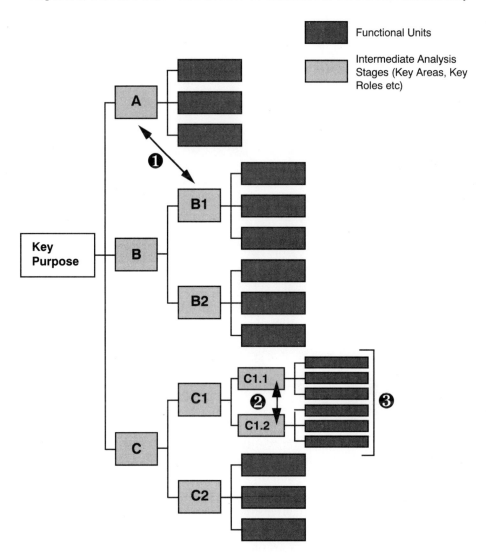

Fig. 8.3 Revising a ragged functional map

represent a logical and coherent disaggregation from C1. If they do not, they can be eliminated, and the group of functional units can be combined and moved left to link with statement C1. If C1.1 and C1.2 are a coherent disaggregation, it is likely that they should be at the same level as statements C1 and C2. This would involve eliminating C1 and moving C1.1 and C1.2 to the left, giving C1 (originally C1.1), C2 (originally C1.2) and C3 (originally C2).

At point 3 the groups of functional units would need to be examined to check that they are at the right level of detail. If they are over-detailed, then it may be that C1.1 and C1.2 are functional units. If they are at the agreed level of detail, attention will need to focus on C1.1 and C1.2, as in point 2.

Of course, these adjustments may generate inconsistencies in other parts of the map which may require further consideration. The object is to produce a finished map with an equal number of analysis levels, with coherent and logical links between the key purpose and the functional units. The only exception to this general rule is the position of the value base, which can often be expressed as a single unit.

THE PLACE OF A VALUE BASE WITHIN A FUNCTIONAL MAP

An additional presentation problem arises when the values which underpin competent performance in an occupation are represented in a separate value base. The conventions of functional analysis suggest that the value base is a key area within a functional map which acts rather like the management roles – it overarches the other standards and has implications for all the standards.

The problem is how to present this concept when the value base is a functional unit. The flat and two-dimensional appearance of the functional map can suggest that the value base has been sidelined somehow as the last set of categories in a list. People often cannot see how this presentation can imply an overarching approach – it looks rather like an afterthought! But there is a second problem, which is that the value base is often confined to a functional unit but is developed at the next level of analysis following the key purpose – which is normally the level associated with the key area. Having a functional unit at the key area level of analysis leads to one of the characteristics of the ragged map. The potential distorting effect of the value base is shown in Figure 8.4.

One way round this problem is to present the value base at the appropriate disaggregation level but this looks odd as well, as Figure 8.5 demonstrates. It also suggests, even more strongly, that the value base is an afterthought.

An alternative is to follow the logic of the value base. We have suggested that the value base has a direct reference to the key purpose and that it overarches all the other standards. The answer, then, is to present it between the key purpose and the key areas, where it truly overarches and impacts on all the standards. This presentation is shown in Figure 8.6. As far as we are aware this approach has not

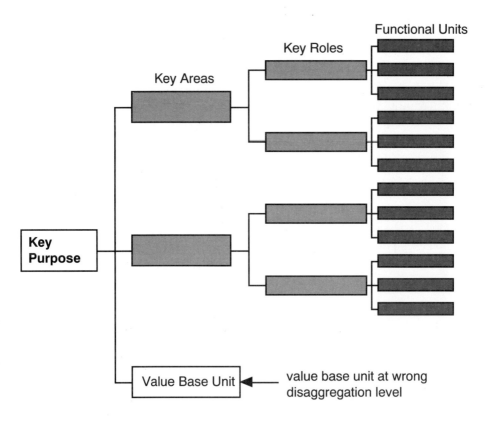

Fig. 8.4 The distorting effect of a value base unit

been tried in any functional maps, but we suggest that it offers a useful way of matching the presentation of the map to the purpose of the value base.

There is one more modification which can be made to improve the general appearance and user friendliness of functional maps. Many people still react unfavourably to the flow-chart appearance of functional maps, so a number of Lead Bodies have decided to present the finished maps in a different format. This usually takes the form of concentric circles representing the different key areas, with key roles represented by arcs in each circle. Examples of these presentation formats are shown in Figures 8.7 to 8.9.

Note that these formats should be developed only when the entire standards development process has been completed. One of the advantages of the tree diagram format is that the relationships between key areas and key roles are much clearer and making changes and adjustments is much easier. The tree diagram is also capable of showing many more levels of analysis than a series of circles. Functional maps are often used to represent all the elements of competence as well as the functional units – a level of detail which would be almost impossible with the circle format.

Now the functional map is complete. The identification of individual functional

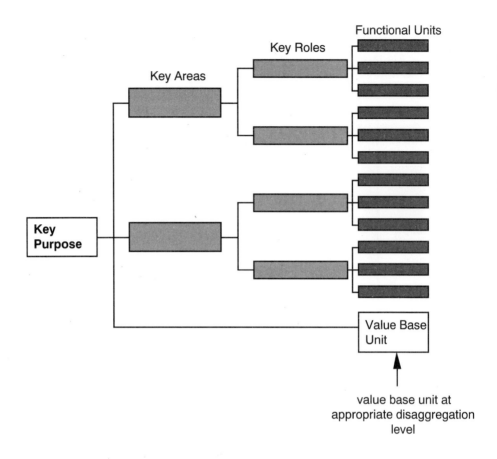

Fig. 8.5 The value base unit at the appropriate disaggregation level

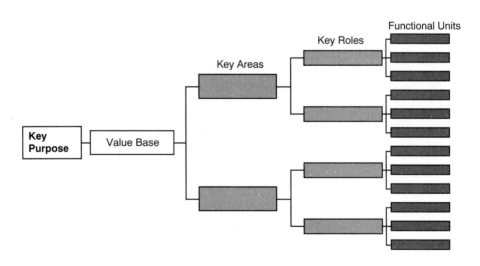

Fig. 8.6 Resiting the overarching value base

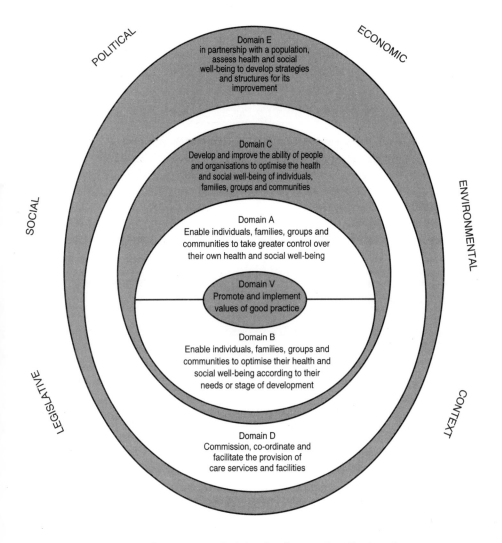

Fig. 8.7 Care sector standards functional map – alternative format

units is the starting-point for the next stage in the standards development process: the elaboration of the individual occupational standards. This is the subject of the next chapter.

NOTES

1. The Employment Department, *Guidance Note 4*.
2. NCVQ and the Employment Department, *NVQ Criteria and Guidance*.
3. PRIME Research and Development and KAP Associates, *Standards for Quality*. Prepared for the Management Charter Initiative.

Extract from the final report

The functional analysis approach generates a 'map' of increasing detail. A broad statement of overall aims and purpose (called the 'key purpose') is successively detailed by posing the question - 'what has to be achieved to enable this to happen?'.

The functional map for quality management has four levels of detail:

- a 'key purpose' statement which describes in very general terms the fundamental purpose of quality management;

- four key roles (A to D) which describe what has to be achieved in order to achieve the key purpose;

- nine units of competence (A1 to D1) which describe what has to be achieved in each of the key areas;

- 24 elements of competence which describe occupational outcomes - ie what someone with quality management responsibilities would need to do to perform this function.

Although the key roles, units and elements are numbered, this is more for identification purposes than to indicate that the functions and activities they describe should be carried out in any particular sequence, or that greater importance is attached to any of them. The units can be seen as part of a quality management cycle - each aspect of which stems from the central key purpose.[3]

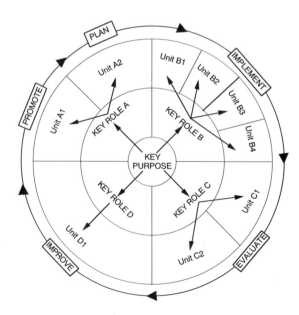

Fig. 8.8 Quality management standards functional map – alternative format

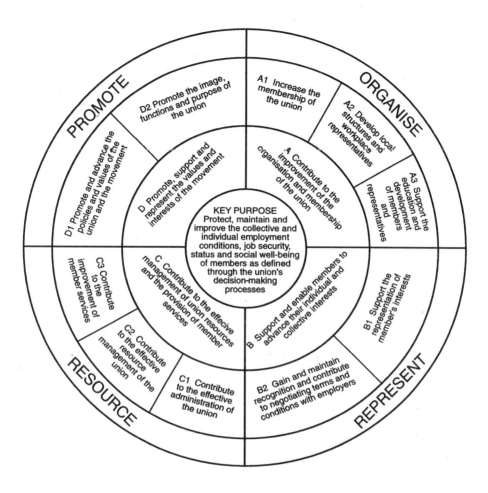

Fig. 8.9 Trade union standards functional map – alternative format

9 Occupational standards – specifications of human performance

Occupational standards are precise descriptions of what a person is expected to achieve in employment within an occupational sector. A standard describes:

- the outcome which needs to be achieved – **what should happen**;
- the quality of achievement expected, applied to both outcomes and processes – **how things should happen**;
- the circumstances under which the outcome is achieved – **the range of applications**.

All three components, taken together, are the **occupational standard**. In the common terminology used in the standards programme the three components are called:

- **the element title**;
- **performance criteria**;
- **range indicators**[1] (when used in occupational standards and range statements in qualifications).

An occupational standard is also called an **element of competence** – the terms are used interchangeably. Because of this common usage we sometimes use one term rather than the other, or show them as a combined term, 'standard/element of competence'. Our preference would be for the term 'standard' to be used within a suite of standards developed through a functional mapping and standards development exercise, and the term 'element of competence' when used in a qualification. However, since the terms are used interchangeably, we accept the dual terminology.

As we have noted elsewhere, the language of occupational standards and NVQs and SVQs often causes confusion. At this level in the analysis even more confusion reigns! We use the term 'competence' as an adjective, as in 'a competent person' or 'the competence of an individual'. However, in some publications the term **'competence'** is used as a noun – as in **'a competence'**. This is usually used as a substitute for an 'occupational standard' or an 'element of competence'. We consider this usage to be extremely confusing because the use of 'competence' as a noun suggests similarities with the personal competences approach described in US management literature, which is based on identifying critical personal characteristics – 'competence**s**' – and other approaches in which 'competenc**ies**' are described as tasks. Neither of these approaches use the same methodology and they are quite different in intent from the standards development approach. This confusion even appears in official literature and guidance.

We will use three examples of complete occupational standards to illustrate the way in which standards are developed and presented (see Table 9.1). They have been chosen deliberately to exemplify three ideal types of standard.

The first deals with an outcome which is mainly product based, ie, the standard describes a tangible outcome which can be examined. Consequently, most of the criteria are detailed descriptions of the nature of the product, or the object.

The second standard describes an interactive process which does not produce a tangible outcome so the criteria have to describe the complexities of human action – the action of the subject.

The third describes the planning of a course of action which contains tangible products which are the results of intangible processes of decision making and evaluation. These products will usually appear as documents (assessments, evaluations, recommendations, plans) which are analyses of information, options and specifications for action. This type of standard is often part of a sequence of 'plan, act, evaluate'. So, for example, the standard 'Prepare drawings and associated graphical information' may be preceded by the standard 'Plan the

---

Example 1. Element title: Prepare drawings and associated graphical information

Performance criteria

(a) drawings and associated graphical material produced are complete, accurate, and comply with design information and relevant documentation
(b) incomplete and inconsistent input information is clarified promptly and appropriate and accurate amendments are made
(c) the type of drawing and associated graphical material produced is as specified and is suitable for purpose
(d) methods and media for production selected are suitable for the drawings required and resources and time available
(e) deviations from current standard conventions are justified and are indicated clearly
(f) registers and records are complete, accurate and up-to-date
(g) checks and approvals regarding content and presentation of drawings and associated graphical information obtained, are necessary and sufficient
(h) production and record keeping is consistent with quality assurance procedures

Range indicators:

1. Type of drawing: location; assembly; component; sketches; working drawings; schedules; presentation drawings
2. Method and medium of production: manual; computer generated
3. Conventions: detailing standards; codes of practice; available products; acceptable current practice
4. Registers and records: incoming and outgoing drawing and document registers; records of document approval and revision.
5. Checks and approvals obtained cover: format; presentation; accuracy; technical content; completeness; referencing; cross-referencing and correlation with associated documents; status; positioning; shape; dimensions; tolerances; composition; fixing; annotation; symbols and conventions

152

Example 2. Element title: Present cases to legally constituted adjudicating bodies

Performance criteria

(a) written submissions are accurate, contain valid and relevant information and follow reasoned arguments which present the case in the most favourable manner
(b) oral presentations are complete, accurate and presented in a pace, style and manner which is intended to maximise the trust and respect of all parties and are appropriate to the level of formality of the hearing
(c) established conventions and procedures are followed
(d) oral presentations are clear and concise, identify the relevant points of the supporting argument and avoid additional information or opinions which have no direct bearing on the current matter
(e) appropriate interventions are made and questions are asked which are designed to present and interpret evidence in the best interests of the appellant
(f) final summaries identify the relevant points of the supporting argument and the major weaknesses in the opposing submission
(g) following a formal case presentation, results are reviewed and assessed with appellants and representatives and key learning points are identified and accurately recorded
(h) in instances where submissions are unsuccessful, clear and justifiable recommendations are made for further appropriate action to determine the case

Range Indicators:

1. Type of adjudicating body: court based; non court based (eg arbitrators, etc)
2. Further action recommended: appeals; reviews; referals to civil courts; no further action

Example 3. Element title: Develop systems for producing plant and animal products

Performance criteria

(a) the aims and objectives of production are identified in sufficient detail to allow planning to take place
(b) the range of potential markets for the products is identified and a realistic assessment is made of market demand
(c) where there is an interest in expanding into new product ranges, a realistic assessment is made of the extent to which the market is capable of influence
(d) opportunities and constraints relevant to the production plan are established
(e) a realistic assessment is made of the feasibility of development options
(f) the option selected achieves the best balance of production aims and objectives, market opportunities and constraints and is sufficiently flexible to meet changing circumstance
(g) the plan includes recording systems necessary for effective implementation and monitoring
(h) plans are presented in ways which are suitable for those who are to use them

Range indicators:

1. Aims and objectives relate to: products – primary and secondary; product mix; methods of production; product timing
2. Markets: sell direct; wholesale; retail
3. Opportunities and constraints: legal; environmental; social, cultural and aesthetic; economic and financial; physical; organisational; timing and seasonality; technological
4. Changing circumstances: market fluctuations; legislation; advances in knowledge and practice; public pressure; operational changes
5. Development options: expand current provision; change current use; move
6. System includes: management of waste; harvesting time; post-harvesting treatments

Table 9.1 Three occupational standards

drawing production requirements of a project'. The standard 'Present cases to legally constituted adjudicating bodies' may be preceded by 'Prepare cases for presentation to legally constituted adjudicating bodies'. Another significant variation in this type is the purpose for the planning: planning action for yourself, planning action for yourself acting with others, or planning actions which others will undertake. This is often associated with different levels of responsibility. In the example shown (Table 9.1), the planning is of a strategic nature and involves planning actions which others will undertake.

The three components which make up a standard have an agreed grammar and syntax designed to make the complete statement as precise as possible, thus minimising ambiguity in interpretation. For this reason the rules of grammar and syntax are quite rigid, as will be noted from the three examples in Table 9.1. It is worth elaborating this point.

THE LANGUAGE OF OCCUPATIONAL STANDARDS

Standards have been criticised for being phrased in such a complex and formal language that they are difficult to access and understand. Indeed, the complexity of the language is often cited as a reason why organisations may be reluctant to use standards.[2]

These concerns are quite legitimate, but need to be placed in context. Standards, to have any practical use, must be precise and unambiguous. This does not just apply to occupational standards but to any standard of performance, service delivery or manufactured product. A standard is a benchmark against which other products, services or aspects of human performance are compared. If the benchmark is not clear and capable of unambiguous interpretation, then we will have a very loose and vague standard which will vary in application.

This often means that standards adopt a very formal language, using defined rather than colloquial terminology. They sometimes include jargon – technical shorthand which is understandable only to occupational specialists. This is essential if the standard is to be used properly by the people who design and implement the systems based on the standards. If the standard is informal and colloquial it may be vague and often useless.

For example, attached to our computers are large colour display screens (technical jargon: monitor). Each comes with a reference manual which helps the user to set it up. At the back of the manual is a short section called 'Specifications'. These are common in many manuals. If you have a computer or car you will find a similar section at the back of your manual. Some of the specifications are quite understandable to the lay person. Here is one: 'Display size: Diagonal; 15 inches. Image size: Horizontal 8.2 inches (208 mm), Vertical 11.0 inches (279 mm)'. This is quite clear – it means that the screen measures 15 inches from corner to corner and is 11 inches high and 8.2 inches wide. The diagonal measurement is an international convention for describing screen size, followed by the width and height measurements. This is an important benchmark. If you use your computer to write text on a standard A4 page (the European standard for describing paper sizes, which is about 11 inches long and about 8 inches wide) this means that you can see a whole page at a time when you are writing and editing. If you mainly use your computer to play arcade games this may be of no interest whatsoever because games are usually configured to use a 14-inch diagonal screen. If you are a graphic designer who needs to see the two-page display of a magazine, this screen is too small – you need a 21 inch diagonal screen.

This specification, or standard, is precise because it enables users to choose the screen size which is most appropriate to their needs. Consequently it is phrased in a language which is precise and unambiguous for the intended audience. If the specification were phrased in simpler language it might read: 'Display size: as big as a sheet of paper'. This colloquial, less formal language would not be very precise because there are different sizes of paper: US letter, US legal, UK legal, A4, etc. You could say: 'Display size: A4', but this is jargon. Some users may not be aware that the European standard paper size is called A4 and many American users would be unfamiliar with the term since American standard paper sizes are different. So the manufacturers use another convention, inches, which allows the user to measure the size of the display they want. Notice also that they helpfully provide a conversion to metric measurements (8.2 inches: 208 mm, 11.0 inches: 279 mm) for users who are more accustomed to the metric system of measurement.

Although this first specification is of use to and understood by most users, some of the specifications for monitors are only understandable to a specialised user of computers. For example, the next specification for our monitors reads: 'Resolution: (h) 640 x (v) 870 pixels; 78 dpi resolution', which is not immediately intelligible to the average or new user. First, there are four jargon terms – '(h)', '(v)', 'pixels' and 'dpi'. The symbols (h) and (v) are easy to guess – they stand for horizontal and vertical. A pixel is jargon for picture element – a single dot on the screen which can be either black or white (for a monochrome monitor), a shade of grey (on a greyscale monitor) or a colour (on a colour monitor). The acronym dpi means dots per inch, which is a measure of how big the dots are.

What does all this mean? Quite simply this is a **standard** which describes how clear the image will be on the screen and how much detail can be seen. The smaller the dots and the greater the number of dots the sharper and clearer the screen image. This is related to cost – more pixels per inch cost more to manufacture. An expanded version of this standard might be: 'Number of picture elements (which are the single dots which make up the image) on the screen: Horizontal 640, Vertical 870. There are 78 picture elements in each inch'.

For some users this is important information. The graphic designer who needs to be able to display colour photographs to edit and place in a publication needs as many dots as they can afford so that precise close-up work is possible. The player of space invaders wants as many as are necessary to make the spaceship visible for the least cost.

Notice what has happened, however. As the information in the standard is required by fewer users (ie everybody is interested in screen size but fewer people are affected by image resolution) it is assumed that more specialised users will know the jargon used in the sector, so this is used – even to the extent of abbreviating words like 'horizontal' and 'vertical'. This makes the specification shorter, and is a common feature of technical specifications.

So far we have looked at two of the specifications for a monitor: size, which is of interest to most people, and resolution, which is of interest to specialists. However, there are some specifications which may be entirely meaningless to the lay person and most computer users. Here is the next specification: 'Video specifications. Video signal: Analog RS-343A; Horizontal scan rate: 68.9 kHz; Vertical refresh rate: 75.0 Hz'.

And if you find that hard to follow, take a glance at the specification for the laser component of the CD ROM which is attached to our computers: 'Type: Semiconductor GaAlAs laser; Wavelength: 790 +/- 25 nanometers; Output power: 0.2 milliwatts; Beam divergence: 55 degrees'.

These standards are totally incomprehensible to most users – which is fine, because the standards tell them nothing that they want to know or could do anything about. These standards are of interest only to technically qualified maintenance engineers or the few technically competent users who have an interest in maintaining their own equipment.

What do we learn from these examples? There are a number of important lessons which can be used as criteria for expressing standards (whether product, service or occupational):

- Standards are phrased at different levels of detail for different users.
- As the audience for standards diminishes in size and increases in technical competence, the language tends to use more technical shorthand (jargon).
- All standards need to be precise and unambiguous, even if they are designed for the lay user.

An analogy may serve to illustrate these lessons and form the link with the language used to express occupational standards.

A motor car has at least four levels of technical specification. In the factory design department is a master computer file which may contain up to 1,000,000 graphic images, component lists and other manufacturing and product specifications – this is the motor car – in all its detail and complexity. At the other end of the scale is a four-page glossy brochure which the interested customer receives when they make an enquiry at a showroom. The brochure contains little more than some nice photographs, an outline of available models, some performance and economy figures, and trim options. Somewhere between these two extremes are two kinds of maintenance manual. One is commercially produced and is sufficiently detailed for the competent and interested amateur to maintain the vehicle. The second manual is more complex and is produced by the manufacturer to enable technically qualified service personnel to maintain the vehicle professionally and provide expertise for the amateur who has exhausted their competence.

None of these documents is of any use whatsoever to a user other than that for which it is developed and intended. The customer wants neither a 1,000,000-file archive nor a 200-page service manual to make a purchasing decision. A designer, production engineer or service engineer, on the other hand, would have some difficulty in recreating or even servicing a motor car from the four-page glossy or the commercial maintenance manual. The amateur mechanic would find a description of the colour options of little use in replacing the clutch.

This analogy allows us to identify four different audiences for standards. These are:

1. professionals involved in the design and implementation of the system;
2. professionals involved in customer service and the maintenance of the operation of the system;
3. lay people who have an interest in the system and limited technical competence;
4. those who may become users of the system but who cannot be assumed to have any existing technical competence or interest in its operation.

For each of these audiences, the criteria described earlier hold true. The standards offer different levels of detail for different users, depending on the user's needs. Designers and production engineers need all the available detail; potential customers need a brief summary. As the audience for standards diminishes in size and increases in technical competence, the language tends to use more technical shorthand (jargon). The language of the professional service manual will have much more technical language and shorthand than that produced for the competent amateur mechanic. But all the standards need to be precise and unambiguous, even if they are designed for the lay user. The potential customer on a tight budget will want to know the miles per gallon the vehicle can deliver – a phrase like 'economical' will not be sufficiently precise.

These audience profiles can be generated for occupational standards as well. For occupational standards the audiences will be:

- professionals involved in the design and implementation of standards and qualification systems – this will include employees of Lead Bodies, Awarding Bodies, advisory staff, specialist consultancies and human resource management professionals in organisations;
- professionals involved in customer service and the maintenance of the operation of the system – those involved mainly in qualification delivery and with the design and delivery of learning and assessment, and people in organisations involved in implementing standards. This audience may also include learners and candidates who have a well-developed interest in the system;

- lay people who have an interest in the system and limited technical competence – those involved with qualifications in a support role, for example, managers and supervisors who may sponsor candidates and provide evidence about their own staff. This audience may also include learners and candidates who have a peripheral interest in the system itself;
- those who may become users of the system but who cannot be assumed to have any existing technical competence or interest in its operation – for example, potential candidates for qualifications, potential sponsors for qualifications and those who may wish to identify the benefits of using standards.

To return to the language of occupational standards we can ask the simple question 'For which audience are occupational standards designed?'. The answer is 'All four – eventually', and this caveat is essential. Eventually, the standards need to be presented with different levels of detail for different audiences. But at the initial design stage we are attempting to produce the most complex and detailed specification possible, from which all other forms of presentation will be derived to meet the needs of different audiences. Thus, the development of occupational standards aims to capture precision and reduce ambiguity by the use of formal structures of grammar, precisely defined terms and the use of agreed conventions – just like a complex product standard – because it will be used by professionals involved in the design of qualifications and other systems for evaluating human performance. Anything less than the maximum possible precision will impact on the systems they develop and allow ambiguity and lack of precision to multiply as the presentation of the standards is modified and simplified for different audiences.

Consequently, since we are in the business of developing complex benchmarks for human performance we need to use a language which reflects that complexity.[3] The next section explains the purpose and rationale for the use of the language used to express occupational standards.

THE ELEMENT OF COMPETENCE TITLE

The first set of conventions applies to the element title **and to all other outcome statements**, including all the statements in the functional map and the titles of functional units. These statements need to be clear to all potential users and to achieve this, the statements have a number of characteristics:

- The statement must describe an outcome (the result of activity) in performance terms. This is achieved by using an **active verb** (or verbs) which describes the action or behaviour which will produce the outcome – *what* happens;
- The statement must describe the focus of the action – grammatically, the **object** of the action – to *what* or *to whom* the action is directed;
- If necessary for clarity, the statement must also describe any **conditions** which

qualify the action – the *context* in which performance takes place.

Quite simply, a statement of competence should be a grammatical sentence which has self-contained meaning within the occupational context and does not have to be interpreted by reference to other statements. This can lead to a degree of repetition within a functional map or when elements of competence are presented together with a unit of competence title, but this repetition is preferable to the statement not making sense in its own right.

This requirement – that each statement should stand alone within the occupational context – is important for subsequent development. Elements of competence defined during the standard development process may be re-allocated to different units of competence when qualifications are proposed. Some may even be used in qualifications in other occupational sectors. If the element of competence has meaning only in relation to the unit title, then re-allocation within the standards or transfer to other occupational sectors can be extremely confusing.

Also, when standards are used by organisations they may be selected and restructured to meet specific organisational requirements. Consequently it is useful to use the convention of stating each statement of competence as a full grammatical sentence at all stages of standards development. The importance of this convention can be illustrated by an example taken from one of the functional units which was used in the previous section.

D111	Prepare and agree the development of a procurement programme
D111.1	Plan and document a procurement programme
D111.2	Specify the work content and duration of a contract

In this unit, the functional unit title and the two element titles stand alone. Each has a separate meaning which is independent of the other statements. However, the functional unit could be expressed like this:

D111	Prepare and agree the development of a procurement programme
D111.1	Plan and document the programme
D111.2	Specify work content and duration

In this presentation the two element titles depend on the unit title for their meaning. If they are subsequently separated from the functional unit title they will not have any immediate meaning and will cause confusion.

Precision is increased and this kind of confusion is avoided by the use of the convention:

active verb
object of the activity } which, taken together, describe the outcome
conditions or circumstances of the activity } or expectation

Here are some functional units and element of competence titles which show how this structure is applied:

- **Present cases to legally constituted adjudicating bodies**

Active Verb(s):	Present
Object:	cases
Condition:	to legally constituted adjudicating bodies

- **Prepare drawings and associated graphical information**

Active Verb(s):	Prepare
Object:	drawings and associated graphical information
Condition:	[Types of drawing are in the range indicator but it could be argued that the conditional statement 'for construction projects' would make the statement clearer]

- **Develop systems for producing plant and animal products**

Active Verb(s):	Develop
Object:	systems
Condition:	for producing plant and animal products

- **Monitor, adjust and control variables to meet production targets and product specifications for board manufacture**

Active Verb(s):	Monitor, adjust and control
Object:	variables
Condition:	to meet production targets and product specifications for board manufacture

- **Negotiate and conclude a contract for financial services**

Active Verb(s):	Negotiate and conclude
Object:	a contract
Condition:	for financial services

To demonstrate that this structure works at every level in a functional map, here is an analysis of a key purpose statement from the training and development standards:

- **Develop human potential to assist organisations and individuals to achieve their objectives**

Active Verb(s):	Develop
Object:	human potential
Condition:	to assist organisations and individuals to achieve their objectives

In attempting to achieve precision, the outcome statements developed using this approach tend to be lengthy and formally stated. But this is preferable to statements which are not clear, like:

- Interpret findings; and
- Report findings.

For many users these statements beg the questions 'what findings?', 'report what findings to whom?'. For the sake of a few additional words, clarity comes cheap. Regrettably, this attenuated approach is quite common and we have seen many functional units, units of competence and element of competence titles consisting of two or three words. We may need to remind ourselves from time to time that one of the purposes of the standards programme is to increase access to these performance specifications as part of the democratisation of the learning process. Oversimplifying to the extent that meaning is lost will cause confusion and restrict access to those who do not have all the information they need to make sense of the standard.

THE ACTIVE VERB

Perhaps the most important component of any statement of competence is the active verb or verbs which are chosen to start the statement. Although the term 'active verb' can imply a physical action, this is not always the case. The active verb may indeed describe a physical activity, as in 'prepare (drawings and schedules)' or 'Dry and reel (formed paper and board)'. But the active verbs may also describe continuous processes, like 'Identify and monitor (instances of aggressive and abusive behaviour)' and cognitive processes, like 'Analyse and synthesise (resource procurement constraints on the development process)'.

The active verbs should be chosen with care to best reflect the outcome and should be used consistently throughout the standards which are being developed. It causes confusion to use a term like 'negotiate' in one standard and 'agree' in another if the intent and the outcome are the same.

As with any document which contains defined terms it is useful to provide users with a glossary so that they are fully aware of the context in which particular words are used and the meanings which are ascribed to them. This is common practice in some standards development projects and our own glossary, taken from numerous projects we have worked on over the past ten years, is given in Appendix 2.

Having chosen the active verb, the object and the conditional statement (if this is necessary to clarify meaning), the process of developing elements of competence is the same as for the development of the stages of detail in the functional map. Each functional unit is disaggregated into component standards, represented in the first instance by element of competence titles, which will take the same form as that which applied to the functional map:

- a linear or sequential process (eg calibrate and set up equipment, manufacture items, check items for conformity and quality);
- a cyclical process (eg develop, implement, evaluate);
- separation of different processes or methods (eg identify information sources, evaluate information sources);
- separation of different products or outcomes (eg test mechanical components, test electrical components).

Groups of standards within functional units may also have hybrid rules where these patterns are combined or where additional standards are added to accommodate contingency or task management components.

Table 9.2 shows examples of functional units with their constituent element of competence titles.

In Table 9.2, Example 1 is a hybrid, combining stages in a process (prepare, present) with different processes or methods 'presenting cases to employers' and 'presenting cases to legally constituted adjudicating bodies'. Example 2 is a very straightforward case of separating different products – drawings and associated graphical information and schedules. This separation is also obvious from the functional unit title 'Prepare drawings and schedules'. Example 3 in the table is a cyclical process: develop systems, establish targets, monitor and review systems and targets.

At this level of detail, groups of elements may also contain elements which are associated with the management of contingency and the management of different activities (task management). The following functional units and elements, developed for the Plant, Animal and Land Sector Consortium, show this pattern.

Example 1
Functional unit title: Provide specialist advocacy services on behalf of members
Element 1 Prepare cases for presentation and representation
Element 2 Present cases to employers
Element 3 Present cases to legally constituted adjudicating bodies

Example 2
Functional unit title: Prepare drawings and schedules
Element 1 Prepare drawings and associated graphical information
Element 2 Prepare schedules

Example 3
Functional unit title: Develop, monitor and review systems and targets for producing animal and plant products
Element 1 Develop systems for producing plant and animal products
Element 2 Establish targets for producing plant and animal products
Element 3 Monitor and review systems and targets for producing plant and animal products

---

Table 9.2 Functional units and elements of competence

Functional unit title: Monitor and co-ordinate the movement of people within sites
Element 1: Welcome and receive visitors to the site
Element 2: Care for visitors
Element 3: Monitor and control unwelcome visitors

In this unit, Element 3 describes a contingency.

Functional unit title: Commission, monitor and evaluate projects
Element 1: Commission projects to enable objectives to be met
Element 2: Monitor and evaluate the process and progress of projects
       against targets
Element 3: Support project teams to enable them to achieve project
       objectives

In this unit, Element 3 is a task management element which provides resources and co-ordination to enable Element 1 and 2 to be achieved.

A point to note is that it is sometimes tempting to develop each analysis as a sequential process, even if this is not the most appropriate method of disaggregation. This is a hangover from task analysis. In task analysis, once a task is broadly described then the analysis proceeds by identifying what happens first, what comes next, and so on until a list of sequential activities is produced. Functional analysis and standards development are not based on task analysis, so a sequence of activity is not always the most appropriate way of expressing the outcome.

The iteration process is concerned with the balance between the functional unit title and the constituent element titles in just the same way that the functional unit and the key roles were considered in the previous section. As element of competence titles are developed they may appear, on examination, to be too demanding or too trivial to justify elaboration as a complete occupational standard, and revisions to the functional units may be required which in turn might impact on higher levels in the analysis. Functional units might be regrouped as elements of competence or proposed elements of competence might become functional units. As with the identification of functional units, this stage of detail is not entirely clear cut. The scope of an element of competence should not be so limited that it starts to appear like a specific task or skill description, nor should it be so broad that it contains a number of different outcomes, each of which require separate elaboration. For example, the element 'Present cases to legally constituted adjudicating bodies' could have been treated as a functional unit and further elaborated as follows:

Functional unit title: Present cases to legally constituted adjudicating bodies

Element 1: Prepare written submissions for legally constituted adjudicating bodies

Element 2: Present arguments to legally constituted adjudicating bodies

Element 3: Ask questions of witnesses in legally constituted adjudicating body hearings

Element 4: Present final summaries to legally constituted adjudicating bodies

Element 5: Review and assess the results of cases presented to legally constituted adjudicating bodies

Element 6: Recommend further action to determine cases rejected by legally constituted adjudicating bodies

---

However, if we examine each statement we find that it concentrates on a single action which will generate only a single evaluative statement (called a performance criterion). Furthermore, the statements, taken separately, do not represent a complete work role. Just being able to 'Ask questions of witnesses' will not impress your client if you are not able to 'Present final summaries'. In this case, the minimum description of the complete work role is the original element title.

COMMON MISTAKES

The format and structure of the element of competence title, although widely described in guidance materials, is often subject to wide interpretation and variation which can create further confusion. The most common errors are described below.

1. Describing knowledge, skill or understanding instead of outcomes – for example

- Understand the principles of …;
- Describe the features of …;
- Demonstrate an understanding of …;
- Use communication skills to ….

The standard (element title, performance criteria and range indicator) describe outcomes and effective performance. Knowledge and understanding underpin and extend performance and are identified at later stages in the development process. This distortion often occurs within disciplines which have been traditionally stated as lists of topics to be learned or learning objectives. It is also a format which may be used automatically by people who have been previously involved in learning design.

The role of the standards developer is to act as an interpreter for such statements to uncover the outcome which results from the application of knowledge and to suggest that important statements about what needs to be known are incorporated into evidence specifications or learning guidelines which occur later in the development process.

The same applies to the use of skill descriptions: it is important to identify what outcome the application of the skill produces. Here are expanded (and hypothetical) versions of the examples given above and suggestions on how they might appear when phrased as outcomes.

Knowledge statement: Understand the principles of double-entry bookkeeping
Outcome: Element title: Enter and process financial information in a double entry bookkeeping system

---

Knowledge statement: Describe the features of different kinds of mortgages
Outcome: Element title: Advise clients on financial products which meet their identified needs

[It would also be necessary to have a range indicator to illustrate different types of financial product, including types of mortgage.]

Knowledge statement: Demonstrate an understanding of database formats
Outcome: Element title: Format and document a database application to meet user requirements

---

Skill statement: Use communication skills to relate effectively with other team members
Outcome: Element title: Establish and maintain effective working relationships with team members

---

2. **Describing outcomes as activities by using verbs which simply mean 'do' – for example:**

- Undertake maintenance activities.
- Carry out a health and safety audit.
- Use equipment to produce finished products.

This structure usually occurs if the functional analysis is, in fact, a task analysis.

The format is similar to a set of task instructions which concentrate on the activity, not the result. Statements like this are quite easy to convert into outcomes because the active verb is usually apparent, although it may have been converted into an adjective or noun.

Task statement: Undertake maintenance activities
Outcome: Maintain plant and equipment to meet operating specifications

---

Task statement: Carry out a health and safety audit
Outcome: Audit and report on health and safety in the work environment

---

Task statement: Use equipment to produce finished products
Outcome: Produce finished products [This would normally require a
conditional statement to indicate context]

---

3. Describing outcomes which are not the responsibility of the individual – for example:

- Ensure that health and safety systems are in place.

The term 'ensure' is sometime used to imply that the expectation involves co-ordinating the activities of others. Whatever the intention, the outcome is not clear. Does this mean 'Monitor and maintain the health and safety of the work environment' (ie the individual is expected to do it), or 'Plan and co-ordinate the implementation of health and safety systems' (ie the individual is expected to provide the resources to enable others to do it)? It is the role of the standards developer to identify what is intended and to suggest an appropriate format.

4. Putting the evaluative term into the statement of competence – for example:

- Continuously maintain the supply of materials.
- Accurately calculate production targets.
- Review methodologies which are appropriate to the investigation.

The evaluative terms which set the standard belong in the performance criteria (explained fully in the next section) where all the critical criteria can be stated. Stating evaluative terms in the element of competence title usually means that one term is selected, whereas in most cases a number of different terms are needed to fully evaluate the outcome. For instance, in the first example above the term 'continuously' has been selected. In reality, the supply of materials needs to be continuous, the materials need to be of the right type, defective materials need to be identified and rejected, and so on. To incorporate all these evaluative terms into the element title would be quite inappropriate, particularly when there are the performance criteria for this purpose. We could end up with a statement like

'Continuously maintain the supply of the correct type of materials which are of the required quality'.

ACTIVITIES AND OUTCOMES

Although these are the most common problems with the phrasing of statements of competence, the overwhelming difficulty seems to be recognising the difference between descriptions of activities (what people do) and the outcomes (what should happen – what people are expected to achieve). Table 9.3 gives further examples of the difference between activities and outcomes.

What people do (activities/inputs)	What people are expected to achieve (results/outcomes)
Interview loan customers	Evaluate the needs, status and creditability of loan applicants
Write technical reports	Evaluate potential solutions against known technical criteria
Obtain patient case histories	Establish patient health status from direct interview and existing written sources
Bath a patient	Enable clients to maintain their physical cleanliness
Operate a chemical spray	Control pests by the application of chemical treatments
Set up and operate an autoclave	Sterilise instruments used in clinical procedures
Conduct a careers interview	Match available labour market opportunities against client interests, abilities, previous learning and qualifications
Carry out a training needs analysis	Identify the learning needs of individuals and organisations

Table 9.3 Activities and outcomes

SUMMARY

Does each element of competence title:

- use language which is precise and consistent with the recommended grammatical structure?;
- represent a distinct work role within the industry or occupation rather than a specific task or component part of a work role?;
- describe outcomes, expectations or results of activity, rather than activities procedures and methods?

Do the element of competence titles within each functional unit:

- identify critical aspects of task management and co-ordination of work roles as suggested by the Job Competence Model?

NOTES

1. Range indicators are developed for occupational standards and tend to be illustrative, ie they describe **all** the significant variables which might be important. When qualifications are developed,

the range indicators take on a different role and are refined to become range statements which specify which aspects of the range must be included in formal assessment. This distinction, that range **indicators illustrate** and range **statements specify**, is important to understand.

2. A Confederation of British Industry report commented 'nearly 100 firms, unprompted, identified jargon as a barrier to implementation. The language used [in NVQs] should be accessible and comprehensible' (Confederation of British Industry, *Quality Assessed*). A report from the Institute of Manpower Studies stated: 'The terminology and concepts used within NVQ/SVQs were perceived to be a major issue inhibiting people's understanding of the standards ... for instance, in Retail, the language used in the ... material was considered to be too complex and long winded.' The figures which support this statement show that only 15 per cent of users reported 'problems in understanding' as a difficulty. The report continues: 'by contrast, some employers using the MCI standards agreed that the language posed difficulties but also believed that having to grapple with it was part of the learning process and would help managers understand what they had to achieve'. Callender *et al.*, *National and Scottish Vocational Qualifications.*

3. As we went to print we started work with a team from the University of Birmingham Language Technology Unit to investigate and report on language difficulties in occupational standards and NVQs. Some of the analyses and recommendations of the team are likely to modify some of our statements on language and structure so we recommend that readers look out for the forthcoming report, which will be published as part of the Research and Development series of Learning Methods Branch and in the journal *Competence and Assessment.*

Occupational standards – criteria for successful performance

10

PERFORMANCE CRITERIA

The performance criteria set the required standard of performance to achieve the outcome described in the element of competence title. This central role means that the performance criteria are the most important part of an occupational standards, and it is here that precision and lack of ambiguity are essential.

But the search for precision has led to criticisms of the way in which performance criteria are phrased because the 'passive voice' used to express the criteria can appear extremely formal, wordy and off-putting.[1] This point is worth examining.

One solution to the formal statements is to write the criteria as instructions to candidates – indeed, this formulation is the one most often used when people 'convert' the standards into what they believe to be a more user friendly format. Another option is to state the criteria as a list of questions, directed as assessors.

We can demonstrate these approaches by examining one of the examples used in the NCVQ Criteria document:[2]

candidate records are complete, legible and accurate

When re-phrased as an instruction, with potentially 'difficult' words replaced by more colloquial terminology, this becomes:

the records which you keep about candidates must be accurate, contain all the information that is required and they should also be easy for someone else to read

When re-phrased as a question to an assessor, this becomes:

are the records which are kept by the candidate for this award, complete, accurate and legible?

The use of the passive voice arises from a simple fact – that standards are statements which are intended to be used by different people for different purposes. This enables the different users: assessors, teachers, trainers and human resource development specialists to use them by interpreting the statements in terms of their own requirements. The expectation is that a statement like 'candidate records are complete, legible and accurate' is interpreted by the assessor as:

I need to gather and judge sufficient, valid evidence to make me confident that the candidate is able to keep records which are complete, legible and accurate

- by the learning professional as:

  I need to develop a learning programme which will enable the learner to produce and maintain records which are complete, legible and accurate

- and by the human resource development specialist as:

  one of the standards we should apply to our evaluation of assessor capability is that the records they keep are complete, accurate and legible; **or**

  one of the criteria we will build into our review and appraisal system is that assessors keep complete, legible and accurate records; **or**

  when we are training and developing assessors one of the programme components should cover the maintenance of complete, legible and accurate records; **or**

  when we are designing the job of an assessor we should include the keeping of complete, legible and accurate records.

The other good reason why standards are phrased in the passive voice is that they do not describe what people should do or what evidence should be collected. They describe **what should happen** in the work environment. This is just the same as a technical specification for a car component. A drawing will be produced which shows the finished component in the form of a diagram. Certain details will be emphasised and various conventions will be used to show detail which would not be visible in the solid component – such as cross sections. Listed down the side of the drawing will be technical information: the type of material to be used, the measuring gauges which will be needed and explanations of symbols. The drawing will be annotated with critical dimensions with tolerances appropriate to each measurement. This is a **specification** – it is the same as an occupational standard in that it describes what the component **should be like** – just as an occupational standard describes what performance **should be like**.

The drawing is not specifically directed at the person who manufactures the component, nor the quality engineer who may examine it. If it did, it would be of little use to the other person. If instead of a drawing we produced the following series of instructions for the manufacturer:

- draw a 30cm billet of mild steel from stores for each component you need;
- place the billet in a three jaw chuck and tighten it;
- start the lathe and take three cuts to produce the first nominal diameter which should measure 10 cms.

This would be of limited relevance to the quality engineer. On the other hand, the single drawing can be used by both manufacturer and quality engineer because it states what the finished result should be like – not what the person has to do. Note however, that this instructional format would be useful for a learner – but that without the 'standard' in the form of the drawing the learning instructions cannot be generated.

This is exactly the reason why standards are phrased as outcomes and performance criteria appear in the passive voice – they state **what should happen**. The two associated questions: how do you acquire the knowledge and skills needed to do it (learning), and how do you know that someone has done it properly (assessment); are questions which can be derived from the description of what has to happen. But this limits the standard to its use within NVQs and we have already suggested that standards are not just NVQ components – they are also intended to be used directly within organisations to support human resource development.

The engineering drawing is not just a set of instructions to a manufacturing engineer and a set of criteria for a quality engineer. It is also a reference document for a systems engineer, who is required to fit together and integrate the operation of different components and systems, to a materials manager who is specifying and commissioning a supplier of raw materials and to the service engineer who needs to know the original dimensions of a worn component. In each of these uses the drawing will be interpreted and used in a different way. This is the same kind of interpretation which has to happen when assessors, teachers, trainers and human resource professionals use the standard for their different purposes.

There may well be a case for changing the language of the performance criteria if the standards are to be used to support learning – because learners are the very people who are not likely to understand the content of the standards. This is not too difficult to do. Table 10.1 shows an example of a standard which was developed for Trade Union Voluntary Officers (shop stewards). The original standard is called a 'training standard' simply because the main purpose of the standard is to support the education and training of voluntary officers – that is, no NVQs are planned. To make the training standard more 'user friendly' we were asked to convert the training standards to learning support materials – the converted example, called a learning module, is shown in Table 10.2.

PERFORMANCE CRITERIA – SETTING THE STANDARD

Performance criteria describe five different outcomes of performance:

1. physical products;
2. interactive processes;
3. planned courses of action;
4. critical stages or overarching requirements of a process;
5. contingent outcomes which only occur if certain conditions apply.

The influence of the Job Competence Model can be seen in these five different outcomes. Physical products are often associated with technical expectations; interactive processes are part of the work environment; planned courses of action are part of task management; critical stages or overarching requirements of a process are part of task management and contingent outcomes are part of contingency management.

▨▨ T H E · T R A I N I N G · S T A N D A R D ▨▨

This page shows the standard, which is part of a unit. The standard describes **what should happen**. On the opposite page is the Learning Module. This describes in more detail **what the steward needs to do and what the steward needs to know** if they are to reach the standard. The standard and the Learning Module are closely related. Either one, or both versions may be used to plan training programmes.

A11.2   Identify, make contact with and recruit potential members

Performance Criteria

(a) in workplaces where recognition agreements are in place, information about potential members are requested in line with agreed procedures

(b) where no recognition agreements exist, alternative and realistic methods of contacting potential members are identified

(c) clear and accurate written materials are made available to potential members

(d) in cases where there may be a conflict of interests, appropriate procedural guidance is sought from relevant specialists and negotiations and agreements are initiated and concluded with other unions which maximise potential membership and retain effective inter-union relations

(e) individual and group enquiries about membership are dealt with promptly

(f) potential members are given clear explanations about the benefits of union membership and negative responses are countered with persuasive arguments and relevant factual information

Range Statements:

1   Alternative contact methods:
   * canvassing;
   * leaflet distribution;
   * advertisements;
   * branch networks;
   * negotiation of access;
   * employer inductions

2.   Written materials provided:
   * union promotional material;
   * locally developed 'welcome pack'

3   Sources of specialist advice for procedural guidance:
   * colleagues;
   * full time officials;
   * research departments;
   * TUC procedures;
   * formal agreements (eg Bridlington agreement)

4   Type of potential member:
   * new recruits;
   * self-employed;
   * contract workers;
   * home workers;
   * non-employed trainees

This standard is part of Unit A11:
Develop, organise and contribute to member recruitment and retention

The standards in this Unit are:

A11.1 Develop a recruitment and retention strategy
A11.2 Identify, make contact with and recruit potential members
A11.3 Prepare and present promotional information to potential members
A11.4 Maintain contact with and information about members

Table 10.1 A training standard

THE·LEARNING·MODULE

The overall aim of this group of modules is: To recruit, retain and organise union members

The aim of this module is: To work out who your potential members are, to make contact with them and recruit them

What you need to do:

1. If your workplace has a recognition agreement, you will be able to get information about **potential members** in line with your agreed procedures.

2. If you don't have a recognition agreement, you will need to choose **ways of contacting potential members**. The method you choose will depend on what is practicable in your workplace.

3. Sometimes there may be a conflict of interest with other unions. If this is the case, get **specialist advice** on the correct procedures to follow. When you are clear about the procedures you can negotiate and agree with other unions and reach a solution which will allow you to contact and recruit as many potential members as possible, whilst at the same time, maintaining good relations with other unions.

4. Deal promptly with any enquiries you receive from individuals or groups of people.

5. When you make contact with potential members, provide them with **recruitment literature**.

6. When you make contact with potential members, explain clearly the benefits they will get from union membership. Give them relevant information about local issues and use persuasive arguments.

What you need to know:

▮▮➡ **What** procedures do you have - what are the procedures?

▮▮➡ **What** contact methods are best for you in your workplace?
▮▮➡ **Why** are the contact methods you have chosen best for you?

▮▮➡ **What** kinds of conflict might there be with other unions?
▮▮➡ **Where** can you get, and who can give you advice?
▮▮➡ **How** will you conduct the negotiation and reach an agreement which allows you to recruit and maintain good relations?

▮▮➡ **What** are your procedures for enquiries - how fast can you process them, could this be improved?

▮▮➡ **What** literature is available and from whom?

▮▮➡ **What** are the benefits of union membership?
▮▮➡ **What** local issues are likely to be important?
▮▮➡ **How** do you phrase and present persuasive arguments?

Notes and explanations:

1. You may have to deal with different types of **potential member**, including:
   * new recruits;
   * self-employed workers;
   * contract workers;
   * home workers;
   * non-employed trainees.

▮▮➡ **How** will you need to modify your approach and contact methods to take account of the needs of these different types of potential member?

2. Different **ways of contacting potential members** will include:
   * personal contact in the workplace or outside the workplace;
   * distributing documents and recruitment literature;
   * advertising on noticeboards or in the local press;
   * working with existing branch networks;
   * negotiating with your employer to get access to new recruits and other potential members;
   * having a slot at the induction programmes run by the employer.

▮▮➡ **Which** of these methods are possible in your workplace?
▮▮➡ **Which** ones seem to work best?

3. The **recruitment literature** you will need will include:
   * union recruitment packs - including any locally produced welcome packs;
   * other materials (ie not official union materials) which may be relevant, like press cuttings, local leaflets etc.

▮▮➡ **Where** or **from whom** will you get recruitment literature?

4. You will be able to get **specialist advice** from:
   * other stewards or convenors;
   * full time officials;
   * your union research departments;
   * advice and guidance from the TUC;
   * any formal agreements which affect your union or all unions.

▮▮➡ **How** will you decide which is the best source of advice for you?

Table 10.2 A learning module

173

Within these five types are a wide range of characteristics which will vary in frequency and significance in different sectors and work roles. These are detailed in Table 10.3.

Here are examples of each type of criterion, taken from the three exemplar standards.

1. Physical products:

- *Drawings* and *associated graphical material* produced are complete, accurate and comply with design information and relevant documentation.
- *Written submissions* are accurate, contain valid and relevant information and follow reasoned arguments which present the case in the most favourable manner.
- *Plans* are presented in ways which are suitable for those who are to use them.

The products shown in italics are drawings, associated graphical materials, written submissions and plans.

2. Interactive processes:

- Oral *presentations* are complete, accurate and presented in a pace, style and manner which are intended to maximise the trust and respect of all parties and are appropriate to the level of formality of the hearing.
- Oral *presentations* are clear and concise, identify the relevant points of the supporting argument and avoid additional information or opinions which have no direct bearing on the current matter.
- Appropriate *interventions* are made and *questions* are asked which are designed to present and interpret evidence in the best interests of the appellant.

The interactions shown in italics are presentations, interventions and questions.

3. Planned courses of action:

- The aims and objectives of production are identified in sufficient detail to allow planning to take place.
- A realistic assessment is made of the feasibility of possible development options.

Both of these statements describe key components of a planning process.

4. Process stages/requirements:

- Established conventions and procedures are followed [*overarching requirement which applies to many of the other criteria*].
- Checks and approvals are obtained at certain stages in the production of the drawings [*critical step in a process*].

5. Contingent outcomes which only occur if certain conditions apply:

- Incomplete and inconsistent input information is clarified promptly and appropriate and accurate amendments are made.

Products

Manufacturing and assembling products from materials and components
Changing the state of products or materials (including chemical treatments, cleaning, sterilising, etc.)
Selecting, processing and analysing data
Originating, formatting and presenting documents
Locating, positioning and arranging objects
Intervening into system operation (calibrating, adjusting etc.)

Interactions

Providing and exchanging information
Providing and seeking support
Promoting rights and values
Directing or controlling others
Persuading and negotiating with others
Empowering and enabling others

Planned courses of action

Identifying opportunities and constraints
Analysing and synthesising information to develop new knowledge
Assessing feasibility
Determining aims and goals
Designing and specifying products and services
Calculating and obtaining resources
Selecting and allocating resources
Developing plans, schedules and targets
Commissioning work (including contracting, tendering)
Monitoring implementation of plans
Evaluating progress against plans and targets
Adjusting targets and plans against monitoring information

Process stages/requirements

Following procedures and methods
Meeting schedules and timescales
Monitoring resource use
Optimising resources
Choosing criteria, methods and alternatives
Maintaining health and safety

Contingencies

Identifying problems (includes hazards)
Diagnosing problems
Generating potential solutions
Evaluating solutions
Restoring systems to an operational state
Passing on information and reflecting to support future action

Table 10.3 The range of outcomes for which criteria may need to be identified

- In instances where submissions are unsuccessful, clear and justifiable recommendations are made for further appropriate action to determine the case.

175

PHRASING PERFORMANCE CRITERIA

Performance criteria are phrased in one of two ways:

- a description of the critical outcome or process plus an evaluative phrase;
- a description of a state which either should or should not occur – usually applied to a critical stage in a process [*this type of criterion is less common*].

THE CRITICAL OUTCOME OR PROCESS

Performance criteria are developed by analysing the element title against the five types of outcome described above. These will not all be present in every element of competence, but it is good practice to consider each in turn. This information must be drawn from occupational specialists, otherwise critical factors may be missed. Here is an example, using the element title 'Prepare drawings and associated graphical information'.

Are there any physical products? Yes, there are:

- drawings and associated graphical material
- registers and records of drawings and associated graphical information

Are there any interactive processes? No, in this particular standard there are none. This is not to say that interaction is not important to the work role as a whole, but for the production of drawings, interaction is not a critical outcome

Are there any planned courses of action? No, in this case there are none, but planning document production will appear in other elements of competence in the functional unit

Are there any critical requirements of a process? Yes, there are:

- the methods and media selected to produce the drawings (overarching – applies to a number of other criteria)
- checks and approvals obtained at certain stages in the production of the drawings (critical step)

Are there any contingent outcomes which occur only if certain conditions apply? Yes, there are:

- incomplete and inconsistent information (which may need to be clarified)
- deviations from standard conventions (which may need to be explained)

A summary of this analysis process would give us a list of all the critical outcomes and processes:

- drawings and associated graphical material;

- registers and records of drawings and associated graphical information;
- the methods and media selected to produce the drawings;
- checks and approvals obtained at certain stages in the production of the drawings;
- incomplete and inconsistent information (which may need to be clarified);
- deviations from standard conventions (which may need to be explained).

The second example uses the element of competence title 'Present cases to legally constituted adjudicating bodies'.

Are there any physical products? Yes, there are:

- written submissions

Are there any interactive processes? Yes, there are:

- oral presentations of the case
- interventions made during hearings and questions asked of witnesses and the appellant
- final summaries of the case

Are there any planned courses of action? Yes, there are:

- reviewing and assessing the case with those concerned after the hearing has finished and identifying learning points for future cases

(*note*: the preparation of the case, which will include data gathering and planning the presentation of the case materials, appears in the preceding element of competence in the functional unit.)

Are there any critical requirements of a process? Yes, there are:

- keeping to established conventions and procedures (overarching – applies to a number of other criteria)

Are there any contingent outcomes which occur only if certain conditions apply? Yes there are:

- recommending what action to take where submissions are unsuccessful

---

A summary of this analysis process would give us a list of all the critical outcomes and processes:

- written submissions;
- oral presentations of the case;
- interventions made during hearings and questions asked of witnesses and the appellant;

- final summaries of the case;
- reviewing and assessing the case with those concerned after the hearing has finished;
- keeping to established conventions and procedures;
- recommending what action to take where submissions are unsuccessful.

The element 'Develop systems for producing plant and animal products' is slightly different in that it consists solely of one of the types of criteria: planning courses of action. Although plans are produced (which are physical products), the plans contain all the analysis, data processing, evaluation and selections which typify the planning process. The processes are:

- aims and objectives for production identified;
- the range of potential markets identified;
- market demand assessed;
- the likelihood of influencing the market for new products assessed;
- opportunities and constraints identified;
- development options assessed and the one option selected.

All these planning processes will appear in a document – a plan, which will have two further characteristics to which criteria must be applied. It will:

- include recording systems which will enable implementation and monitoring of the success of the plan;
- be presented with regard to the users of the plan.

Because the three example standards were deliberately selected to demonstrate ideal versions of different types of standard (products, interactive process and planning courses of action) it is not surprising that they tend to match the different types of criterion. In Example 1, the most important criteria concern the product (drawings). In Example 2, most criteria are to do with interactions. In Example 3, nearly all the criteria describe planning processes.

This pattern is not uncommon. Elements of competence are often focused on one of these three different outcomes. However, some elements combine all three, as is shown in Table 10.4. In this example, some of the criteria describe products in the form of written documents:

- written submissions and claims provided to the employer;
- written responses and proposals compared and clarified;
- written refusals to employers;
- summaries of points of agreement and the results of negotiations.

The example also contains a number of interactions:

- claims presented (orally);
- information and arguments offered (orally);
- probing questions asked to test consistency and resilience;

Element B13.3. Contribute to negotiations

Performance criteria

(a) A negotiating strategy, based on a realistic assessment of the power and influence base of the membership, is agreed with the negotiating team

(b) The strategy identifies realistic and acceptable best results, opening offers, team roles and responsibilities and identifies appropriate practices and tactics for negotiations

(c) Complete and accurate written submissions are provided to the employer to agreed timescales and present a clear rationale

(d) Written submissions contain justifiable claims for maintaining and improving existing conditions which are compared and quantified against favourable, relevant and valid comparative data

(e) Written responses and proposals from employers are compared with anticipated best results and accepted if they fully meet expectations

(f) Written refusals to employers are drafted in a language and style which clearly indicates refusal but is designed to maintain trust and respect

(g) Claims are presented which are matched to favourable comparative data and based on agreed demands and expectations

(h) Negative employer responses are clarified and countered with relevant additional information and arguments

(i) Appropriate questions are asked which are intended to test the consistency and resilience of the employer's position and to probe for possible movement

(j) Established negotiating conventions are adopted and are only broken in instances where alternative action is likely to further the claim and is agreed in advance with the team

(k) Points of agreement are summarised and accurately recorded

(l) Temporary adjournments are suggested at appropriate points in the negotiation and additional information, support and advice is obtained from relevant people

(m) Strategies and tactics are modified and alternative strategies developed to take into account agreements already made, the teams' assessment of the likely outcome of the process and the likely response of the employer and members

(n) In instances where the team judge that no additional offers are available and the agreement is not within acceptable parameters, additional action within the terms of the procedure agreement and union policy is recommended to representatives and members

(o) Results of negotiations are accurately summarised and passed on promptly to all relevant parties

Range indicators

1. Type and subject of negotiation: claims for/alterations in terms and condition; recognition; representation of group grievance; redundancy; equal opportunities; privatisation; training and education; changes at work (including work organisation, investment policy, etc); rights to information, consultation and participation

2. Roles adopted in negotiating teams: participant; lead negotiator

3. Sources of information to support claims: labour market information; company reports and accounts; economic indicators (eg inflation, retail price indices, etc); national wage rates and averages (including comparative data); union policy and rules; procedures; social trends (including trends in Europe)

4. Criteria for calling temporary adjournments: deadlock; mistakes/errors in presentation and discussion; needs for additional information; unanticipated responses and developments

5. Negotiating conventions: make-up of team (including seniority, number); format for meetings; venues; recognised meeting protocols; established informal channels of negotiation; established feedback practices; established timescales

6. Options for further action in case of failure to agree: negotiations at higher levels of authority; referral to senior union officials; conciliation services; ballots and consultations with members

7. Relevant parties: members; representatives; senior union officials; employers/employer representatives; other unions; media

Table 10.4 A standard which incorporates products, interactions and planning processes

- points of agreement summarised (orally);
- temporary adjournments suggested.

The example also describes a number of planning processes:

- agreeing a negotiating strategy and tactics;
- assessing the likely outcome of the process and the likely response of the employer and members;
- modifying strategies and tactics and developing alternative strategies;
- identifying and recommending additional action.

The example may also be analysed against the five categories of criteria:

1. Are there any physical products? Yes, there are:

   - written submissions and claims;
   - written refusals;
   - summaries of points of agreement and the results of negotiations.

2. Are there any interactive processes? Yes, there are:

   - claims presented (orally);
   - information and arguments offered (orally);
   - probing questions asked to test consistency and resilience;
   - points of agreement summarised (orally);
   - temporary adjournments suggested.

3. Are there any planned courses of action? Yes, there are:

   - agreeing a negotiating strategy and tactics;
   - assessing the likely outcome of the process and the likely response of the employer and members;
   - modifying strategies and tactics and developing alternative strategies ;
   - identifying and recommending additional action.

4. Are there any critical requirements of a process? Yes, there are:

   - presenting submissions to agreed timescales (critical stage in the process);
   - adopting established negotiating conventions (overarching – applies to a number of other criteria);
   - modifying strategies and tactics as conditions change.

5. Are there any contingent outcomes which occur only if certain conditions apply? Yes there are:

   - breaking negotiating conventions;
   - calling temporary adjournments;
   - recommending action if offers are not acceptable.

This analysis process, using the five types of criterion, is more comprehensive than the simpler approach of identifying just the three types of outcome (products, interactions and planning processes). The more detailed analysis picks up important contingencies, critical stages and overarching requirements which affect other criteria. As can be seen in Table 10.2, the first analysis fails to identify the important criteria of keeping to negotiating conventions, breaking them where this may offer an advantage and the various judgements and decisions which have to be made as the negotiation proceeds.

SETTING THE STANDARD

Some performance criteria are unconditional, that is, they describe a state which should either occur or not occur. Most criteria are conditional, so the outcome or process described in the criterion is qualified by an evaluative phrase. The evaluative phrase, when added to the critical outcome or process, sets the level of performance which is expected in employment. Because the evaluative phrase describes the quality of performance it needs to be as precise as possible to offer a benchmark for the evaluation of performance. However, it should not be over-specified to the extent that it might constrain action in circumstances where alternatives or options are an integral part of the outcomes required.

Where performance criteria are unconditional they may be either critical stages in a process or outcomes which are related to existing conventions or specifications which have national applicability. Examples are:

- **conforms to** ... (specifications);
- **is consistent with** ... (codes of good practice);
- **meets** ... (legal requirements);
- (conventions) ... **are followed**;
- (surfaces are) ... **free from** ... (contamination).

In these five examples the criterion is unconditional. In the first four this is phrased as an outcome or processes which *must* happen. The fifth describes something which *must not* happen. Note that references should only be made to conventions and specifications which have national applicability. Specifications or procedures which are specific to one organisation are not an acceptable benchmark for a performance criterion.

Where the outcomes or processes are conditional or qualified the criterion should contain an evaluative phrase. There are three ways of expressing evaluative phrases. Each depends on what it is the criterion relates to.

1. Where the criterion relates to an observable outcome, like a physical product, an action or a document, the outcome is phrased as a noun so we use **adjectives to qualify the noun**. Examples are:

   - **relevant** (information);

- **appropriate** (action);
- **justifiable** (conclusions);
- (dimensions are) **accurate**.

2. Where the criterion relates to a process, like analysing data or modifying a presentational style, the process is expressed as a verb, 'to analyse', 'to modify'. In these cases we use an **adverb to qualify the verb**. Examples are:

- presentational style is **appropriately** modified;
- data is **accurately** analysed.

3. Where the criterion relates to an intention to affect the action of others, but the person to whom the standard applies has no actual control over the action of others, we use **a passive verb to indicate the degree of influence** which is possible. This often occurs where an individual is in an advisory relationship. So, for example, a trade union officer may encourage voluntary representatives to consult with their members. They cannot do the consulting themselves, nor may they be in a position to direct representatives to consult. Rather, they must use persuasive arguments to achieve the intended result whilst at the same time maintaining a good relationship with representatives. We would phrase this intention as:

- representatives are **encouraged** to consult ...

Equally, a guidance counsellor may believe that a client would be best advised to seek additional specialist assistance. The counsellor may make this suggestion, offer encouragement, offer resources and even assist in the process, but they would not actually get the advice and then present it to the client. We would express this intention as:

- the client is **supported** in seeking assistance ...

In these two examples we have described interactive processes. The trade union officer will not simply recommend consultation and then 'give in' if the representatives decide against it. The officer will continue to encourage the action by offering positive arguments and clear reasons to try to gradually persuade the representatives to do what the officer thinks is right. Similarly the counsellor will engage in a number of processes and actions to support the client. If the client is willing but not able to take advantage of additional assistance the counsellor may offer additional support by engaging in an informal rehearsal of an interaction which the client is worried about. They may suggest reference sources if the client does not know who to contact. They may offer to accompany the client to an interview. In both these cases the trade union officer and the counsellor have opportunities to adjust and modify their behaviour during the processes of 'encouraging' and 'supporting'.

Sometimes, however, there is no opportunity to adjust and modify behaviour. If the trade union officer is presenting a written grievance on behalf of a member they will need to bear in mind that, although they are in potential conflict with the employer, they will need to maintain a good relationship for the future. Thus, we would describe the style and tone of the written case as:

- documents are drafted in a style and manner which is **designed to** maintain the trust and respect of the employer.

This formulation is also used where all the factors which may influence the intended result are difficult to influence directly or to predict. For example, in creating a healthy environment for an animal, we might phrase the criterion as:

- accommodation **is designed to** promote the health and well-being of the animal.

However, this would not stop a cow from hurting itself if it kicked a hole in a wall and injured its leg.

As with the active verbs used to signal the action or behaviour in element of competence titles, evaluative terms should be used consistently and with an agreed meaning. Appendix 3 is a glossary of the evaluative terms which we have incorporated into performance criteria over the past eight years, together with our interpretation of their meaning.

The way in which evaluative terms are used is closely related to the components of the Job Competence Model which, in turn, have a link with the five types of outcome we identified above. This relationship is shown in Table 10.5, which charts the focus of each type of criterion against the type of evaluation appropriate to that focus. The table also gives examples of the kinds of evaluative phrases which might be used.

It should be noted that this Table 10.5 is not intended to be exhaustive; it merely shows **examples** of the evaluative terms that might be used for a particular focus and criterion. In practice, other terms might be more appropriate, including specialised and technical terms which are part of the technical language of the occupational sector.

We can apply this chart to some of the critical outcomes we have already identified above to see how the complete performance criterion – the critical outcome or process and the evaluative phrase – are developed.

In Example 1, 'Prepare drawings and associated graphical information', we identified these critical outcomes and processes:

- drawings and associated graphical material;
- registers and records of drawings and associated graphical information;
- the methods and media selected to produce the drawings;
- checks and approvals obtained at certain stages in the production of the drawings;
- incomplete and inconsistent information (which may need to be clarified);
- deviations from standard conventions (which may need to be explained).

FOCUS OF CRITERION	FOCUS FOR EVALUATION	EXAMPLES OF EVALUATIVE TERMS AND PHRASES
Products		
Manufacturing and assembling products	Dimension, finish, fitness for purpose	Correct, accurate, capable of ... meets specification, free from ... (blemishes etc)
Changing the state or shape of products or materials	Finish, appearance, composition, fitness for purpose	Free from (blemishes, etc), meets specification, appropriate, sustainable, avoids hazards
Selecting, processing and analysing data	Origin of data, fitness for purpose, interpretation, conclusions	Relevant, correct, accurate, complete, justifiable, realistic, appropriate, sufficient, valid, reliable, current
Originating, formatting and presenting documents	Origin of data, appearance, structure, content, fitness for purpose	Relevant, accurate, complete, clear, logical, coherent, meets specification, appropriate to (purpose)
Locating, positioning and arranging objects	Position, security, safety, appearance, relationship	Correct, accurate, avoiding hazards, coherent, symmetrical
Intervening into system operation (calibrating, adjusting)	Fitness of end product, maintain in operational state	Correct, accurate, confirmed, sufficient to (maintain operational state), operates as specified
Interactions		
Providing and exchanging information	Content, type, fitness for purpose, access/disclosure, obstacles	Correct, accurate, appropriate, concise, clear, confidential, realistic, modelling behaviour
Providing and seeking support	Content, tone, style, method (of communication), relationship	Encouraged, confirm, supportive, minimise, proactive, realistic, free from ... consistent with ... modelling behaviour
Promoting rights and values	Behaviour, tone, style, method (of communication), relationship	Encouraged, appropriate, supportive, minimise, preferred, non-condoning, free from ..., consistent, modelling behaviour
Directing or controlling others	Content, tone, style, method (of communication), relationship	Required, are followed ... consistent, safely, (conflict is ...) diffused, conforms to ..., without delay, modelling behaviour
Persuading and negotiating with others	Content, tone, style, method (of communication), relationship	Relevant, accurate, valid, timely, realistic, agreed, justifiable
Empowering and enabling others	Content, tone, style, method (of communication), relationship	Encouraged, supportive, appropriate, realistic, consulted
Planned courses of action		
Identifying opportunities and constraints	Fitness of source material, interpretation	Relevant, accurate, appropriate, justifiable, sustainable, valid, reliable, current
Analysing and synthesising information to develop new knowledge	Fitness for purpose, interpretation, nature of conclusions	Relevant, accurate, appropriate, justifiable, realistic, valid, reliable, innovative
Assessing feasibility	Fitness of source material, interpretation, analysis process	Relevant, accurate, appropriate, justifiable, realistic, valid, reliable, current
Determining aims and goals	Fitness for purpose, interpretation, nature of conclusions	Relevant, accurate, appropriate, justifiable, realistic, valid, reliable, current

Activity	Focus for evaluation	Examples of evaluative terms
Designing and specifying products and services	Fitness for purpose, content, achievement of outcome	Relevant, accurate, innovative, realistic, valid, justifiable, meets specification of needs
Calculating and obtaining resources	Content and results of calculations, fitness for purpose	Accurate, sufficient, appropriate, realistic, cost effective, capable of
Selecting and allocating resources	Fitness of resource, quantity, fitness of allocation	Relevant, sufficient, appropriate, optimise, cost effective, capable of
Developing plans, schedules and targets	Fitness to achieve aims	Accurate, relevant, realistic, justifiable, appropriate, schedule, timing, capable of
Commissioning work (eg contracting, tendering)	Selection process and fitness of outcome	Accurate, appropriate, relevant, suitable, capable of
Monitoring implementation of plans	Frequency, interpretation, analysis	Regularly, agreed schedule, optimise, accurate, justifiable, capable of
Evaluating progress against plans and targets	Fitness of analysis and conclusions	Accurate, relevant, justifiable, valid, reliable
Adjusting targets and plans against monitoring information	Achievement of outcome	Accurate, sufficient, justifiable, capable of

Process stages/requirements

Activity	Focus for evaluation	Examples of evaluative terms
Following procedures and methods	Conformity, fitness of selection	Correct, conforms to ... are followed ..., relevant, appropriate
Meeting schedules and timescales	Conformity	To schedule, immediately, as soon as possible/practicable, in time, in sufficient time, realistic, reasonable
Monitoring resource use	Frequency, analysis process, fitness of conclusions	Regular, accurate, sufficient to ...
Selecting and optimising resources	Fitness of selection, amount of waste, added value	Accurate, appropriate, sufficient, sustainable, minimise (waste), optimised
Choosing criteria, methods and alternatives	Fitness of choice to achieve outcome	Relevant, realistic, appropriate, suitable, capable of ... sufficient to
Maintaining health and safety	Degree of hazard and risk	Avoided, minimised, eliminated

Contingencies

Activity	Focus for evaluation	Examples of evaluative terms
Identifying problems (includes hazards)	Critically, retrievability, representation of problems	Accurate, timely, before breakdown is irretrievable, realistic, justifiable
Diagnosing problems	Analysing process, conclusions	Accurate, relevant, realistic, likely, appropriate
Generating potential solutions	Analysis process, fitness of options	Relevant, realistic, justifiable, appropriate, likely to ...
Evaluating solutions	Analysis process, fitness of selection, affect on outcome	Accurate, relevant, realistic, likely to ... sufficient to ...
Restoring systems to an operational state	Fitness of end product, return to operating state	Operates as specified
Passing on information and reflecting to support future action	Content of information, fitness for user, conclusions	Accurate, timely, complete

Table 10.5 Focus for evaluation and examples of evaluative terms

We can take each statement in turn, match it to the chart and then select the most appropriate evaluative terms.

The first critical outcome describes products: drawings and associated graphical material. The products are documentary information (expressed as nouns) so, reading from the chart (Table 10.5), we would expect them to have characteristics to do with origin of data, appearance, structure, content and fitness for purpose. The evaluative terms used to express these characteristics are adjectives like relevant, accurate, complete, clear, logical, coherent, appropriate to (purpose), and terms which are unconditional, like conform to ….

The complete performance criterion, produced by the specialist team which developed this standard, is:

> Drawings and associated graphical material produced are *complete, accurate, and comply with design information and relevant documentation*

The evaluative phrase is shown in italics. The developers have chosen 'complete', 'accurate', 'comply with design information and relevant documentation' (meets specification) and 'relevant' (applied to the origin of the information) as the appropriate evaluative terms in this instance. The reasons why they did not choose the other possible terms ('clear', 'logical,' 'coherent', 'appropriate to users') are easy to infer.

Drawings used for the construction of buildings are produced according to precise guidelines and conventions which are set nationally (sometimes internationally) and which allow little room for interpretation. This is referenced in the range indicators for the standards which identifies 'detailing standards' and 'codes of practice'. The purpose of these conventions is to produce documents with a standardised appearance which are 'clear, logical and coherent in style and content'. Consequently, these evaluative terms are not necessary because the existing standards and codes of practice already fix these possible variations.

But the first full criterion is not sufficient to fully define the characteristics of the drawings and associated graphical information. Referring back to the full standard (Table 10.4) we see that there are different types of drawing which are used for different purposes. This is not captured by the first criterion, so we need an-other criterion which links together the type of drawing produced and the pur-pose of the drawings. This is done by linking the type of drawing with the specification which would be issued to start the production process and using the evaluative term 'suitable' to match the type of drawing with the purpose of the drawing.

> The type of drawing and associated graphical material produced is *as specified and is suitable for purpose*

Both these terms equate to the example terms given in Table 10.5 ('meets specification' and 'appropriate to purpose').

There are four more criteria which are also associated with the drawings:

1. the methods and media selected to produce the drawings;
2. checks and approvals obtained at certain stages in the production of the drawings;
3. incomplete and inconsistent information (which may need to be clarified);
4. deviations from standard conventions (which may need to be explained).

The selection of methods and media selected are associated in Table 10.5 with 'choosing criteria, methods and alternatives'. The term selected for this criterion is the adjective 'suitable' – one of the examples given in the table. A condition is added because the suitability of the method **selected** is related to two other factors, the type of drawing and the time and resources available.

This second factor – time and resources – is an important characteristic of the construction sector. Drawings may be modified and developed on-site to meet emerging or changing requirements as construction operations progress. There may not be time available to return to the design office to produce a finished drawing on a CAD system, so a drawing is produced on the spot. At the extreme, this may be an outline sketch on the back of an envelope! However, even if the drawing is an impromptu sketch it must still be 'complete, accurate and comply with design information and relevant documentation'. This gives the complete criterion:

> Methods and media for production selected are *suitable* for the drawings produced and resources and time available

From time to time it is necessary to obtain checks and approvals at particular stages in the production of the drawings and for particular aspects of the drawing. This criterion is not so clear cut as the first two examples. One reason for this is that it is not immediately clear whether 'checks and approvals' are products (which would be phrased as nouns – **a** check, **an** approval) or processes (which would be expressed as verbs – **to** check, **to** approve). In fact, they are nouns – checks and approvals are physical documents.

The criterion appears to relate to a critical stage in the process of producing drawings. This would normally suggest unconditional terms which describe 'conforming to procedures' or 'meeting schedules and timescales'. However, in this instance the checks and approvals are obtained only when they are necessary. The individual is expected to make a judgement about which aspects of the production process require checks and approvals. Simply following a procedure and having every stage and detail checked would slow down the production schedule and waste resources. This is an example of where we would not wish to constrain action to slavish conformity to a procedure.

This means that although the criterion appears to describe a stage in a process, the action which is required is a choice: whether to submit for and obtain checks and approvals (and only doing so where necessary). This locates the criterion in another part of the chart (Table 10.5) – 'choosing criteria, methods and alternatives' – and the foci of the criterion are the nouns – checks and approvals. The full criterion is:

Checks and approvals regarding content and presentations of drawings and associated graphical information are *necessary and sufficient*

The developers have chosen the adjective 'sufficient' from the category on the chart (Table 10.5) and added the term 'necessary', which indicates choice.

Obtaining checks and approvals depends on a choice made by the individual and there may be some drawing schedules which do not require this outcome. This raises a problem for the design of standards – how to include 'optional' or contingent outcomes which may not arise in every performance.

One solution, which is still widely practised, has the effect of making the entire criterion optional. This involves the use of the term 'where necessary', as in:

Sufficient checks and approvals regarding content and presentations of drawings and associated graphical information are obtained *where necessary*

Since we are trying to achieve precision and reduce ambiguity, this is not a helpful way of describing this contingent state. The standard will eventually be incorporated into a National Vocational Qualification where it forms an important specification for the assessment process. The criteria identify those outcomes which **must** be assessed. Where it is valid and feasible, evidence of performance is collected from the work environment for employed candidates. What, then, does the candidate do if this condition does not arise because the production process which they have chosen to use for presenting evidence contains no instances where they judge that a check or approval is necessary?

The solution is to describe the criterion in the way used in the example, ie by applying the evaluative term 'necessary' as a qualification of the nouns 'checks and approvals'. In this structure, checks and approvals **are** obtained, and those that are obtained are sufficient and necessary. This phrasing **requires** that the candidate obtains checks and approvals. If these are not available as part of the candidate's work role, then alternative sources of evidence must be tapped. The candidate might be given access to work where checks and approvals are likely to occur, or a realistic simulation in the form of a case study might be devised to give the candidate the opportunity to identify and select those aspects of content and presentation which require approval.

This distinction in phraseology may seem petty, but it is fundamental to understanding the nature and purpose of a standard. A standard is not intended to be a complete reflection of every workplace. It describes best practice and often incorporates aspects of practice which are not present in all workplaces because it refers to anticipated future requirements. Thus, some workplaces used to gather evidence for NVQs may not contain all the conditions described by the standard. The answer is not to make the standard conditional on one workplace. Rather, the standard should state unambiguously what is required nationally, in the context of the occupation as a whole. If evidence is not available from a particular workplace then other methods of evidence collection must be used.

Two further criteria in the example standard describe contingencies which may arise in the production of drawings: having incomplete and inconsistent information available and the occasional need to deviate from standard conventions.

Input information (that is, the information which is available from which the drawing will be produced) which is inconsistent must be clarified and the drawing may then need amending. The clarification of the information is a contingency – 'identifying problems' on the chart – and the requirement is that the information is clarified promptly to avoid holding up the production process. The amendments to the drawing are not a contingency; they are part of 'formatting and presenting (documentary) information'. The amendments need to be appropriate (related to the information provided) and accurate. This gives the criterion:

> Incomplete and inconsistent input information is clarified *promptly* and *appropriate and accurate* amendments are made

Note that this is also a criterion which could have been phrased using the ambiguous 'where necessary' format – for example:

> Incomplete and inconsistent input information is clarified *promptly* and *appropriate and accurate* amendments are made *where necessary*

The second contingency involves circumstances in which it is necessary to deviate from standard conventions. There may be many reasons for doing this which need not be our concern, and such deviation is acceptable provided the reasons are justified and the deviation is clearly indicated. Two of the categories shown in Table 10.5 are relevant here. The first is the contingency category of 'identifying problems' – in this case a problem in design or presentation which requires a deviation from normal conventions. The second is to do with 'providing and exchanging information' – how the deviation is identified on the drawing. In both cases evaluative terms from the appropriate categories have been chosen: 'justifiable' and 'clear'. The criterion is:

> Deviations from current standard conventions are *justified* and are indicated *clearly*

The final criterion for the products identified in the analysis process describes registers and records of drawings and associated graphical information. These are physical products (expressed as nouns) so we will use adjectives to qualify them. At first glance this appears to refer to the routine storage of documents – a rather grand description of filing – in which case we would examine the category 'locating, positioning and arranging objects' on the chart (Table 10.5). However, the registers of drawings and graphical information in a design office are rather more complex than simply keeping a file. It involves the entering, processing, updating and categorising of information, so it is really part of the category 'selecting, processing and analysing data'. The key factor in maintaining records and registers is that they are complete, accurate and up to date ('current' on the chart). This gives the criterion:

> Registers and records are *complete, accurate* and *up to date*

This completes the development of criteria for the critical outcomes and processes identified in the earlier analysis. However, there is one remaining criterion which has an overarching function and applies to all other criteria.

Documentary production and registration is a key part of the quality assurance procedure in building design and construction so this needs to be referenced to cover all stages in the production process and all the outcomes. Quality assurance is achieved by conforming to externally specified procedures, so we need to examine the 'following procedures and methods' category in Table 10.5. What is required is conformity to an external standard, so the unconditional form applies. The criterion is stated as:

> Production and record keeping is *consistent with* quality assurance procedures

All that remains is to place all the criteria in an appropriate order which reflects the normal sequence of operations. This is not strictly necessary because the criteria are not a sequential analysis of a task, but sequencing the criteria assists users in identifying the normal steps in the process. The contingencies are inserted into the sequence at the point at which they normally occur. By convention, criteria which apply to all other criteria are placed last. The final version of the standard with all of the criteria is shown in Table 10.6.

This process of identifying what is to be evaluated and then selecting suitable evaluative terms applies to all performance criteria except those which simply state whether a condition should or should not exist. Table 10.7 shows a number of performance criteria taken from the three example standards with the evaluative phrase shown in italics and the type of evaluative phrase in brackets.

There have been many concerns expressed by critics of this methodology that

(a) Drawings and associated graphical material produced are *complete, accurate* and *comply with design information* and *relevant* documentation

(b) Incomplete and inconsistent input information is clarified *promptly* and *appropriate* and *accurate* amendments are made

(c) The type of drawing and associated graphical material produced is *as specified* and is *suitable for purpose*

(d) Methods and media for production selected are *suitable* for the drawings required and resources and time available

(e) Deviations from current standard conventions are *justified* and are indicated *clearly*

(f) Registers and records are *complete, accurate* and *up to date*

(g) Checks and approvals regarding content and presentation of drawings and associated graphical information obtained, are *necessary* and *sufficient*

(h) Production and record keeping is *consistent* with quality assurance procedures

Table 10.6 Performance criteria for the element 'Prepare drawings and associated graphical information'

the precise specification of performance at this detailed level is reductionist and therefore fails to account for the richness and complexity of human action. We disagree with this view. To analyse in detail does not mean that the only point of concern is the individually detailed item. Most of the words in this book were chosen with care and precision. An iterative editing process modified and adapted words, phrases, sentences, paragraphs, sections and chapters. The meaning conveyed by the book cannot, and is not intended to be, expressed in a single word or

- Written submissions are *accurate*, (adjective qualifying noun – submissions) contain *valid* and *relevant* (adjective qualifying noun – information) information and follow *reasoned* (adjective qualifying noun – arguments) arguments which present the case in the *most favourable manner* (intended effect of action)
- Oral presentations are *complete, accurate* (adjective qualifying noun - presentations) and presented in a pace, style and manner which is *intended to maximise the trust and respect* (intended effect of action) of all parties and are *appropriate* (adjective qualifying noun – presentations against level of formality) to the level of formality of the hearing
- *Appropriate* (adjective qualifying noun – interventions) interventions are made and questions are asked which are *designed to present and interpret evidence in the best interests of the appellant* (intended effect of action)
- Final summaries identify the *relevant* (adjective qualifying noun - points) points of the supporting argument and the *major* weaknesses (adjective qualifying noun – weaknesses) in the opposing submission
- In instances where submissions are unsuccessful, *clear* and *justifiable* (adjective qualifying noun – recommendations) recommendations are made for further *appropriate* (adjective qualifying noun – action) action to determine the case
- The aims and objectives of production are identified in *sufficient* (adjective qualifying noun – detail) detail to allow planning to take place
- The range of potential markets for the products are identified and a *realistic* (adjective qualifying noun – assessment) assessment is made of market demand
- Where there is an interest in expanding into new product ranges, a *realistic* (adjective qualifying noun – assessment) assessment is made of the extent to which the market is capable of influence
- The option selected *achieves the best balance* (intended effect of action) of production aims and objectives, market opportunities and constraints and is *sufficiently* (adverb qualifying verb – flexible) flexible to meet changing circumstances
- Plans are presented in ways which are *suitable* (adverb qualifying verb – presented) for those who are to use them

Table 10.7 Performance criteria – the evaluative phrase

191

sentence, and extracting a single word or sentence out of context would not help anyone to understand what the whole book is about.

We offer this analogy as an expression of the purpose of occupational standards. Within the overall context of a functional analysis all the words and phrases which are in the performance criteria, the elements of competence, the functional units – all the way up to the key purpose – express the total meaning of the occupation, what it exists for and how it operates. To understand each item, or performance criterion, as one might wish to understand a single sentence in this book, it is necessary to read it and extract meaning in the context of the whole message. That is what a performance criterion is intended to do: to convey precise meaning within the context of the whole occupation. It does not, and was never intended to, stand alone as an atomised specification of performance requirements.

In this context the performance criterion is a sentence in a paragraph (the occupational standard). The paragraph does not usually make any sense without all its sentences. Equally, a paragraph cannot tell you the content of the chapter – you need all the paragraphs. With a standard, you need all the standards in a functional unit, the constituent elements and the performance criteria to make full sense of what is being described and you need all the units to understand the nuances and complexity of a complete key role.

Even within this attempt to reach a precise specification, the limitations of our rich language in expressing fully the complexities of human action are evident. The evaluative phrases are chosen to be as precise as possible without unnecessarily constraining action. Yet look at the evaluative phrases. Some **are** constraining – the term 'correct', for example, gives little opportunity for leeway. Some require conformity to procedures. But most are far from precise. Terms like 'relevant', 'appropriate', 'justifiable', 'clear', 'logical', 'innovative', 'supporting', 'encouraging' and 'realistic' are hardly the stuff of absolute precision and offer little succour to those who accuse the standards approach of reducing human action to measurable outputs. And these are the more commonly used evaluative terms. Most of the evaluative terms used in performance criteria require careful human judgement and consideration – and that is as it should be. The evaluative terms provide a benchmark which prompts participative discussion, negotiation and judgement – human attributes for a humane system. This is a far cry from any claims to measurability and rigid objectivity.

This is the intent and purpose of the approach – not to impose specifications on people, but to encourage them to participate in the judgement of performance. If we recall once again the origins of this method, it was designed to enable trainees to participate in learning and assessment processes. That purpose has not changed. It was designed as an alternative to imposed and authoritarian systems of learning design and assessment which were based on the assumption that learners were in subordinate relationships and received both wisdom and judgement from teachers and trainers. Learning, then, was a process of revealing truths from a curriculum which was owned by the teacher. Assessment was the application of mysterious processes of judgement which converted three hours of examination work into a single mark or a pass against criteria owned by the examiner and not revealed to the candidate.

A standard opens the process to both the provider of the learning and assessment resource and the learner/candidate. For perhaps the first time in the history of education, the learner/candidate has access to the specification of performance and in many sectors will also be involved in the participative process of setting the specification. This access locks the learner into the learning process. They can see what they are expected to be able to achieve and they know the criteria against which their performance will be judged. They can participate in the assessment process by planning the collection of evidence, deciding what evidence should be presented, and participating in the evaluation of the evidence and the interpretation of the criteria. This is, potentially, a profoundly democratic process, and it is only made possible by the detail of description which allows the learner access to the performance specification.

PERFORMANCE CRITERIA – COMMON MISTAKES

It is at the level of the performance criteria that precision and careful choice of evaluative terms is critical. Without care and precision, ambiguities will emerge which will cause problems of interpretation. Despite guidance being available since 1988, there are still some recurring mistakes in phrasing performance criteria:

1. Listing stages in a task – eg a set of instructions:

- Produce drawings and associated graphical materials.
- Clarify and amend incomplete or inconsistent information.
- Produce drawings and associated graphical material as specified.
- Use suitable production methods and media.

In these cases it is necessary to start the criterion with the noun rather than the verb and then to develop the most appropriate evaluative phrase. Because this approach usually stems from a task analysis approach, the criteria as a whole may need to be re-examined to identify any contingency and task management components which may have been missed.

2. Describing all outcomes as 'correct' or in terms of a procedure:

- Drawings and associated graphical material are correct.
- The correct procedures are used to clarify and amend incomplete information.
- The type of drawing and associated graphical material conform to given procedures and instructions.
- Correct methods and media of production are selected.

This usually indicates that the concept of competence which underpins the standard is based on a procedural and conforming view of human action. The evaluative terms need to be unpacked to determine the standards of best practice within the occupation and to express a broader view of occupational competence.

3. Referencing the criterion to the procedures of an organisation:

- Drawings and associated graphical material are produced according to organisational procedures.
- Organisational procedures are followed to clarify and amend incomplete information.
- The type of drawing and associated graphical material conform to organisational procedures and instructions.
- Methods and media of production are selected which conform to organisational procedures and instructions.

This format was very common in many of the first occupational standards – indeed there were some early NVQ accreditations in which every criterion was expressed in this way. This stems from a fundamental misunderstanding of the nature of standards, which is that they are independent of the methods and procedures by which individual organisations choose to carry out their activities. The procedures of an individual organisation are not national standards. This format results in descriptions where the only outcome is that organisational procedures are followed.

Correcting this format involves examining the focus and evaluative terms chart (Table 10.5) to select the most appropriate term by which to set the standard applying to the outcome or process.

Referencing to external standards is acceptable if external standards, like legislation, national or international conventions or codes of practice already exist. These should always be referenced in a note or in the range indicator.

4. Describing processes and activities without an evaluative phrase (only acceptable where a critical stage in a process is described or when a condition or state should occur or not occur):

- Drawings and associated graphical material are produced.
- Action is taken to clarify and amend incomplete information.
- Different types of drawing and associated graphical material are produced.
- Methods and media of production are selected and applied.

This is also a frequent mistake and means that the development process has not been completed. The critical outcomes and processes have been identified, but the evaluative phrase is missing. This is also typical of a task analysis approach and is close to a series of task instructions. The analysis process which we recommend to identify the evaluative phrase simply needs to be applied to each statement.

5. Offering options, alternatives or conditions:

- Drawings and associated graphical material produced are complete, accurate and comply with design information and/or relevant documentation.
- Where appropriate, input information is clarified and necessary amendments are made.
- The type of drawing and associated graphical material is as specified and is suitable for purpose where necessary.
- Methods and/or media of production selected are suitable for the drawings required and resources and/or time available.

We have already discussed the problems of offering options in standards, and particularly the 'where necessary' format. However, this can appear in a number of different guises, as shown in the examples above. There are a number of simple rules to overcome this problem:

- If you are tempted to use 'and/or', simply change to 'and'.
- If there are real alternatives or options, develop separate criteria for each one.
- If the criterion refers to a contingent action, phrase the action to describe what needs to occur **when** it happens, not **if** it happens.

6. Describing criteria which are not within the control of the individual:

- Drawings and associated graphical material produced are complete, accurate, and are understood by all users.
- Where input information may be incomplete or inconsistent, prompt clarification is sought by an appropriate authority.
- Instructions to drafting technicians ensure that the type of drawing and associated graphical material is as specified and is suitable for purpose.

Criteria can describe only outcomes which are within the control of the individual, and should be rephrased to meet this requirement. Here are modified versions of the examples given above:

- Drawings and associated graphical material produced are complete, accurate and in a style and format appropriate to the needs of all intended users.
- Where input information may be incomplete or inconsistent, prompt clarification is sought from an appropriate authority.
- Instructions to draughting technicians are clear, unambiguous and capable of interpretation by an experienced practitioner.

PERFORMANCE CRITERIA – SUMMARY

Is each performance criterion:

- composed of a critical outcome and a clear evaluative statement, rather than a description of a process or instruction (except where a critical stage or a state is described);
- expressed in a language which is as precise as possible without unnecessary constraints?

Do the criteria, taken as a whole:

- describe what needs to happen when contingencies arise;
- avoid descriptions of procedures and methods except where there is no other practical reference;
- describe only those outcomes which are essential for successful performance;
- identify critical contingencies and variances?

NOTES

1. The most recent criticism of the complex and passive language of standards can be found in Beaumont, G. *Review of 100 NVQs and SVQs, A Report Submitted to the Department for Education and Employment.* No date or place of publication given but assumed to be London 1996.
2. National Council for Vocational Qualifications (1995), *NVQ Criteria and Guidance*, London: National Council for Vocational Qualifications.

11 Occupational standards – specifying the range of performance

THE ORIGINS OF RANGE STATEMENTS

Occupational standards describe **what** a person is expected to achieve (the element of competence title) and the quality of achievement expected (the performance criteria). In the early developments in standard setting this specification appeared to be sufficient to define both learning and assessment.

The arrival of the National Council for Vocational Qualifications in late 1986 changed this picture quite dramatically. Now there were to be truly national qualifications based on demonstrated competence at work. And to be national the assessment processes needed to be consistent and coherent, drawing evidence from different workplaces and matched to a common benchmark, the occupational standard.

One of our first industry-wide standards projects was in the building society sector where we worked with the newly formed Building Society Lead Body. This was the first general application of a functional approach and we were asked to modify a number of existing competence objectives to meet the new criteria and guidance which were in the process of development within the Technical Advisory Group and NCVQ. The project specification required that we identify the performance criteria and specifications of underpinning knowledge. Underpinning knowledge became an issue for standards development following the report of the Review of Vocational Qualifications. The first guidance issued by NCVQ[1] stated:

8.1 An accredited qualification is a statement of competence which will incorporate assessment to specified standards of:

skills;
relevant knowledge and understanding;
ability to use skills and apply knowledge and understanding to the performance of relevant work-related activities.

8.2 It is not necessary for each and every assessment to embrace all the above three elements. However, it will be necessary for the totality of the assessment upon which an award is based to demonstrate that the successful candidate is competent according to the level of the qualification, in skill, knowledge, understanding and ability in application.

The specification and assessment of underpinning knowledge and understanding has been an important debate in the development of occupational standards and National Vocational Qualifications. It is too complex a matter to be dealt with in this book, but suffice it to say that the issue was largely ignored before 1987 because the drive towards specifying performance was seen as an alternative to knowledge-based curriculum design. The whole idea of knowledge testing was treated with suspicion based on a concern that this might lead to a reversion to what were regarded as outdated practices, including written examinations. But the specification of knowledge and understanding became an important issue, intended to bridge the gap between the more generalised outcome descriptions which emerged from the functional analysis approach and the process of assessment in NVQs.

The move away from detailed task analysis to describing broad outcomes required that variations in occupational context be accommodated in the standards. A simple example taken from our work on the Building Society sector illustrates this problem.

One of the standards developed for the sector was concerned with providing information to customers about products and services. The element title was:

Inform customers about products and services on request

This outcome statement immediately begged the question, 'Which products and services?'. Initially it was thought, rather naively, that the specification of the different products and services did not really matter, and that the candidate would simply need to cover all the products and services which their particular branch or society offered. For a locally assessed and certificated qualification this may have been sufficient, but for a national qualification this level of potential variation was clearly not acceptable.

The standard task approach which we described in Part 2 would have solved this problem by generating a standard task for each variation. If the products were classified as investments, lending and insurance, then standard tasks would be defined as:

Inform customers about investment products on request
Inform customers about lending products on request
Inform customers about insurance products on request

There would be additional standard tasks for the services which might be classified as foreign currency, travellers' cheques, credit cards and share dealing. This would result in four more standard tasks:

> Inform customers about foreign currency services on request
>
> Inform customers about travellers' cheque services on request
>
> Inform customers about credit card services on request
>
> Inform customers about share dealing services on request

Thus, instead of a single outcome statement, the sector would have been faced with seven standard tasks, each with rather similar performance criteria. More standard tasks would have to be added from time to time as the sector developed and offered new products and services.

Since this development route had been rejected, a solution was needed which accommodated the different variables and circumstances. Specifying underpinning knowledge and understanding was identified as the most likely solution.

The idea was simple. The outcome statement would be qualified by a statement of underpinning knowledge which required that the candidate demonstrate their knowledge of the different kinds of services and products. They would also be assessed through a limited number of work observations on their ability to inform customers about products and services in general, plus a knowledge test. The combination of performance assessment and knowledge testing would be sufficient to demonstrate competence. The content of the performance observation would be based on serendipity, consisting of those customers, products and services which the candidate happened to encounter during the observation period.

To signal that the general term 'products and services' would be qualified within the standard, the titles of elements which would require underpinning knowledge statements were modified by the insertion of the term 'a range of ...', to give:

> Inform customers about a range of products and services on request

But this approach quickly floundered for the simple reason that 'knowledge of ...' is not the same as 'being able to ...'. This became particularly important as further variations were identified which also required qualifying knowledge statements. For the example element title above, it quickly became apparent that products and services were not the only changing variable. There were also different categories of customer.

Investigations within the sector identified a number of different categories of customer, each of which was seen as significantly different because they needed different kinds of information and different styles of interaction:

- minors;
- teenagers;
- 16+;

- middle-aged;
- pensioners;
- rude and abusive;
- physically disabled;
- visual or auditory impairment;
- confused;
- foreign language speakers with limited command of English.

Continuing with this development path would have resulted in the element title changing again, to:

> Inform a range of customers about a range of products and services on request

The other disturbing result would have been that a customer adviser who had been observed informing a pensioner and a minor about a savings account would be deemed capable of informing a rude and abusive adult with a limited command of English about share dealing services. This was clearly stretching what could be inferred from a knowledge test.

The eventual answer was to incorporate these significant variations into the specification of the standard. The final project report describes this development:

As work proceeded it became increasingly apparent that the … element of competence, which is deliberately generalised and based on 'outcomes', fails to tie down particular contexts (or applications) with sufficient precision to give clear guidance to subsequent practitioners.

This means that when devising or evaluating assessment practice … the elements and performance criteria on their own do not provide sufficient information on the 'content' of the field – the content and the range of situations to which they were expected to apply are implicit.

This need for contextualisation led to the development of the concept of **range statements**, which are the **application of standards in context**. The notion of 'range' was slipped into the standards development language in a paper written by Bob Mansfield for the Technical Advisory Group in February 1988. In this he suggested that 'this may well require the addition of a separate knowledge element which details the **range** of products which need to be incorporated into the competence'.

Range statements provide details of the context and content to which the standard applies. That is, they should exemplify the range of conditions in which companies and employers in the occupational sector expect an individual to be able to perform. The standards (ie the element of competence and the performance criteria) are the outcome statements - they describe the result of competent performance. The range statements define the **coverage** of the element in terms of the context and content (activities) to which those outcome statements have to be applied.

Range statements do not exemplify or illustrate the content and context. They define it by inclusion. Consequently this means, in practice, that when a range statement has been defined for an element, the accreditation process should ensure that the individual accredited is capable of performing across the range so defined.[2]

The concept of range, therefore, was used to provide a context for the occupa-

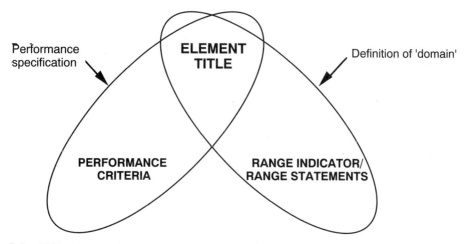

© David Mathews and reproduced with his permission

Fig. 11.1 An occupational standard – specification and domain

tional standards for the explicit purpose of assessment within NVQs by setting the scope or domain of the standard. This was helpfully illustrated by David Mathews and is shown in Figure 11.1. But the report goes on to identify another important function for range statements:

> The decisions which have to be made [about range statements] represent current good practice in the industry. For example, it is not possible to prescribe criteria which would determine whether a particular investment product should be included in the range. Rather, it is necessary to draw from informed practitioners, and especially those who are forward thinking and likely to be slightly ahead of traditional practice, a representation of current good practice in the industry.
>
> This requires a balance between products and services which are emerging, and in which the candidate will need to be competent, and the existing availability of the products for training and assessment. These issues become more complex in nationally-recognised standards as they are often the base by which different sections of the industry see the industry developing. **Emerging practice should be the key principle** due to the time lag between the descriptions of the standards and the development of the qualification – plus the fact that the purpose of linking qualifications to employment-led standards is to increase the competence of the work force to enable the economy to be more competitive now and in the future. Range statements, therefore, have a strategic role within an industry.[3]

We saw this 'strategic role' as the most important function of the range statement – that it existed to exemplify current best practice and to signal anticipated future requirements in employment. We recognised that it also had an important technical role to play in specifying the scope of assessment, but the concept of range offers much more to the standards development process. In effect, it gives a longer shelf-life to occupational standards.

One of the early criticisms of task analysis was that analyses could quickly become out of date in sectors in which technology or methods of work were rapidly changing. In 1982, when our previous company was involved in the Youth Training Scheme, we considered using the services of a particular awarding body which had started moving into the performance assessment arena by developing a number of office task descriptions. We decided not to use the awarding body because the task descriptions which made up the qualification contained such descriptions as:

- type duplicator stencils;
- set up and operate a spirit duplicator;
- repair a paper file.

Even in 1982, spirit duplicators were well on their way into industrial museums. We certainly didn't have one and none of the employers with whom we worked could even remember having one. Enquiries confirmed that the last surviving manufacturer in the UK had stopped producing them a year before and were now involved in the manufacture of photocopiers.

We fed this information back to the awarding body who responded with sympathy but firmness. They conceded that spirit duplicators were not exactly the cutting edge of technology, but they pointed out that they had commissioned an expensive task analysis exercise three years before, when such equipment was apparently to be found, and they did not intend and could not afford to change all their systems every time a piece of equipment changed. They also advised us that we could probably buy a second-hand machine from an office suppliers and that many schools still used them so perhaps we could contact a school which was upgrading to photocopiers and make them an offer for their duplicator.

The irony of this situation was lost on the awarding body, so we offered to deliver the qualification using photocopiers instead of duplicators or to develop an analysis of photocopier operation which we would gladly offer to them. Both suggestions were declined – so we looked for another awarding body.

This story has a number of lessons apart from the obvious futility of training young people on equipment which is obsolete. It demonstrates a serious problem with specific task analysis: the analysis can outdate quickly. It also shows that there is a time delay between the emergence of new technologies and work methods and their expression within vocational qualifications.

One of our early claims for outcome-based descriptions was that they did not outdate as quickly as task analyses. Reproducing documents and information (the outcome of photocopier and spirit duplicator operation) could cover both task descriptions and any subsequent developments in technology. But until the concept of range emerged this claim rang a little hollow because if a candidate had been assessed on a spirit duplicator they might find some difficulty in coping with a photocopier without further training, so confounding any claims to transferability. The standard itself contained nothing which could describe such an important difference.

Range resolved this difficulty. The type of reprographic equipment could be specified in the range to give a context to the outcome description. This also meant that the range could be updated easily to identify changes in technology and working methods, which would not necessarily impact on the content of the performance criteria and element titles. This offered the possibility of accelerating the process of expressing new and emerging requirements in qualifications since only the range, not the entire standard, would require revision.

We realised that, over time, performance criteria would have to be modified as changes became so significant that critical outcomes and processes changed, but that many new developments could be accommodated by range statements. This was a key feature in the second extract from the Building Society report, that the sector could use range strategically to identify current best practice and emerging practice as investment products changed.

Regrettably this strategic aspect of range statements was not taken up by NCVQ. In the two guidance documents which describe range statements NCVQ take a bureaucratic view of the concept, identifying only its technical contribution to qualification design and assessment.

> A range statement must accompany each element. This should express the various circumstances in which the competence must be applied, and may detail, for example, differences in physical location, employment contexts or equipment used.[4]

> A range statement defines the range and scope of an element and its performance criteria ... define[ing] ... the breadth of competence required for an individual to be considered occupationally competent. Range statements should clearly identify critical categories to be covered in assessment ... The Lead Body *must ... be selective when constructing range statements, including only that which is common and critical* in establishing transferable competence [our italics].[5]

The Department for Education and Employment guidance, on the other hand, stresses the strategic contribution which range statements can play:

> A range statement is a description of the range of application to which a standard is intended to apply. A standard is deliberately broad in scope and does not specify particular equipment, materials, methods or processes – rather it identifies outcomes. The range statement identifies particular and significant ranges of variation which fix the domain of the standard by identifying how the element may be interpreted in terms of *current good practice in the industry.*

> *It is intended that the range statement is regularly updated to keep the standards up to date* in terms of technology, processes and methods ... in this way, *the range statement is an important barometer in the process of updating and changing standards.* New applications and methods are introduced into range statements as they emerge and can suggest a change in standards (by the addition of new performance criteria or the development of separate elements) [our italics].[6]

This guidance document also signalled a further development in the range concept. In a footnote to the chapter, the possibility of there being two types of range statement emerged:

> there are two types of range information; range statements, which identify classes for assessment and broader information which we call range indicators ... [where] ... more general standards are developed ... range indicators are used.

Range statements were developed at a time when the distinction between occupational standards and National Vocational Qualifications was more theoretical than real. We showed in Part 2 that the competence, standards, assessment, learning model established that standards and qualifications were separate and that standards development preceded qualification design.

But in 1987, when range statements were first suggested, standards and qualifications were pretty much a seamless robe. Most publicly funded development was designed to produce qualifications, standards were seen as simply a stage on this route. Projects started from the point of view of designing a qualification and the early functional analyses were of the work roles which had been selected as the target for qualification design.

Only as functional analysis emerged as a more robust model was it applied to whole occupational sectors and the relationship between occupational standards and qualifications become clearer. A functional analysis could generate many qualifications as elements from functional units could be recombined into units of competence in NVQs. Standards could exist and be used separately – the design of qualifications was the only use which required the development of an assessment process. And it was a problem in the assessment process which range statements were developed to solve.

Range statements then, have a technical role **only in qualifications** because they are specifications for assessment purposes. Where standards are used for purposes other than qualification design, a different kind of description of context is needed. This description of context is not a specification, because the only reason for precisely specifying a range statement is to identify what aspects and contexts **must** be included in assessment. Standards, in themselves, are not related automatically to an assessment process; they only perform this function in a qualification.

In a standard, a user needs an indication of what the **total** range of variables might be to which the standard is **intended** to be applied. We call this description a range indicator. Notice the significant difference. A range statement in a qualification **specifies** critical categories to be covered in assessment, a range indicator **illustrates** all the variables which could apply.

A range indicator, therefore, is not a specification but a series of descriptions of different and significant circumstances and contexts. Range statements in qualifications specify the different contexts which **must** be sampled in assessment. In general, range indicators are much broader than range statements and one of their functions is to provide a starting-point for refining into range statements. But another important function is the strategic contribution which we described above. The range indicator can be used by a Lead Body to signal important changes in technology, methods and processes which may subsequently be incorporated into range statements in qualifications.

This is a further reason why we consider it to be critical to separate occupational standards from National Vocational Qualifications. If a standard effectively disappears when it is incorporated into a qualification, then modifying it in order to update it becomes extremely difficult. Once the standard has been incorporated into the mythical realms of the NVQ Framework and the NCVQ database, then changing it requires changes to the whole qualification, the delivery system and assessment processes. This is not likely to happen on a monthly basis. But if the standards are recognised as having an independent life, further development, change and modification can continue in the light of changes in existing good practice and anticipated future requirements. Then, at agreed intervals, the standards can be used to inform modifications to the qualification to keep it up to date.

DESCRIBING RANGE INDICATORS AND RANGE STATEMENTS

Both range indicators and range statements are structured in the same way. They comprise a number of range dimensions, each of which should be as similar as possible to the terminology which appears in the standard. Conventionally, the range dimensions are listed in the order in which they appear in the standard, and are numbered.

Next to the range dimension, each significant class is described. Each variation is called a range class. Here is an example:

1.   Customers: retail customers; wholesale customers

The range dimension is 'customers'. The range classes are 'retail customers' and 'wholesale customers'. The example shows two more conventions. The range dimension is followed by a colon and each range class is separated by a semi-colon. These are not fixed rules – it is simply important to indicate clearly the difference between the dimension and the classes and to separate clearly each class. The following formats are equally acceptable:

1. Customers
   •   retail customers
   •   wholesale customers

or

1. Customers
   (i)   retail customers
   (ii)   wholesale customers

If the first format is used it is advisable to use a semicolon to separate classes rather than a comma. Using a comma can cause confusion, as may be seen in the following, more complex example:

> 1. Customers: retail customers, with credit facilities, wholesale customers

Is this three range classes, or two? When punctuated using semicolons, this becomes a lot clearer:

> 1. Customers: retail customers, with credit facilities; wholesale customers

There are two classes in the example: retail customer with credit facilities and wholesale customers.

Care should be taken to avoid mixing up dimensions. This usually results from specifying the range dimension too broadly, as in the following example:

> 1. Customers: minors; adults; employed; unemployed; physically disabled; impaired sight

This example actually has three different dimensions: the age of customers, the employment status of customers and the special needs of customers. Mixing them up in this manner causes confusion, particularly when used to guide assessment. For example, for a criterion describing the content, style and tone of communication used with customers, the age of the customer might be significant. Explaining a savings account to a child of ten will be quite different from explaining an investment policy to a mature adult. However, the employment status of the potential investor is irrelevant. If the criterion describes the assessment of credit-worthiness, the employment status of the applicant will be significant, but their special needs will not. If the criterion describes the presentation and location of promotional information, the special needs of a customer may be an important factor but age and employment status will not be significant. If all three criteria appear in the same standard, each mentioning customers, the result is confusion. The range dimensions in this case would require modification and separation:

> 1. Customers for whom the style of communication may need to be modified: minors; adults
> 2. Assessment of the credit-worthiness of customers: employed; unemployed
> 3. Positioning of promotional materials should take account of: customers with physical disabilities; visually impaired customers

There are additional confusions and errors which can be included in the specification of range and these are covered next.

DEVELOPING RANGE INDICATORS AND RANGE STATEMENTS

The development of range indicators and range statements is quite straightforward. When developing the element title and the performance criteria any description (usually a noun) which is likely to contain variations should be highlighted and listed beneath the performance criteria. Table 11.1 shows the element 'Prepare drawings and associated graphical information', with potential range dimensions italicised.

Range dimensions need to be detailed only where the different classes affect the performance of the standard. This means that only those dimensions which might require a modification to the method used or the outcome achieved should be included. So, for example, 'type of drawing' is included in the range because different conventions and formats apply to different types of drawing. The term 'drawings' in the element title might also provide a clue that a range dimension is needed, particularly when the noun is a plural implying that different types may be involved.

The methods and media of production are included because producing a drawing on a computer-aided design system requires different methods and processes to manual drafting. Conventions are included because the different conventions apply to different types of drawing and different applications. Records and registers are included because there are different quality assurance procedures and storage requirements for different types of record. Checks and approvals are identified because many different types may be required and there are different

---

Element title: Prepare drawings and associated graphical information

Performance criteria

(a) Drawings and associated graphical material produced are complete, accurate, and comply with design information and relevant documentation
(b) Incomplete and inconsistent input information is clarified promptly and appropriate and accurate amendments are made
(c) *The type of drawing and associated graphical material* produced is as specified and is suitable for purpose
(d) *Methods and media for production* selected are suitable for the drawings required and resources and time available
(e) deviations from current standard *conventions* are justified and are indicated clearly
(f) *registers and records* are complete, accurate and up to date
(g) *checks and approvals* regarding content and presentation of drawings and associated graphical information obtained, are necessary and sufficient
(h) production and record keeping is consistent with quality assurance procedures

Range dimensions

1. Type of drawing
2. Method and medium of production
3. Conventions
4. Registers and records
5. Checks and approvals obtained

Table 11.1 Identifying range dimensions

procedures and processes for each type. Another clue is where the potential dimension is qualified by an evaluative term which indicates choice. Terms like 'suitable' and 'appropriate' often suggest variations which require a range dimension.

Some statements may appear to require a range dimension but in practice do not. In the example above it might appear that 'design information', 'relevant documentation' and 'incomplete and inconsistent input information' would benefit from expansion through a range dimension. However, none of these statements is a variable which requires a different application of the standard. In criterion (a), drawings and graphical materials **must** comply with design information and relevant documentation, whatever the nature of that documentation. Different types of design information and documentation will not make any difference to the fact that the drawing must comply with them. What they may trigger is different types of drawing – identified as a range dimension. Equally, inconsistent input information is not a range dimension. Whatever the type of information, it **must** be clarified, and the process of clarification will not vary with the type of information.

This is an important point in developing range dimensions and their related classes. If the factor chosen does not change the application of the standard, it is not a range dimension.

This can lead to the rather contradictory range statement which identifies 'all' as the range class, as in:

Type of customer: all

This is not a range. If the requirement is to be able to perform the standard with all types of customer, and an example of one is no different from any other, then there is no variable and no range. If it is necessary to explain that the standard is designed to be applicable to all customers, then this should be included in an explanatory note.

When the range dimensions have been identified the range classes are developed. Range classes identify different applications of the standard. It is important that the classes should be neither too broad, in which case significant differences will be obscured, or too narrow, in which case effort will be wasted in collecting evidence for what is, in effect, the same performance. This is best illustrated by an example. The first range dimension from our example 'type of drawing' contains seven range classes:

1. Type of drawing: location; assembly; component; sketches; working
    drawings; schedules; presentation drawings

Each of these has different characteristics, uses different conventions, has a different purpose and uses different methods and media for production. Each requires a different application of the standards specified in the performance criteria.

- Location drawings show where things should be, to scale.
- Assembly drawings show how things are put together, so they highlight fastening systems and the relationships between components. Assembly drawings will also show components which are inside each other. Overall dimensions are usually shown.
- Component drawings show single components, usually in the form of a manufacturing specification. All the dimensions in every plane are shown, tolerances are identified and other specifications, like material type, may be included.
- Sketches are simplified representations of any kind of drawing which are not to scale. They may be produced to give an impression or produced in response to a contingency.
- Working drawings show general arrangements of related systems within a structure.
- Schedules are a graphical method of tabulating and categorising components and elements.
- Presentation drawings show overall external and internal impressions (shape, colour, etc) of finished structures.

Because of these differences in characteristics, methods and conventions, each class is quite separate. If this were a range statement in a qualification it would be necessary for a candidate to demonstrate evidence of competence for each type of drawing. As a range indicator it shows the range of significant types of drawings in the occupational sector.

The range classes could be specified differently – for example, by identifying just three classes: formal scaled drawings, presentation drawings and sketches – but this would obscure important differences between different types of scaled drawings. The classes could also be stated in more detail – for example, by distinguishing between presentation drawings of exteriors and presentation drawings of interiors. This would make little sense because the methods, media and conventions used for interiors and exteriors are the same.

The decisions on what constitutes range classes should be the subject of detailed consultation because it is in this level of development that technical expertise in the occupational sector is of critical importance. Participants should be encouraged to identify factors and criteria for separating range classes, otherwise incoherent and inconsistent lists can result from this process. The listing of all factors can be a useful starting-point, but attention should quickly be concentrated on factors which involve a significant change in the way in which the standard is delivered.

For example, in the element 'Prepare cases for presentation and representation', one criterion specifies that appropriate sources of advice should be consulted where specialist advice and guidance on a case is needed. This required a range indicator because the way in which advice is sought and the credibility of the advice received might vary. The first draft of the range indicator involved listing all the sources of advice normally used by officers:

- internal union;
- legal specialists;
- conciliation agencies;
- the Commission for Racial Equality (CRE);
- the Equal Opportunities Commission (EOC).

When this indicator was examined again, however, it quickly became apparent that the only difference between the last three classes is that they specialise in different issues. The processes involved in contacting them, the way in which requests should be stated and the credibility of the information provided is the same. What makes them similar is that they are all regulatory and advisory bodies which are external to the union, and it is this difference – internal union sources and external agencies – which makes the difference.

The separate class of 'legal specialists' is redundant because legal specialists will either be employed by the specialist department within the union or by one of the regulatory and advisory agencies. The removal of this redundant class and the combination of the three regulatory and advisory bodies gives a much simpler range indicator (which is also the range statement in the proposed qualification):

Sources of advice

- internal union
- regulatory and advisory bodies (eg CRE, EOC, ACAS)

Notice that the second class contains examples in brackets. It is quite acceptable to illustrate or give examples of what is intended by the class in this way.

RANGE INDICATORS AND RANGE STATEMENTS

Range indicators are usually the starting-point for the development of range statements and they also form an important focus for qualification design. When qualifications are developed a number of considerations will be brought into play which do not apply to the identification of occupational standards.

A qualification is a compromise between the ideal specification contained in the standards and what is practical in terms of current working practice. In general, it is expected that most NVQs are developed for people in work and the preferred source of evidence is that collected as part of normal work performance. Consequently, if the qualification requires outcomes and contexts which are quite rare in current practice, few candidates will be able to achieve the qualification.

We have our own views on the nature of qualifications which we hope to address in more detail in a subsequent publication, but the simple fact is that qualifications may be less demanding and strategic in orientation than can be achieved with occupational standards. Consequently, the breadth of the range indicator needs to be refined into a more precise specification of what must be required for assessment purposes. There are three ways in which the range indicator may relate to the subsequent range statements.

The first possibility is that the range indicator may transfer completely to the qualification and become the range statement. For example, the second range indicator from the worked example above:

2. Method and medium of production: manual; computer generated

is likely to remain the same when a qualification is developed. CAD systems are now so commonly used in the sector that it would be difficult to imagine competence in producing drawings which was solely restricted to manual drafting methods.

The second possibility is that certain range classes are very densely packed and require further development and elaboration to provide sensible range classes to target assessment. For example, the range indicator:

3. Conventions: detailing standards; codes of practice; available products; acceptable current practice

will require refinement. It is quite likely that this would have to be specified in much greater detail for assessment purposes. In particular, the broad statement 'acceptable current practice' requires elaboration. Here is a more specific version of the range indicator:

3. Conventions: BS 309 detailing standards; BIATT and RIBA codes of practice; recognised current practice as described in ICE/RIBA practice handbooks

The third possibility is that the range indicator may provide a context for further disaggregation of the element titles. For example, the worked example we have used in this section may be considered to be far too demanding within a qualification because of the wide range of different types of drawing which are referenced in the first range indicator:

1. Type of drawing: location; assembly; component; sketches; working drawings; schedules; presentation drawings

This single range indicator may provide the context for separating different elements of competence within a qualification, or even in different qualifications. For example, two elements might emerge from this process:

> Element 1: Prepare location, assembly and presentation drawings and associated graphical information
>
> Element 2: Prepare working drawings and associated graphical information

Note that in this example the range indicator has been used to develop conditional statements for the element title. This is not uncommon. The range is closely associated with defining the domain of the standard.

The definition of range indicators completes the process of standards development. Remember, though, that even at this level of detail the process of iteration is still important. When developing performance criteria and range indicators we still identify areas where the coherence of the analysis is called into question, which means that we may need to track back the analysis to look at adjacent elements of competence and even adjacent functional units.

When range statements are developed for the formation of qualifications, this signals the start of a different process – the development of evidence requirements and assessment guidance to inform the assessment process. This is beyond the scope of this present book, although we hope to return to this issue in a later publication.

Standards are a modest contribution to the description of human behaviour. They are complex in structure – but then, so is human action. Their purpose is to exemplify the description of competent performance in a manner which reflects the original vision of NTI: flexibility and adaptability to meet the challenges of changing markets and work requirements.

As we have noted earlier, all methods of analysis of human performance are partial. Functional analysis and occupational standards are equally partial, although they both claim to offer more than previous methods. But the critical question is, how universal are these methods in describing the enormous variety of different work roles? This question forms the basis of the next chapter.

NOTES

1. NCVQ, *The National Vocational Qualification Framework*.
2. Mitchell, L. Mansfield, B and Leigh, A., 'Understanding knowledge'.
3. Ibid.
4. NCVQ, *Criteria for National Vocational Qualifications*.
5. NCVQ, *NVQ Criteria and Guidance*.
6. Mansfield, 'Deriving Statements of Competence'.

Part 4
APPLYING THE METHODOLOGIES

12 The limitations of analysis – a universal model?

Functional analysis and the standards which are derived from this method claim to offer a more comprehensive description of work roles than could be obtained from previous methods of occupational analysis. We have already described how practitioners of previous approaches recognised the gaps in the descriptions of competence and a number of different constructs were adopted to give a more rounded and holistic model of capability, often by the addition of common skill categories to descriptions of activity. In Chapter 3 we referred to this as the 'bolt-on' approach.

One of our claims is that functional analysis and occupational standards do not suffer to the same extent from this lack of coherence and coverage; rather, through the method we have described we can capture all significant aspects of work roles.

Despite this claim it was only at the later stages of standards development that the question of whether standards and functional analysis could provide complete coverage of all occupations and levels of responsibility within occupations was properly tested. Early standards-setting exercises tended to concentrate on roles which were mainly characterised by tangible and routine activities. This was largely due to the policy surrounding the introduction of youth training and the developments connected with the Youth Training Scheme.

As attention turned to so-called higher level roles, claims emerged concerning the inability of functional analysis to capture non-tangible aspects of work roles – without, it should be added, any real attempt to apply the full power and potential of the method. Not surprisingly, many practitioners fell back to the comfort of the 'bolt-on' approach. This arose from the view that functional analysis was adequate for the description of tangible routine work activities but could not capture the important and critical aspects of competence which did not generate tangible outcomes and which tended to be concentrated in higher-level roles. Since functional analysis, as widely practised, was often little more than hierarchical task analysis, this misinterpretation is quite understandable. This view also links with the models of competence we discussed in Chapter 3 where we suggested that hierarchical models of competence propose that different types of work role require different methods of description and specification.

The basis of the argument was that people in higher-level roles needed a set of personal competences or personal attributes and capabilities which appeared to be indefinable except in the most general terms. Possession of these attributes, when combined with the more mechanistic functional analysis, would be the necessary ingredients of standards for groups such as managers and personnel professionals. We firmly believe that part of this debate concerned issues of power and status, expressed through a hierarchical model of competence.

The issue centred on the single most important principle of standards development: whether standards should describe what people are like or what they are able to do. Standards, unequivocally, describe the latter. In their guise as public qualifications, standards have no business commenting on what people are like. No such descriptors have ever appeared on publicly certificated qualifications – and NVQs, in this respect, are no different from and have no more authority than any other public certification.

In some occupations the issue of creativity was used to beat the mechanistic Gorgon of functional analysis. 'How', we were asked, 'would the creative genius of Michelangelo have fared in the NVQ system?'

The trite answer is that if NVQs had existed at the time of Michelangelo it is unlikely that the possession of an NVQ would have played any part in his selection as the right person to paint the ceiling of the Sistine Chapel. As a mature professional, he would have an existing body of work to demonstrate his competence, references from previous employers and an established reputation – all of which would provide far better evidence of competence than an NVQ.

This attempt to extend the standards model into descriptions of what people are like also raised the issues of values and ethics. It is quite clear – and the mature versions of functional analysis recognise this – that all occupations operate within a context of values and ethics. In some, the relationship between values and practice is clear and explicit. The care sector is a prime example. In others, like in construction and engineering, the relationship is less obvious, but it nevertheless exists.

Once again the solution to these issues was to attribute the applications of values and an ethical base to the personal attributes of the individual. Rather than try to express the **outcomes** which such values and ethics might produce it seemed easier to attribute (and judge) people against the attitudes and values of 'caring', 'honesty', 'probity', and 'environmental awareness'.

The basis of this attack on the functional analysis approach rests, then, on the supposition that functional analysis is partial – that it is not capable of describing critical components of human action and consequently deficient as a method for defining occupational standards for all work roles.

The description of human action may take many forms and have a number of different purposes. There is no single form of analysis which exhausts all aspects of human behaviour. It is the **purpose** of the analysis which determines which methods of analysis will be appropriate. In this sense functional analysis is not different from any other form of analysis. It is appropriate only for its stated purpose: to describe the outcomes of human action in work environments.

TYPES OF ANALYSIS

It may be useful to note the main types of analysis which are used to describe human behaviour. These have been usefully summarised by David Mathews, drawing on the Work of Fleishman and Quaintance, and are shown in Table 12.1.

Although some of these types of analysis may be superficially similar, they are all significantly different and they are used for different purposes. It is quite clear that the form of analysis appropriate to the development of occupational standards and NVQs is type 5 in the table – the analysis of the intended effects of activities – of which one important derivation is functional analysis. However, there have been numerous attempts to introduce analyses based on type 3 – ability requirements.

1. **Behaviour description**
   demonstrated behaviour or skills

2. **Behaviour requirements**
   behaviours or skills which should be used or are assumed to be needed

3. **Ability requirements**
   abilities needed by the individual to maximise performance

4. **Task characteristics**
   features of task, activity or job

5. **Outcome expectations**
   intended effects of activities - functions

© David Mathews, after Fleishman and Quaintance, 1984

Table 12.1 The analysis of human behaviour

A SHORT HISTORY OF ANALYSIS

Methods of analysis and descriptions of human action are closely associated with developments in other branches of science which are themselves strongly influenced by cultural values and mores. One significant trend is for methods of analysis to change over time towards stressing the **outcomes** of activity rather than the *underlying states* or *dispositions* which determine activity. Functional analysis is part of that trend.

In the nineteenth century deterministic theories of human action were commonplace. The 'sciences' of phrenology and physiognomy (analysis of lumps on the cranium and categorisation of facial features) were used to account for differences in personality. Criminal behaviour, in particular, was extensively studied using these methods on the assumption that criminal tendencies were internal states which could be assessed by outward physical signs. Vestiges of this approach survive in the enduring belief that people with close-set eyes are shifty and not to be trusted!

Character was classified against simplistic scales using terms like 'melancholic', 'choleric' and 'sanguine'. Learning disability was attributed to psychological states described as 'idiocy' and 'cretinism'. Lest we become too complacent, these latter descriptions were in common use in psychiatric hospitals in the 1960s.

The underlying principle of these approaches is the view that human nature and capability is relatively fixed and largely determines behaviour, and that this nature can be described by a series of constructs, may have visible outward signs and may be revealed by a variety of subtle or not-so-subtle tests. These approaches have their twentieth century counterparts – the widespread adoption of intelligence testing and the development of deviance theory are two examples.

The tendency for such approaches to give way to outcome-based descriptions of action is well documented. What used to be described as 'mental illness' is now described in terms of the behavioural outcomes which it produces – for example, 'difficulty in maintaining emotional relationships', or 'learning difficulties'. Criminality is described in terms of its outcomes – evidence of theft is required before someone can be called a thief – not the reading of bumps on the head or the measurement of the length of the nose. In all areas of human description this tendency is apparent. The description of disability is radically changing as we move to describing the result rather than the person. The partially blind are visually impaired. The label applied to the person – blind – is replaced by a description of the outcome – visual impairment.

In describing human capability the same tendency is evident. We no longer attempt to find direct measures for, or label people as, 'numerate', 'dexterous' or 'literate'. Rather, we describe what people can do. As in all developments in analysis and scientific thinking the previous models are still used in an *ad hoc* manner, so we still, for example, describe people as 'literate' or 'illiterate' in everyday speech, using the labels as a linguistic shorthand.

For certain purposes we still use these labels as rough measures. Schools, for example, continue to use for formative purposes concepts like literacy and numeracy as global indicators of ability. The point, however, is that we now seek more precise instruments to identify and report on these characteristics. Children's literacy is assessed against a series of complex attainment targets – educationalists do not try to score literacy, based on informal and arbitrary assumptions. In other words, judgements which may be conveniently phrased in highly generalised terms are now based on evidence which is matched to clear criteria. The constructs – literacy, numeracy – are inferred from evidence. A person is literate because they are able to produce outcomes which are independently defined as literate. We also know that literate, in itself, is not a useful criterion for describing achievement. The concept will need to be further analysed to generate a number of precise descriptions of discrete outcomes.

It is also worth noting that the meaning of terms like literate and numerate are historical and cultural, and will change radically over time. In the 1990s to be literate includes the ability to interpret tax forms, computer manuals and other complex instructions as well as the recitation of poetry. 'Numerate' will include the ability to use a calculator as well as being able to use the four operators. Such expectations would not have existed at the end of the last century or even midway through the twentieth century.

A person is literate if they can achieve attainment targets – outcomes. A person is not seen as literate because:

- they were born literate;
- they are from a social class which is naturally literate;
- there are external features and indicators (a literate brow, an educated manner, a studious demeanour) by which literacy can be directly inferred.

Different forms of language and description are appropriate to different circumstances and purposes and, as a result, different rules and norms apply. Thus, among colleagues we might use terms like creative, honest and professional, but these are not terms which stand up to the rigour, accountability and scrutiny required for public authoritative statements about a person's capability.

Public statements about capability are the business of NVQs. These statements are given authority by the systems of assessment which are an integral part of the NVQ system, and although we do not intend to discuss assessment in detail in this book, we do need to consider it in this context.

Occupational standards and the NVQs developed from them are accredited and become public statements through the **assessment of outcomes** – the results of activity. The term 'assessment of outcomes' can be somewhat misleading since it suggests that only tangible and observable outcomes – objects or artefacts – may be assessed (**what** has been done). In many instances, of course, it is also necessary to assess the process – **how** something is done – by direct observation or the tapping of the underlying cognitive processes through forms of knowledge testing.

The basis of assessment for an NVQ is two-fold:

1. **The outcomes of performance must be potentially demonstrable.** This does not mean that all evidence must be physically observable, nor does it mean that actual performance in the work environment is the only valid source of evidence. It means that any evidence collected potentially must be capable of **demonstration** and that a number of assessors, using the same criteria, should be able to agree on the quality of the outcome and should be able to come to the same conclusion based on the same evidence.

2. **The outcomes and the criteria for judgement must be capable of being described independently of the candidate.** In medical diagnosis it is the consistency and accuracy of the **diagnosis** that is judged, not the quality of the doctor. The capability of the doctor is inferred from the evidence of a number

of accurate diagnoses. In setting an assessment specification, therefore, it is necessary to describe the evidence which, when taken as a whole, would indicate a successful diagnosis. The specification does not describe the personal characteristics of the doctor.

This means that personal attributes which may underpin competent performance are not in themselves directly assessed, since they are not directly demonstrable.

This position is similar to the legal system. A jury or magistrate does not judge whether a person is evil or good, a thief or a murderer. They judge independent evidence, against stated criteria of validity and reliability of evidence, about what the person has done and infer from it, beyond reasonable doubt, a state of guilt or innocence. A thief is a person who is guilty of theft, and theft is an outcome which can be described independently of the individual who is guilty of the crime. The outcome, theft, may also be described by the application of a criterion like 'any act or failure to act which is intended to permanently deprive an individual or corporate body of property'. It is a description which is independent of any individual who commits the act. The separation of the act and the nature of the individual is so important in the legal system that evidence of an individual's previous behaviour which might lead a jury to infer a tendency to act in particular ways is specifically excluded from the evidence which is presented.

In assessing the competence of candidates for NVQs, assessors compare evidence against criteria of successful performance (the performance criteria) and then judge whether a person is competent or not competent. As with the legal analogy, the criteria for judgement must be independent of any individual who may perform the act. The general disposition of the candidate must not influence the judgement. Judgement is made only against stated criteria. This is called **criterion referenced assessment**, and it is the foundation of the standards programme and NVQs. The boundaries and limits of criterion-referenced assessment is shown in Figure 12.1.

Personal characteristics or qualities – or any other description of what people are **like** – are not therefore admissible as evidence of competent performance. There are good reasons for this which are bound up with the rationale of introducing NVQs and occupational standards in the first instance.

Assumed internal states, like honesty, concern for quality and creativity, defy precise definition and consensus and are unreliable assessment benchmarks. For example, in a survey undertaken by Stewart[1] 75 managers were asked to list 15 qualities required by successful managers. Twenty-five per cent of respondents identified the same 15 characteristics as indispensable, but when asked to define those qualities they offered 147 different definitions.

Assessors will also vary widely in their definition of assumed 'states' or personal 'qualities', so they will generate their own rules of evidence and their own specifications for acceptable evidence, most of which will be unstated and unconscious. This is unacceptable in a system which is publicly accountable and which claims

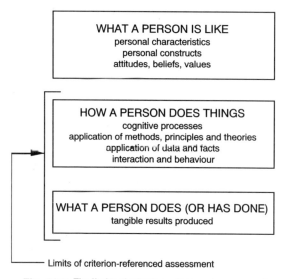

Fig. 12.1 The limits of criterion-referenced assessment

to make valid and reliable statements about a person's capability on which future judgements about employability may depend.

The generation of arbitrary and unstated criteria allows assessor preference to influence the judgements which assessors make. This reduces the reliability of assessment below acceptable limits. It also raises an associated problem: what to do if a candidate fails an assessment. In NVQ assessment a failure to meet the standard is not recorded and is assumed to infer a requirement for further learning and development. Failure to score on a test for 'reliability' presumably infers that the person is 'unreliable', a negative label which might be judged libellous if publicly stated.

The rules of evidence which may be used for some purposes, like internal appraisal or selection judgements, are less rigorous than those which must apply to publicly validated assessments which appear on a public document. Within legal constraints concerning gender and racial equality, judgements about a person's suitability for employment are for selectors to make and take responsibility for. They are not made available publicly as reliable inferences of current and future capability. Thus, a selector may judge that *by his/her standards and criteria* a portfolio or performance indicates that a candidate possesses 'creativity', or that certain other indicators offer the same indication. This is fine, it is a personal judgement. But public assessment is not a personal judgement; the assessor is a representative of everyone. Public accreditation assumes that all assessors, given the same evidence, will come to the same conclusion within the known limits of reliability.

Methods and techniques used to assess directly personal qualities, usually referred to as psychometrics, are norm referenced (ie based on average scores for

221

candidate populations, not independent criteria) and not sufficiently reliable and valid for public assessment purposes, although they may offer applications for other purposes.

Standards need to generate descriptions of human capability which can be independently judged against clear criteria. This does not imply that the descriptions of outcomes and the assessment specifications must be immediately understandable to the layperson, nor that any person may act as an assessor. Simplicity is not a requirement. In the assessment of roles which are highly complex and technical it is inevitable that assessors will be experts in their field and, as such, will share a common language of expression and meaning. These linguistic communities may use language in different ways and may use terms and an understanding of terms which cannot be understood easily by the layperson.

This is likely to be more common in occupations and roles where much of the capability is to do with process and cognitive processing. In occupations which tend to be judged on artifacts which can be precisely described, then everyone can, potentially, be an assessor. If an outcome describes the dimensions of an artefact, then any person who can use the measuring instrument can assess the result. But if we start to use criteria like 'polite', 'justifiable', 'realistic' we are describing processes and outcomes which may require expertise in the field to judge validly and reliably.

It may appear to be a small step from using terms like 'polite' and 'justifiable' to using terms like 'integrity' and 'creative'. But there are key differences. To refine the term further would lead to extremely detailed and complicated descriptions of action which will add no value to the description. So a criterion like:

> Recommendations are justifiable against agreed criteria for choice

could be expanded with much greater detail:

> Potential recommendations are accurately matched to appropriate criteria for choice
>
> Each criterion is accurately assessed for its potential contribution to a successful outcome
>
> The relationship between each assessment and its criterion is accurately identified
>
> Those recommendations which clearly meet the criteria and which are positively assessed are selected for presentation

This level of detail adds enormous complexity to the expression of the standard but may add little value for comprehension or assessment.

A second reason why further detailing is not necessary is that we have reached a point where people who are competent in this outcome can achieve an agreed meaning on the evaluative term. This is what we mean by 'value'. Since an agreed meaning can be achieved, further detailing will add nothing in terms of precision, only detail for detail's sake.

Terms like 'justifiable' and 'realistic' are usually matched to other conditions to help assessors and candidates make judgements. For example:

> Recommendations are justifiable **against agreed criteria for choice**
>
> Options selected are realistic **in terms of the resources available**

In each case, the evaluative term is referenced to specific conditions. Recommendations are not justifiable in any global sense, but specifically against 'agreed criteria for choice'.

There are instances where the evaluative term carries the meaning without a reference point or condition:

> Customers are served promptly and politely

This form only works in instances where the terms 'promptly' and 'politely' have the potential to be commonly understood without further qualification. Concepts like integrity and creativity, however, describe aspects of behaviour which are capable of considerable further refinement before agreement over meaning can be achieved. In this sense their use and retention for inclusion in criteria is not legitimate because they can be further unpacked to obtain more precise descriptions which are more amenable to assessment. As in the example of the concepts of literacy and numeracy, there are further stages of analysis which can unpack and make such concepts more precise.

The personal constructs which operated as a language of capability in the past are fast being unpacked by the proper application of functional analysis. The constructs may be useful starting-points for thinking through the outcomes which we need to describe within occupational standards – so the concept of literacy helps us describe what a literate report would be like in the context of a report of a scientific experiment. But could we imagine a performance criterion like: 'The report is literate'. Clearly this is quite inadequate. We need to use this type of phrase merely as a first step to trigger thinking about the outcomes we require. A proper analysis would dig deep into the concept within the context and emerge with criteria like:

> Data and summaries of data are complete and accurate
>
> Graphical information and diagrams are accurate, conform to presentational conventions and are designed to enhance the clarity of the presentation

Inferences drawn from data are matched and justified against appropriate theoretical models

The style and structure of the report is within accepted conventions and formats and the language is appropriate to the intended audience

An example of this unpacking process can be seen in the development of standards in the construction sector sponsored by the Construction Industry Standing Conference. Early in the project the Construction Industry Council Education and Training Committee, an influential constituent member of the Lead Body, stated that: 'The CIC Education and Training Committee is of the opinion that NVQs, particularly at level 5, must take into consideration ability relating to flair, creativity, judgement and quality.' If we examine the qualities described by the CIC committee we find that it contains two distinct groupings:

1. performance characteristics (what people can do – judgement and quality);
2. personal characteristics (what people are like – flair and creativity).

This is the first key distinction: some of the qualities to which people refer are, in fact, outcomes – they merely require further elaboration and unpacking to make them usable as performance criteria.

The performance characteristics described by the CIC require further expansion. Is 'judgement' the ability to make realistic and valid judgements? If so, about what and in what circumstances? Is 'quality' the ability to produce work consistently to recognised standards of quality? In both instances these performance descriptors, once elaborated, are perfectly capable of being incorporated into the standards since they are performance standards.

The characteristics of creativity and flair, however, are not performance characteristics since they describe what people are like. Within the remit of the standards programme and the criteria for the design of NVQs, they are not capable of separate description or assessment.

Much can be done, however, to develop descriptions of the outcomes and performance characteristics which result from the application of these personal qualities or characteristics.

THE UNPACKING PROCESS

First, it is necessary to expand and unpack the concepts. It is unlikely that the concepts of creativity and flair have common meanings throughout a single profession, let alone in different occupations. A measure of agreement on meaning – or a series of descriptions which address potentially different meanings – is an essential foundation to any subsequent work to develop useful descriptions which can be used to set standards.

The unpacking process involves two stages:

1. separating contributions which are already performance related (to be logged for development of the standards);
2. grouping the remaining concepts into categories for further consideration.

As an example, a working group might produce the following list of concepts:

- flair;
- creativity;
- working to schedule and time constraints;
- originality;
- concern for quality;
- leadership;
- concern for the environment;
- pride in appearance;
- reliability/honesty.

The first step would be to eliminate and log those attributes which can be expressed as performance standards, when suitably modified:

- working to schedule and time constraints;
- concern for quality (converted to: able to work to quality standards);
- concern for the environment (converted to: able to identify and meet requirements for environmental conservation and regeneration);
- pride in appearance (converted to: personal appearance in x contexts).

The remainder, which are constructs, might be grouped into the following categories:

1. Attributes related to quality/production of work:

    - flair;
    - creativity;
    - originality;
    - concern for quality;
    - reliability.

2. Attributes related to relationships with others:

    - leadership;
    - pride in appearance;
    - honesty.

3. Attributes related to professional position in the community:

    - creativity;
    - originality;
    - concern for quality;
    - concern for the environment.

The next stage of analysis involves describing how the concepts support critical outcomes. This can be done by inviting experts to give clear examples of how these attributes are expressed and demonstrated in different work roles. Exploration involves a questioning approach which seeks to express the construct in outcome terms and also identifies boundaries to the construct – opposites, similar states, etc.

The approach involves taking each attribute within its context and asking questions like:

- How do you know that a piece of work is creative?
- What is the opposite of creativity?
- How does creative work differ from work which is judged to be the opposite of creative?
- Think of a specific example of work that has the quality of creativity. What particular characteristics do you notice and how would you describe them to a layperson?
- Which people/roles need to have this attribute? Is it the same for (say) an architect as it is for (say) a civil engineer; or, in other occupations, for a set designer or for a performer?
- How do people acquire creativity?
- What conventions or principles in the discipline are used to make judgements about creativity?
- What conventions or principles in the discipline are taught to students to encourage them to develop creativity?
- What examples are used as benchmarks for creativity?

Different kinds of responses will emerge from this approach to questioning, such as:

1. Performance characteristics – answers like:

- using conventions in unusual and novel contexts;
- modifying conventions to meet new requirements;
- knowing and applying principles which are generally recognised as contributing to novel and creative solutions;
- using personal styles and formats which are developed by the individual.

These responses can be developed into performance criteria which can be incorporated into standards.

2. Additional attributes – answers like:

- creativity is the application of flair and originality;
- having a creative sense;
- having an extrovert personality.

In these responses, references to other attributes ('flair', 'originality') can be explored in the same way to generate performance statements, but if the approach simply generates circles of cause and effect (like, 'flair depends on creativity and vice versa') then further exploration is fruitless.

3. Claims for unique recognition – answers like:

- I know it if I see it;
- you can't describe it;
- it can't be defined;
- creative work is simply creative – there is nothing else to add.

These responses suggest that there are categories of judgement which can be made only by individuals and which are the responsibility of individuals to make for whatever purpose they intend to use them. They are not sufficiently precise to be included in standards or to be the subject of assessment for public certification. Put quite simply, if it is impossible to describe or illustrate a construct in terms of outcomes, it cannot be assessed by criterion-referenced assessment.

The purpose of this stage is to extract as much performance information from the attribute as is possible, isolating personal and professional judgements and assumptions which individuals may still choose to adopt. Having extracted the performance information there are a number of ways in which these performance characteristics, derived from personal constructs, may be embedded directly into the standards.

The standards themselves consist of:

- an element title;
- performance criteria;
- a range indicator (in standards) or a range statement (in NVQs).

Additionally, when standards are formed into qualifications, the following components are added:

- evidence specifications and guidance;
- descriptions of underpinning knowledge and understanding (often categorised as data/information; routine knowledge and procedures and principles/methods; theories and processes).

At each of these levels of detail the performance content of personal attributes may be embedded. The following examples are illustrations of what can be done at the different levels of detail offered by the standards format.

ELEMENT TITLES

It can be difficult to express the performance aspects of attributes in elements titles since they do not contain qualitative or evaluative information – the very aspects which many personal attributes aim to describe. However, elements can be developed which clearly imply coverage of many of the personal attribute descriptions. For example:

- Establish and maintain relationships with (customers/clients/members of the public, as appropriate to the sector).
- Monitor and maintain the quality of work in progress.
- Contribute to the improvement of product quality and customer satisfaction.
- Identify and disseminate advances in professional theory and practice.
- Contribute to the development of novel approaches and solutions.
- Investigate and recommend new ... materials, practices, methods (as appropriate to the sector).

All these elements titles have been used in developing standards.

PERFORMANCE CRITERIA

Performance criteria are a main focus for embedding performance descriptions which are related to personal attributes. Examples are:

Criteria associated with integrity, honesty and duty of care

- Customers and clients are treated politely and in a manner which promotes goodwill and trust.
- Funds held on behalf of contracting parties are separated from the personal and organisational funds of the practitioner and any gains resulting from the temporary investment of contracting party funds are paid in full.
- Offers and contracts which are illegal and which may generate conflicts of interest are declined.
- Information is only disclosed to those who have a legal right to receive it.
- The confidentiality of client information is maintained.
- Advice given to clients is based on a valid and comprehensive evaluation of available information and services, conforms to recognised codes of practice and constitutes the best advice available within the judgement of the adviser.
- The criteria adopted for evaluating information and selecting recommendations are based solely on furthering the interests of the contracting party within the constraints of statute law and recognised best practice.
- Where an individual communicates information to the worker which indicates that the individual or others may be put at risk, a clear explanation that the information may need to be shared with others is given in a manner appropriate to the individual.
- Individual's expression of feelings and needs are responded to in a manner which supports the right to such expression provided that it does not adversely affect the rights of others.
- Animals are treated in a manner which complies with relevant legislation, minimises any likelihood of stress and injury and optimises the health and well-being of the animals, self and others.

Criteria associated with quality and improvement

- Work is completed to schedule.
- Recommendations for improvement to systems are planned, implemented and monitored and improvements are accurately documented.
- Individuals and teams are given appropriate support to design systems for controlling processes which deliver products and services consistent with quality strategies and policies.
- Clear, relevant and assessable standards of quality are clarified and agreed with users.
- The role of each individual in the organisation's drive for quality is highlighted and s/he is actively encouraged to take responsibility for her/his function.
- Promotional methods and messages are improved to achieve the best balance between feedback, perceived take-up and presentation and the organisation's aims and vision for the future.

Criteria associated with creativity and innovation

- Design and presentation conventions are suitably modified and adapted to meet technical and client requirements.
- Form and colour styles are adopted which improve and enhance the appearance of the design.
- Existing, novel and innovative solutions to problems are identified and the characteristics, methods of generation and processes adopted are accurately analysed and summarised.
- Modifications to standard solutions which are realistic in terms of the criteria and which offer the potential to develop novel solutions are identified and applied.
- The results of testing novel solutions are evaluated against overall success criteria and are referred to appropriate specialists for comment and feedback.
- Associated innovations and developments, consequent upon the development of each product, are realistically predicted.

Criteria associated with contributions to teams

- Appropriate and timely help and assistance is offered to other team members.
- Appropriate and positive contributions are made to working groups.
- Language and behaviour is suitable to a team environment and contributes to the establishment and maintenance of effective working relationships.
- Appropriate self-development and training is undertaken which is sufficient to enable the individual to maintain professional standards of practice.
- Employed staff who are to work with volunteers are provided with appropriate information and opportunities for discussion on the potential contribution of volunteers.
- Conversations and contacts with patients are conducted in a manner, expression and tone which is supportive of that individual and is likely to promote her/his confidence in the care team.

- Effective communication is maintained between the animal and the person in a way which promotes their confidence and competence.
- Instruments are arranged in the order of use according to the operator's requirements.
- The preparation is paced with the operator's requirements.

Criteria associated with environmental concern and awareness

- Significant factors which may have environmental implications are identified and clear recommendations made to reduce negative environmental impact.
- Realistic recommendations are made to replace energy forms which have negative long term effects on efficiency or environmental pollution.
- Waste is disposed of in a safe manner and place.
- Working methods and systems allow for waste and by-products to be dealt with in a manner which minimises the effect on the surrounding environment.
- Where accidental damage or pollution to the site or environment occurs, action is taken to minimise its effects and appropriate persons are informed without delay.

RANGE STATEMENTS

Range statements are used to indicate that candidates for qualifications are required to apply their competence in different contexts and to adopt a range of methods and approaches. An inclusion of a class in a range statement means that samples of evidence must be generated for **each** class – range statements are not options. Examples which specify circumstances which may provide evidence associated with personal qualities include:

- *Range of design briefs:* Pre-existing products; new and innovative products not previously manufactured and constructed.
- *Range of performances:* Performances which follow the recognised conventions of style and content; performances which modify and adapt existing conventions.
- *Range of styles/formats:* Standard conventions; (specific) technical conventions; styles developed by the individual.
- *Range of clients:* Clients with detailed specifications; clients with no clear specification; clients requiring conventional, cost-sensitive solutions; clients requiring novel and innovative solutions.
- *Range of information:* public information; confidential information.

EVIDENCE SPECIFICATIONS

Evidence specifications are used to indicate the type and amount of evidence required to cover all the performance criteria and the range of a standard. The specification can also detail the non-routine, new and innovative contexts which are to be included in the evidence collected. For example:

230

Performance and knowledge evidence, taken together, should cover at least one instance in which a convention is modified within technical constraints to meet a unique client requirement.

Clearly, this specification might not arise in normal working conditions, in which case it would be necessary to simulate the condition and generate evidence from a project or assignment specifically designed to test the ability to develop an innovative solution by changing a known convention.

UNDERPINNING KNOWLEDGE

Descriptions of knowledge and understanding are used as a tool for designing evidence specifications and learning programmes. At this level of analysis the theories, principles, practices and conventions which underpin occupational competence can be stated. These descriptions may be extremely detailed and may cover more than one element or unit of competence. This is to be expected in higher-level occupations. An example, developed for the Chartered Association of Certified Accountants, is shown in Table 12.2.

Principles, Methods and Theories

- interpreting and applying:
- monitoring, analysing and assessing implication of changes in:
- evaluating and promoting changes in:

} rules and ethics of professional practice and conduct

Information, data

- the nature and purpose of rules and ethics of professional practice and conduct, such as:

  - integrity
  - independence
  - objectivity
  - impartiality
  - public and social responsibility
  - confidentiality
  - quality of work
  - competence
  - negligence
  - liability

- the nature and role of the bodies which set professional rules and ethics
- the nature and scope of financial accounting and the reason for its current state of development
- the purpose of final accounts/financial statements of limited companies and the relationship of this to the regulatory framework (eg Companies Act and the role of the auditor)
- nature, purpose and role of accountancy within organisations as 'financial and related information processing' profession

Source: 'Knowledge and Understanding Specifications', produced for the Chartered Association of Certified Accountants by PRIME R&D Ltd. © ACCA 1992

Table 12.2 Knowledge and understanding relating to professional membership and practice

NOTE

1. Stewart, *The Reality of Management.*

13 The human dimension – values and ethics

THE VALUE BASE

Another way of extending the method of functional analysis has been the development of value base units and codes of practice. These approaches do not embed into individual standards performance characteristics derived from personal qualities – rather, they state essential performance characteristics separately as an overarching requirement which sets the context of the standards.

The first clear expression of a value base in a functional map was in the functional analysis which resulted in standards for those who support the delivery of health and social care.[1] Such individuals are expected to support client rights, to treat clients with respect, maintain their dignity and to promote non-discriminatory practice.

These capabilities were often described in terms of personal qualities and attributes. Care workers were expected to have a 'caring attitude', a 'belief in the rights of service users' and a 'positive attitude towards anti-discrimination'. These descriptions, of course, describe what people are like, and are consequently not directly assessable within the remit of NVQs and occupational standards.

This did not mean that these matters were ignored, however. Considerable innovative work was undertaken to describe the **outcomes** which such personal qualities would generate in terms of performance expectations in the workplace. The care worker standards have specific performance criteria in elements which relate directly to these important issues, plus a separate unit of competence which is a mandatory part of any qualification derived from the standards. The unit is called the Value Base Unit and labelled as the 'O' unit as it **O**ver-arches all the standards to which it relates. Thus, in any care setting, such as enabling service users to maintain their physical cleanliness and appearance, the client's dignity and respect must be optimised through offering individuals their personal choice and preference. An example of one element from the 'O' unit is shown in Table 13.1.

The performance criteria of the Training and Development Lead Body standards use specific performance criteria to express values as described in the previous section. Thus we find criteria such as:

233

UNIT 01 Promote equality for all clients

Element title: Promote and support individual client choice and preference

(a) Clients are encouraged to be as self-managing as possible, to express their needs and preferences and to exercise informed personal choice on all matters consistent with the plan of care

(b) Where there are difficulties in communication, the appropriate support is given or sought

(c) Information given by the client is confirmed by the worker and appropriate modifications made where necessary

(d) Clients are offered appropriate support on matters in which they express concern

(e) Clients are provided with freedom from unwanted observation, communication, contact and interruption, consistent with the individual's wishes and needs and within organisational constraints

(f) Problems in granting client choice from the worker's or the service's angle are explained in a manner, and at a level and pace, appropriate to the individual

(g) Where there are risks to the client from the choices made, these are explained in a manner which is supportive of the client whilst outlining the risk

(h) Where client informed choice is restricted by others, this is recorded/reported in the required format

(i) Where a client is unable to exercise their rights personally, his/her interests are represented clearly and accurately to others in a manner which is consistent with the plan of care

(j) All agreements made, decisions taken or actions planned on behalf of the client are in his/her best interests and consistent with his/her preferences

(k) Confidential information from a client is only disclosed to those who necessarily require it following confirmation from that client

(l) The necessary records relating to client choice and preference are accurate, legible and complete

Range statements

1. Type of rights: personal; legal (eg Mental Health Act, Health Authority Rights Charter, Data Protection Act, Children's Act)
2. Rights include: right to make a complaint; right to give informed consent to care and/or treatment; right to obtain information on care policies and services available
3. Space: physical; personal.

Note: Provision of privacy is within environmental and care requirements and constraints; deprivation of rights may be apparent or reported

Table 13.1 Value base element from the standards for care workers

> Negotiations and agreements are conducted and concluded in a manner which promotes and maintains goodwill and trust

which specify and limit the strategies an individual should use. Others, such as:

> Confidential information is stored securely and made available only to those who have a right to it

and

> Decision makers are given opportunities to ask questions and seek clarification

specify how power should be exercised in relation to others.

The TDLB also chose to amplify and express the values in the form of a Code of Practice (Table 13.2).[2] This was also the choice of the TUSDB in the standards for

Five value statements

The standards rest on five general expressions of value, each of which requires people to achieve specific outcomes. These are:

1. Promote and support individuals' choices and preferences
2. Promote, support and provide training and development that offers the best opportunity of meeting organisational needs
3. Acknowledge the identity and values of others
4. Communicate effectively
5. Provide and promote equality of opportunity

Table 13.2 The TDLB value statements

This value base underpins trade unions' reason for existence and should inform the behaviour of trade union members, their representatives and officers. People will have differing views on what constitutes the whole spectrum of trade union values and it is unlikely that unanimous agreement would be reached on a single, fully comprehensive list of such values

Trade union values imply behaviour and attitudes which reinforce these values; for example, in an officer's dealings with members, representatives, colleagues and staff, employers, the public and the world at large. There are also practical outcomes to applying trade union values – in education, organisation and agreements

Set out below are those basic underpinning values which inform the behaviour and attitude of trade union officers and which would command the greatest possible agreement among trade unions and trade unionists. They are, in fact, objectives in their own right

Justice and Fairness
Demonstrably fair treatment in all aspects of work with open and just procedures for dealing with complaints and grievances from individuals and groups

Equality and Equity
Equality of opportunity and equity of treatment requires the elimination of prejudice and procedures which openly or covertly discriminate against people on the grounds of gender, race, religion and sexual orientation

Democracy
The greatest possible involvement in decision making at work and participation in the activities of the union by members. Advocating and implementing procedures and practices and providing information which encourages such participation

Unity
Maintaining cohesion between members and groups of members in working towards trade union objectives. Having regard to the legitimate needs and aspirations of all members as well as those of the majority.

Table 13.3 The TUSDB value base statement

professional trades union officers – embedding values in performance criteria and adding a separate commentary on the value base. The TUSDB statement[3] is shown in Table 13.3.

THE FINAL FRONTIER – THE ETHICS OF ANALYSIS

Finally in this discussion of personal attributes it is worth examining the proposition that the question of 'can we assess?' should be predicated by 'should we assess?'

235

Standards and NVQs are designed to generate valid and reliable public statements about a person's capability which are in the public domain. They are not individual opinions or even the sum of a number of individual opinions. They claim to be authoritative, based on evidence and intended to offer valid and reliable information to decision makers.

These characteristics place constraints on the kind of information which should appear on public certificates. This argument has been live in government-sponsored training schemes for many years. In the early years of YTS a number of systems were introduced which attempted to assess and grade personal attributes like reliability, punctuality and self-discipline. All were firmly rejected on very much the same grounds that we have proposed. But we believe that there is an additional reason why such approaches are unacceptable: they are morally indefensible.

NVQ criteria encourage open access to qualifications and specifically de-bar discriminatory practices in both the content of standards and the arrangements for implementation. It is a distortion of power if assessors make global judgements based on no other evidence than their interpretation of a construct and they have the associated right to label individuals against the construct. Such assessments are not made against commonly understood criteria, they are not amenable to valid justification and they are not open to challenge by the candidate, because they represent the power of those in authority to label people.

If we introduce the notion that personal attributes are valid targets for assessment, how long will it be before we are faced with demands to assess directly people's attitudes, values and beliefs – and to make public statements about them? We do not make this point lightly. Once we accept the idea that assessors have the power to label individuals we remove all the checks and balances that exist in robust quality assurance systems.

COMMONALITY AND THE ISSUE OF TRANSFERABILITY

Commonality and transferability are key themes in the standards programme and the development of National Vocational Qualifications. The notion of transfer was raised as an important policy issue in the early 1980s and underpinned many of the developments in the early Youth Training Scheme, even appearing as a key outcome for youth training.

The notion of commonality is linked to transferability in two ways. First, it is argued that common descriptions of activities which are functionally similar enable practitioners, learners and candidates to understand the common skills which underpin apparently different activities. This was one of the purposes of core skill analysis: to uncover core skills which were common to many different work tasks.

The second link involves the proposition that if common skills can be included within common functional units these can be applied in different sectors, thus providing clear links between occupations. Thus people would be able to transfer from occupation to occupation through the achievement of common units and elements of competence, which would offer coherence in the national system and framework of NVQs.

There is also an extremely practical reason why identifying commonality between occupations can be useful. Quite simply, it saves resources in standards development and qualification design. If there is a bank of common, transferable units of competence, standards developers and qualification designers can simply select from the bank and then add any specific requirements which are unique to the occupational sector. This has the potential to save resources, both time and public funds.

Although the notions of commonality and transferability may be extremely attractive they need to be balanced against what is feasible. At one extreme it can be argued that competence in particular occupations and jobs within occupations have no transfer value whatsoever, and that every time we move to different activities and achieve different outcomes we need to re-learn from scratch. This is clearly not so. There are many fundamental skills and capabilities which can be adapted and modified to meet the challenges of new and unfamiliar situations and work roles.

The other extreme is the argument that we can unpick all the common underpinning skills which exist and then identify them in different tasks, work roles and occupations to give a matrix of transferability. This can be an extremely useful exercise for some limited purposes, but it can also be extrapolated beyond credibility.

This issue, how far can the possibility of transfer be extrapolated, almost pushed the ESF Core Skills Project into a number of fruitless directions. The core skill keywords were used to restate tasks in a common language with the assumption that this would produce a map of transferability. It was quickly discovered that this works only if the context in which the skill is deployed is common as well.

For example, one of the core skill key phrases 'Find out information from written sources' has high transfer potential so long as the information is non-technical in nature. We hit problems when the indexes and references are occupationally specific and expressed in dense technical terminology. However, underpinning capabilities like using indexes, glossaries and references are common to many work roles and many occupations.

The term 'diagnose' (applied to fault finding), on the other hand, has nothing like the same potential transfer value. There may be common models of fault finding, but without the additional capabilities expressed by the technical expectations of the Job Competence Model the chances of transfer between occupations are extremely limited. An accountant competent in tracking audit trails will have little hope of diagnosing a fault in a turbine engine. In this instance, occupational context is a critical factor.

The approach reached its extreme when applied to manual skills. To suggest that the ability to operate a word processor has any transfer value to operating a centre lathe – apart from purely reflex actions like switching on the power – is to stretch credibility to its limits.

The problem is linked to semantics. There is a view that the semantic link created by the use of common active verbs like 'diagnose' or 'operate' forge links of commonality between apparently different activities, which is clearly not so. Yet versions of this somewhat unrealistic view still exist in the VET system and have led the search to identify common units of competence which have all the attractive attributes of signalling potential transferability, providing coherence across qualifications and saving resources.

There is already a considerable consensus in the standards programme about common units. The standards identified for managers and training and development practitioners are used widely in different sectors. There have been some complaints about problems of contextualisation and over-generalisation which have led to major reviews of both sets of standards, but there is a growing consensus that general management and training and development processes are common to most occupations.

There are, however, increasing pressures to extend this notion of commonality to other areas in occupational standards. These are not based on a common skills approach; rather, it is argued, there are common **processes** like negotiating, advising and informing which can be used to develop common units for use in different sectors.

The question is whether these common processes can be stated in a manner which allows them to be applied meaningfully in different occupational contexts. The danger is that they become so generalised that they have little specific meaning and do not contain precise descriptions of outcomes.

Clearly a balance needs to be struck which maximises transferability where it is feasible but eliminates spurious connections between outcomes which are significantly different. We have suggested that occupational standards, when derived from a rigorous functional analysis process, group into five categories or key areas, each of which, we suggest, have different implications for transferability. The five key areas are:

1. **The strategic key area** – standards which describe the strategic decision-making processes which involve organisational planning, setting targets and direction.
2. **The operational and technical key area** – standards which are specific to the occupational sector and deliver the operational component of the key purpose statement. These standards distinguish the occupational area from all others.
3. **Operational management** – standards which enable the operational standards to be deployed and delivered effectively. They are usually drawn from

the 'Manage Operations' units of the MCI standards and are often supplemented by operational management standards (like project management) which are more directly linked to the operational and technical components.

4. **Organisational management** – standards which describe the contribution which individuals make to the general management and overall efficiency of an organisation. These standards are usually derived from the remaining units of the MCI standards: 'Managing Finance', 'Managing People' and 'Managing Information' and are relatively independent of the operational standards and the key purpose statement.

5. **The value base** – those standards which, together with the operational and technical standards, represent the core values, ethics and behaviours which underpin good practice in an occupation. They also clearly distinguish the occupational sector from all others.

It should not be assumed that all functional analyses will show these key areas in the same way. Often the strategic key area is embedded in operational and organisational management standards. Some functional analyses have no separate value base – it is embedded in other parts of the analysis. Nevertheless a functional analysis of whole occupational sectors will include these five key areas and in each of these key areas the expectation of transferability will vary.

Strategic outcomes are likely to be common within a broad occupational sector and may well transfer to related occupational sectors. However, more research evidence is needed before this can be established with any degree of validity, but the recently published Senior Management standards,[4] which cover this key area, are certainly predicated on the view that strategic outcomes are common and transferable.

Technical and Operational standards are specific to the occupational sector. When standards are detailed to form NVQs they are specific to occupational work roles. This, of course, is as it should be. People in occupations do deploy specific skills to achieve specific outcomes, that is what makes occupations different. Grave mistakes can be made in trying to force transferability in this area. Semantic similarities can be used inappropriately to gloss over clear differences in purpose, method, process and outcome to the detriment of proper skill development and the achievement of significant and credible performance standards. The fact that the mixing and application of plaster can be described in general process terms in the same way as can mixing and applying icing to a cake does not make it the same activity and the same standard. We could force a spurious transferability by developing a standard entitled 'Mix and apply protective and decorative surface finishes', but this will not make a plasterer into a cake decorator. It might be convenient to use such a general template to derive standards in different occupations where there are apparently similar processes, but this should not lead us into the *non sequitur* that the two occupations are the same and that any transferability between them should be expected.

Operational Management standards may contain two kinds of standard with different transfer potential. Some aspects of operational management may transfer within an occupational sector. For example the ability to recruit and manage a design team is a common standard within the construction sector, independent of the disciplines of architecture, structural engineering and civil engineering. However, the outcomes, methods, processes and context makes this category of operational management quite different from recruiting and managing a primary health care team.

By contrast, the negotiation of a contract for materials, goods and services (the purchase and supply function) may have cross-sectoral transferability because the context does not affect the fact that the outcomes (obtaining necessary services of the required quality), methods (supplier selection and development) and processes (specification, negotiation, agreement, ordering, feedback on quality) are substantially the same.

Organisational management is expected to transfer to all occupational sectors – indeed, the MCI model is based on this premiss. Thus, we would expect system administration, information management, financial management and human resource management to be substantially the same in terms of outcomes, methods and processes in all occupations. Differences in context are already recognised within the MCI model and can be accommodated. However, organisations in different sectors may apply these outcomes in quite different ways. The financial management of a construction company may differ quite radically from that of a retail organisation, so any claims for commonality may be more apparent than real.

The value base is the ethical and value context which describes good practice in an occupation. In this part of the functional map the **purpose** of activity is all important. Methods and processes may be the same, but if the purpose is different this creates a different environment of values and ethics. To take an example: one of the value base standards in the professional trade union officers' standards, 'Promote equality of opportunity and treatment for all members' is based on one of the core units from the care sector awards 'Promote equality for all clients'. The standard has been modified to take account of the difference in role, but most of the unit remains the same. What is critically different is the ethical purpose. The care sector standards are predicated on an ethic of recognising the rights, beliefs and value systems of all clients – individuals, families, groups and communities – with the aim of enabling them to optimise their health and social well-being. Equality of opportunity and treatment is designed to achieve this purpose. Clients' views are listened to and it is acknowledged that all individuals have the right to their own beliefs and preferences. Care workers, however, also have a duty of care to others in the care setting where they work and to the community at large. This means that they are also expected to challenge expressed views when they adversely affect the rights of others.

In the trade union sector the ethical base is different. Equality of opportunity is not concerned with recognising the rights, beliefs and value systems of **clients** but focused on promoting the fair and just treatment of **social groups** who are disadvantaged by differential power relationships. At the most general level this means promoting the interests of organised labour to gain maximum benefits from collective bargaining with employers who represent the capital resources of the economy. This involves promoting and protecting the interests of specifically disadvantaged groups as a key part of everyday functioning. Whilst there are similarities between the trade union sector and the care sector in their ethical base, therefore, there are also key differences related to whose rights are being promoted and the context of that promotion. In the care sector, it is the rights of all, especially those who are permanently or temporarily unable to promote and protect their own rights. In the trade union sector there is a focus on the rights of employees in work contexts where power relationships are unequal.

The implication is that we should not expect value base standards to transfer completely between occupations, although they may be common within an occupation. This fits with existing examples, of which the care sector value base is perhaps the most developed. The value base in the care sector qualifications is common to all the qualifications and is identical in each. However, the value base does not transfer even between qualifications. If an individual with a care qualification wishes to access another care qualification, the value base is reassessed because it is seen (and assessed) as a **context** for all the operational, technical and operational management standards.

This analysis gives us a number of clues about what aspects of competence we might expect to transfer and what factors enable transferability. Purpose, outcomes, methods and processes (**what** is achieved, **how** it is achieved and **why** it is achieved) should be the same for transfer and commonality to be achievable and practicable. In summary:

- **Strategic** standards have transfer potential within an occupational sector and may transfer to other sectors.
- **Operational and technical** standards are likely to be specific to the sector and may be specific to individual work roles.
- **Operational management** standards which have the same outcomes, methods and processes as those of other sectors may transfer across sectors. Those with outcomes, methods and processes confined to the occupational sector are only likely to transfer within the sector.
- **Organisational management** standards have the potential to transfer across occupational boundaries but the nature of application may vary quite widely.
- **Value base** standards are likely to be common only within the occupational sector.

The following case study shows how this approach is applied to the standards for professional trade union officers. (The standards are shown in Appendix 1, Figure A3.)

The standards for professional trade union officers may be analysed as follows:

Key area A. Contribute to the maintenance and improvement of the organisation and membership level of the union

Key area B. Support and enable members to advance their individual and collective interests

These key areas represent the operational and technical roles of the officer. They are specific to this occupational sector and no significant transfer to other occupational sectors would be expected. However, embedded within the operational roles are some standards which could have potential transferability to occupations with a similar purpose.

Key role A1. Maintain and increase the membership of the union is one such case where occupations which recruit members who then have power within the recruiting organisation would have similar standards for recruitment. This might apply to some organisations in the voluntary sector.

In this occupational context, recruitment is more akin to the sale of a service, rather than the alternative meaning of the term, that is, to engage people for employment. The term 'recruit' in this context is quite different from the use of the same term in the management standards. Without the object, 'recruit **members**', the active verb has no meaning in context. This might suggest that the Trade Union Sector Development Group could have adopted a standard from a sales occupation. Apart from political reasons which would probably make this unacceptable within the sector, there are clear differences between the purpose and outcomes involved with the sale of a service and recruitment to trade union membership.

The purpose of trade union recruitment is not solely to offer a service in return for a price. Trade unions do offer many valuable services to their members, but one consequence of joining a trade union is the strengthening of representation, the local power base and the opportunity for the member to participate in the decision-making processes of the union. This is quite different from a commercial sales relationship.

The outcome is also different from commercial sales. The outcome of trade union recruitment is membership; services are only accessed by choice and as required. This is similar to membership of a club, and the standard for trade union recruitment would apply to some degree to similar arrangements where members group together in common to achieve mutual benefits.

Key role A2. Develop and support local structures and workplace representatives is occupationally specific. The purpose, outcomes, methods and processes described in the key role are different from any other sector.

Key role A3. Support the active participation and education of members and representatives does have similarities with occupations where people are expected to contribute to education and training activities as a supporting function to the main operational and technical roles. In original drafts this role was drawn from appropriate TDLB units but it was firmly rejected in the consultation process as being too detailed. We suggest that the issue here is one which the TDLB itself is facing: the recognition of the cross-sectoral role of the part-time trainer who only **contributes** to training and education as part of a broader role.

Key role B1. Negotiate and improve terms and conditions to meet an agreed collective bargaining agenda has three different functional units:

1. B11   Gain and maintain recognition with employers.
2. B12   Contribute to the formulation and implementation of a collective bargaining strategy.
3. B13   Contribute to the negotiation process.

Functional units B11 and B12 are occupationally specific. No other occupation negotiates recognition as described in B11, with the possible exception of marginalised governments seeking international recognition with other governments and inter-governmental bodies. Even in this exceptional case the purpose of recognition is different. B12 is also specific because of the context in which it applies. Seen in isolation the outcome described in B12 could apply to a personnel professional advising a board on negotiation tactics and strategy. However, the professional trade union officer is not advising senior people who employ them, nor contributing to a team agreement. Ultimately the professional officer can only advise. The strategy will be determined by local elected representatives and the members within the context of union policy, both of which are outside the control and influence of the professional officer. Consequently the purpose and processes are different.

B13 is a different case. The negotiation of terms and conditions could equally apply to any occupation where the following purpose, outcomes, methods and processes apply:

- The **purpose** of negotiation is to optimise benefits for others; the benefits to others are the main target and the results will be judged and confirmed by others.
- The intended **outcomes** of negotiation are improvements in the environment and the well-being of the people the negotiator represents, plus an agreement which has long-term viability.
- The **methods and process** of negotiation in the context of collective bargaining cannot be described in terms of common negotiating skills like those which might apply within a sales relationship. Collective bargaining is more complex because it involves the use of two complementary strategies – adversarial and co-operative – which are chosen against a series of judgements about the short- and long-term balance of power;
- Different **methods** are also used to manage failures in achieving the intended outcome. There are legal procedures to be followed and a series of tactics and strategies which may lead, ultimately, to **outcomes** which involve forms of industrial action.

243

This is different from a sales negotiation. Any common standards drawn from a sales occupation would have little meaning for a trade union negotiator. But, it might be argued, negotiations and agreements made between counsellors and their clients to agree treatment plans or other courses of action, or those between trainers and learners to agree learning contracts, could provide a common model which might apply to trade unions. In these two cases, however, the purpose, outcomes, methods and processes are entirely different. This is a further example of where a process verb – 'negotiate' – cannot be taken to imply similarity and transferability as it will not stand up to any form of rigorous analysis.

The negotiations we have described could be applied to any occupational area (with appropriate contextual modification) in which the purpose, outcomes, methods and processes are the same. Consequently we would expect the standards for negotiators representing employers to be broadly the same; contract negotiation would also have substantial similarities.

To demonstrate this potential connection, the Construction Industry Standing Conference have adopted a contextually modified version of unit B13 to cover standards for contract negotiation and arbitration, and have acknowledged the contribution of the TUSDB. Thus there is limited transferability to sectors where the operational requirements are the same, but only where clear links can be identified in the purpose, outcomes, methods and processes.

Key role B2. Support the representation of members' interests is also occupationally specific but could apply to other instances of representation and advocacy where the purpose and outcomes were the same.

Key area C. Contribute to the effective management of union resources and the provision of member services comprises the MI standards from the MCI model with the term 'manager' changed to 'officer'.

Key area D. Promote, support and represent the values and interests of the movement represents the value base but also contains the strategic key role as it applies to professional officers. This might be common to occupations which involve representation and promotion of particular interests.

Functional unit D11. Implement and contribute to the policy making processes of the union is occupationally specific since the relationships in this functional unit are found in no other occupation. However, some parts of the standards in this unit might be applicable to associations which make their own policy – although these are not likely to be occupations – rather, they are usually voluntary associations.

Functional unit D12. Support political activities within the policies of the union is also specific but could apply to certain other sectors: political parties and certain voluntary organisations such as those which engage in lobbying and pressure group activities.

Functional unit D13. Promote equality of opportunity and treatment for all members is a clear value base unit which is specific to the key purpose of trade unionism and would not be expected to have any transfer potential to other sectors. It is drawn from another sector but has been modified as we described earlier.

Key area D2. Promote the image, functions and purpose of the union is an operational management function which might have significant transfer potential in other sectors.

The purpose of this example is to demonstrate that commonality, however convenient it might be both for claims of transferability and administrative tidiness, has strict limits. For standards to be commonly applied they need to be stated in very general terms, and this threatens their credibility within occupations because the outcomes which characterise the occupation are not clearly addressed. By contrast, we do not want standards to be so specific that they will only apply to individual tasks and jobs – that is why a functional approach is used to tease out common outcomes which can be expressed in a common format. We do not want each standards-setting body to reinvent common outcomes like 'reproducing copies of documents and information' by specifying spurious contexts to establish a difference which does not exist. A single common format will suffice.

For these reasons we believe that the identification of common standards needs to proceed by a process of careful analysis rather than allowing semantic similarity to generate assumptions which may not reflect occupational reality. This can be done, as we have shown, by an analysis of the similarities in purpose, outcomes, methods and processes.

NOTES

1. Known as The Integration Project, this project was set up to integrate the work of two previous projects, Health Care Support Workers project and the Residential, Domiciliary and Day Care project. A key issue for the development work was the extent to which values were common across health and social care and how the values could be described in performance terms. See: Care Sector Consortium. *National Occupational Standards for Care.*
2. Training and Development Lead Body, *TDLB Implementation Guide.*
3. Trades Union Congress, *National Standards for Full Time Trade Union Officials.*
4. Management Charter Initiative, *Senior Management Standards.*

14 Quality and standards – evaluating the product

QUALITY AND STANDARDS

You cannot have quality without standards. Because standards are so central to any notion of quality it is essential that the designers and users of standards can discriminate between standards that are fit for purpose and those that are not. This applies as much to national occupational standards as it does to any other sort of standard. The fact that considerable amounts of public money have been spent on developing national standards is not in itself a guarantee of their quality – nor is the fact that they are endorsed by Lead Bodies. As we have suggested throughout this book, the process of standards development has been allowed to follow a number of different directions, some of which involve the application of approaches which, we believe, are not consistent with the aims of the programme.

What we need, then, are standards for standards to allow developers and users to evaluate the fitness for purpose of standards developed by Lead Bodies and the qualifications accredited by NCVQ. An evaluation process is useful for judging the quality of standards and qualifications already developed. This is called **summative** evaluation. But the framework can have a useful role to play, during the development process, for **formative** evaluation. The different purposes of formative and summative evaluation are shown in Figure 14.1.

The most useful form of evaluation for people involved in developing standards is formative evaluation. Formative evaluation is part of the iteration process which is integral to functional analysis. Iteration is normally used to correct and adjust the functional analysis against technical criteria to do with the coherence of disaggregation rules but other quality criteria can also be applied as part of the formative evaluation process.

Summative evaluation tends to have an inspectorial function. It may be used by public agencies to check whether standards and proposed qualifications conform to national criteria and by organisations who may wish to use the standards and qualifications as part of a human resource development strategy. Organisations may wish to evaluate standards against their own mission and goals.

Type	Stage	Purpose
Summative	At the end of the development process	To find out what has happened or been produced and to comment on or review the outcome
Formative	Continuously, throughout the development process	To inform the outcome and influence current and future development

Fig. 14.1 Evaluation processes

AN EVALUATION FRAMEWORK FOR STANDARDS AND NVQS

There are three factors which need to be taken into account when evaluating standards and NVQs. The factors are:

1. **Policy factors.** Standards and qualifications should represent the policy commitments which they are intended to deliver. This involves examining the central thrusts of policy as expressed in the guidance offered by the bodies whose role it is to interpret policy – the Department for Education and Employment and NCVQ.
2. **Technical factors.** Technical factors are those which influence the content, presentation, format and language of the standards – the subject of much of this book. The technical structure is not just a set of rules designed for bureaucratic convenience. The technical structure, we have argued, should be designed to support the policy of developing a more competent workforce.
3. **Implementation factors.** Finally, we should consider the ways in which standards will be implemented and used: how they are structured and presented so that users are clear about their intended use and are able to use them to contribute to the achievement of the policy objectives.

The three factors interact and create a number of tensions which must be resolved as the standards are developed, formed into qualifications and implemented. Figure 14.2 shows the nature of the tensions between the three factors. The positions numbered 1 to 3 represent the distorting effect which can arise if any one of them is permitted to dominate development.

The tension between policy and technical factors concerns the technical feasibility of policy. Quite simply, a minister, government department or even a project steering group may **assert** that something should be accommodated by the standards programme but it may not be technically possible to achieve it. Perhaps the most significant and recurring example of this is the requirement to include personal attributes in standards. As we have shown, this requirement is constantly

248

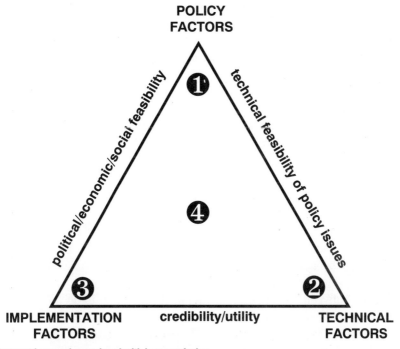

© Margaret Levy and reproduced with her permission

Fig. 14.2 The interaction between policy, technical and implementation issues

resurrected and restated in yet another guise – whether as personal effectiveness, enterprise characteristics or personal competence. It is normally, quite properly, linked to the policy requirement that people need to be competent and flexible. At each resurrection, the technical support system is put into gear and a fruitless search begins for ways of expressing the construct of the month, embedding it, or bolting it on to standards and assessing it. Each time the fundamental technical limitations confound the new enterprise: criterion-referenced assessment cannot accommodate norm-based descriptions, and standards describe what people are expected to achieve, not what they are supposed to be like.

This does not mean that the technical feasibility of policy requirements simply refutes and pushes back the policy to the policy makers. Despite a number of false starts and wasted resources, answers are usually found which reflect the **intention** of the policy if not the letter, leading to new developments through which policy intentions can be restated in a way which the standards programme can accommodate. This is what happened with the development of the value base to accommodate concerns about values and ethics. The work which sought to embed the outcomes of personal attributes and professional competence within standards is another example.

Between the technical and implementation factors the tensions of credibility

249

and utility provide a brake to the enthusiasm of the technical specialists involved in standards development. The standards must be used, so they must be understandable by users and provide a basis for action. This is why standards are sometimes deliberately modified to meet implementation concerns and keep practitioners on board, and also why qualifications are sometimes designed to meet current needs – because if they were too future focused they would not be within the reach of most potential candidates.

The balance is difficult to strike. Since standards and NVQs are intended to **improve** practice they must of necessity be challenging, but if they are too challenging there is the risk that candidates and other users will be demotivated because they will not be seen as relevant. This does not mean, however, that current practice should drive the standards programme and that all the products should be simple and non-threatening to users. The language of the standards is formal and precise, and users may need education and support to enable them to make full use of them. It would not be acceptable to modify the language, and lose precision, simply because the language is unfamiliar and unusual and creates difficulties with certain categories of user.

The balance between implementation and policy factors is to do with feasibility – political, social and economic. There have been many instances where this tension has threatened to both dominate and destroy the programme, particularly in the area of funding. The gradual changes in funding of the YTS programme brought it near to destruction, and current arguments about output-related funding are also causing difficulties. Tension between different policies may also create problems for implementation. A classic example is the issue of the target population for NVQs. Here, two policy criteria seem to be contradictory.

NVQs, state the NVQ criteria, should be 'free from unnecessary barriers … available to all those who are able to reach the required standards by any means'. This is widely interpreted to include those not in employment, whether unemployed or employed in different occupations. This interpretation is encouraged by the fact that the Department for Education and Employment requires providers of youth training schemes, which recruit unemployed people, to offer NVQs. Increasingly, full-time further education students also are able to choose NVQs.

But NVQs are clearly targeted at those who are **in work**, as these statements suggest[1]:

NVQs are qualifications for work …

the NVQ should be relevant to their current work, it should also show that they can transfer their competence to new jobs and different organisations

NVQ assessment is most effective where it is integrated into human resource development practices …

NVQs are work based qualifications, and much of the evidence required for assessment arises from workplace performance

Yet NVQs are widely available to unemployed people who have limited access to workplaces unless their provider is able to arrange work placements. Even where placements are arranged, they may be of short duration and the trainee may not be exposed to many of the normal pressures of employment. Consequently, many training scheme providers use simulations to provide opportunities for assessment. This can be interpreted as being contrary to the requirement that much of the evidence required for an NVQ should come from the workplace.

This is a vicious circle which comes close to the dilemmas of *Catch 22*! On the one hand, the provider must offer an NVQ which is predicated on assessment evidence collected from the workplace. The provider may not be able to provide sufficient work placements for reasons of local unemployment and recession, declining industries or because of involvement in an occupational area which is nationally significant but not well represented locally (like an emerging technology, for example). The provider does the next best thing and uses simulations. It may be suggested that this is not appropriate because of NVQ criteria and the regulations of the Awarding Body (which often specifically precludes simulation or sets strict upper limits to its use). But the hapless provider must offer an NVQ to attract funding. And so the circle continues to turn.

These tensions are not always to do with funding. The requirement for occupational breadth can be challenged by corporate interests who would prefer NVQs to be narrow and specific to particular jobs. And these interests, having the ears of ministers and other powerful lobby bodies, can be very influential.

All these tensions are part of the dynamic of change and power relationships and, as we claimed in our introduction, such tensions require recognition and balance, as in all mature democracies. Figure 14.2 shows three extreme positions, labelled 1, 2 and 3, with 4 representing the position of balance. We would argue that position 4 represents the optimum position for democratic change where the different tensions are recognised, addressed and resolved. The extremes produce distortions in the system which result from the inappropriate application of power and can lead to increases in tension which can threaten to undermine the system.

Policy-driven systems – position 1 – run the risk of being completely out of touch with what is possible in the real world by ignoring all technical constraints and implementation problems. All practicality is thrown by the wayside as policy imperatives are generated and positive feedback is demanded. At worst, feedback systems are modified to generate and publicise only good news, completely disregarding what is actually happening. Many critics of the VET system have made this charge from time to time and many of the matters which they have identified provide evidence of such distortions. Examples are:

- the requirement that all YTS schemes in the early 1980s were obliged to offer 'a vocational qualification or a credit towards one' when some occupational sectors had no qualifications at all;
- statements in government documents like 'NVQs are a guarantee of competence to do the job.'[2] The notion of a 'guarantee' is far in excess of the type of

claim which NCVQ might wish to make for NVQs and the use of the term 'job' effectively contradicts the NCVQ statement that 'specifications (should not) focus on narrow, specific job roles'.

Technically driven systems – position 2 – run the risk of alienating practitioners who are expected to implement the systems. Over-concentration on technical issues can also result in a drift away from policy imperatives as technical problems are resolved for the convenience of the developers. Responses to this tendency include:

- claims that NCVQ constantly moves the goalposts by changing criteria and inconsistently interpreting criteria – an often overstated but widespread perception;
- complaints that implementation is being swamped by paperwork systems which threaten the credibility and cost effectiveness of assessment – a major concern of a recent CBI report;[3]
- complaints about the complex language of occupational standards, NVQs and associated guidance materials.

If implementation factors – position 3 – are allowed to dominate, the tendency is for all change to be resisted and undermined. Practitioners simply change the language of existing approaches and systems, but nothing actually changes. This has also been a key tension throughout the standards programme. Examples are:

- education providers describing full-time courses as NVQs;
- NVQs being achieved through course attendance with little or no workplace learning or evidence gathered from a workplace;
- awards being achieved in such short time-scales that the validity of assessment practices are open to question;
- standards and qualifications being locally modified and redefined to meet institutional or organisational requirements.

The evaluation of standards, therefore, has to balance and optimise these three factors so that policy requirements are challenging and realistic, technical requirements are valid, precise and credible, and implementation requirements are coherent, understandable and robust. This is not a choice. All factors must be addressed to achieve a total quality system.

Based on our own interpretation of national policy, the technical requirements for standards and the needs of implementation, we offer the following criteria for the evaluation of occupational standards.

The four key **policy factors** which integrate all the White Papers and initiatives from 1981 to date are:

1. commonality and coherence – the whole system needs to be coherent, integrated and should identify links within and between standards and qualifications;

2. breadth of competence and transferability – occupational competence should be a broad concept and should incorporate those skills and capabilities which encourage and enable people to transfer to different work roles and meet the challenges of new and emerging work roles;
3. a strategic and forward looking focus – standards and qualifications should be based on current best practice **and** anticipated future requirements;
4. access and equality of opportunity – participation in learning and the recognition of achievement has become a democratic right for all our citizens.

There are two areas where **technical factors** are used to provide a benchmark of competence which delivers the policy requirements:

1. the nature and purpose of the functional map which starts the process of standards development;
2. the structure of the standards themselves.

For **implementation**, there are three ways in which the standards and qualifications can be presented to assist in the processes:

1. the structure and format of the standards;
2. the language of the standards;
3. guidance and support documentation which explains and offers help in implementing standards and qualifications.

These sub-points can be used to develop clear criteria for both standards and qualifications and provide a complete framework for the evaluation of standards and NVQs. The evaluation framework is shown in Table 14.1.[4]

NOTES

1. Extracts taken from: National Council for Vocational Qualifications *NVQ Criteria and Guidance*.
2. HMSO, *Education and Training for the 21st Century*.
3. The Confederation of British Industry, *Quality Assessed*.
4. This evaluation framework was developed from a series of frameworks produced by participants on the Standards Training Programme, a learning programme which the authors ran on behalf of the Department for Education and Employment in 1993–4. It is also informed by the work of participants who attended a series of seminars they designed for the Engineering Training Authority. The authors would like to thank all those who contributed to the development of the framework.

A. Policy criteria

Policy criteria are concerned with the function and purpose of standards and qualifications – what they are intended to achieve

A1 Commonality and recognition
A1.1 Standards are developed from a functional analysis of the occupational area, thus avoiding overlap and giving coherence to the qualification structure within a sector
A1.2 Common standards are used where available and appropriate to work roles in the sector, saving resources and showing the common links between different occupations

A2 Breadth and transfer
A2.1 Technical and operational standards are sufficiently general to enable mutual recognition between closely related occupations and sufficiently specific to be credible with, and usable by, practitioners
A2.2 Standards and qualifications address all the components of competence expressed by the Job Competence Model, including the ability to cope with failures and breakdowns in systems and procedures, working relationships and the management of different activities to meet overall occupational requirements and priorities
A2.3 Standards are designed to encourage the development of individual flexibility and adaptability by including the ability to work in a variety of contexts and to respond to changes in work practices

A3 Strategic focus
A3.1 Standards and qualifications incorporate foreseeable future requirements with regard to technology and work organisation
A3.2 Standards and qualifications clearly describe quality improvement functions and responsibilities
A3.3 Standards and qualifications incorporate a value base which describes best practice, key ethical issues and significant tensions within the occupation
A3.4 Standards and qualifications are benchmarks for excellence, reflecting best practice in the occupation

A4 Access and equality of opportunity
A4.1 Standards and qualifications do not pose any artificial barriers to access and encourage participation by disadvantaged and under-represented groups
A4.2 Where standards and qualifications are restricted to particular groups or individuals there are valid and justifiable reasons for it
A4.3 Qualifications are available to persons not employed in the occupational sector where it is possible to offer valid, reliable and cost effective assessment
A4.4 The overall framework of qualifications identifies clear progression routes between different levels and related occupational areas

B. Technical criteria

Technical criteria are concerned with what standards and qualifications should be like – their structure, format and content

B1 The functional analysis and functional map
B1.1 There is a functional map with a key purpose statement, a number of key areas and key roles. The map ends at a level of detail which approximates to a unit of competence, called a functional unit, which describes an outcome which an individual is expected to achieve
B1.2 Statements in the functional map do not overlap or repeat and statements at the final level of detail are approximately equal in weight and scope

B2 Occupational standards
B2.1 Statements of competence (functional units, units of competence and elements of competence) are clear and precise descriptions of the outcomes which have to be achieved and focus on a critical aspect of performance
B2.2 Statements of competence describe outcomes, not tasks, specific work activities or jobs
B2.3 The titles of statements of competence comprise an active verb, an object, and a conditional statement

where necessary for clarity. Titles should not include evaluative phrases or conditions which would be better described in the range

B2.4   Standards (and the units and elements of competence in a qualification) should be of a size and scope which is realistic (neither too demanding nor too trivial)

B2.5   Performance criteria contain a critical outcome and an evaluative phrase and avoid references to other criteria which are not available for examination or specific organisational requirements

B2.6   Standards contain range indicators which **describe** the kinds of context which the standard is intended to cover. Elements of competence in qualifications contain range statements which clearly **specify** different classes which are significantly different and which must be separately assessed. Both range indicators and range statements use a consistent convention (either punctuation or layout) which clearly separates each class

C.   Implementation criteria

Implementation criteria are concerned with the ways in which standards and qualifications are presented to users and how they are intended to be used

C1   The presentation of standards and qualifications

C1.1   The presentation and layout of standards and qualifications is logical, straightforward, self-explanatory and maximises access for users

C1.2   Standards are accompanied by a commentary, preferably at unit level, which gives a simple and clear description of the scope and content of the standards

C1.3   Standards and qualifications are self-contained within a single document. Where this is not feasible because of the size of the standards, different documents are cross-referenced and a functional map showing the whole framework of standards is placed in each document

C1.4   Standards state the origin, date of issue and the issue or draft number

C1.5   Where an element of competence in a qualification has been developed from an occupational standard, but differs from the original standard, the origin is clearly indicated

C2   The language of standards and qualifications

C2.1   The language of the standards is sufficiently precise to describe the outcome and processes required with minimum ambiguity

C2.2   The language of the standards can be interpreted by all potential users, including assessors and learners, although users may require briefing and training on the purpose and structure of the standards and the language used to express them. The unnecessary use of technical terminology is avoided and any potentially confusing terms are referenced in a glossary

C2.3   The language of the standards, including the performance criteria, follows normal grammatical conventions

C3   Accompanying documentation

C3.1   The documentation describes how the standards have been developed and verified by practitioners

C3.2   Standards and qualifications are supported by appropriate guidance materials and explanatory promotional materials

C3.3   Arrangements for the implementation of qualifications clearly indicate the opportunities for unit accreditation

Table 14.1 An evaluation framework for occupational standards and NVQs

15 Towards implementation

IMPLEMENTATION – STANDARDS WITHOUT QUALIFICATIONS

In Chapter 4 we showed how standards could be seen as separate from qualifications and could be used independently within organisations. In this final section we will discuss, albeit briefly, the ways in which standards can contribute to the improvement of organisational performance.

In our view, rather too much has been claimed for the uses of occupational standards in organisations. Many guidance documents simply offer a list of potential uses without showing how standards might work as part of a wider human resource management strategy. There is a tendency to suggest that standards simply need to be imported into systems and all will be well. Alternatively it is assumed that human resource professionals will implicitly know what to do with them.

Neither approach, in our view, has much to offer the busy human resource professional. For what it is worth, we have also developed our own list of what can be done with occupational standards, following a challenge to identify 101 uses for standards. In the event we only managed 78, three of which are concerned with NVQs. Although such lists are useful **illustrations** of what is possible, they are hardly **illuminating**. Our list is shown in Table 15.1, with the three NVQ applications highlighted.

There is little doubt that a framework of occupational standards offers an important benefit to the development of human resource development systems and processes which contribute more to the achievement of business and organisational goals. However, the relationship between standards and organisational goals is mediated by both the human resource development processes themselves and the ways in which the organisation mobilises human resources to gain external recognition of achievement. Figure 15.1 illustrates this relationship.

The rationale of Figure 15.1 is as follows.

1. Occupational standards used by, or developed within, an organisation should be influenced in their content and overall purpose by the strategic goals of the organisation, which are a reflection of the organisational mission, so that the

Recruitment and selection
1. preparing recruitment specifications
2. preparing job advertisements/details
3. a format for collecting information from referees
4. identifying the required components of a current role/job
5. identifying the required components of an anticipated/future role/job
6. an interview checklist for selectors
7. advance information to job candidates/interviewees
8. specifying induction and initial training

Job design and evaluation
9. development of job/role specifications
10. regular updating of job/role descriptions
11. monitoring the pattern of role/job responsibilities in sections/organisations
12. job design and redesign
13. criteria for job evaluation
14. criteria for the grading of staff
15. criteria for payment and reward systems

Assurance of product and service delivery
16. quality specification for work processes/outcomes
17. structuring and 'loading' production systems
18. monitoring of work processes
19. guaranteeing customer service quality/standards by licensing job holders
20. specification for contract tendering
21. monitoring contract delivery/compliance
22. evidence of competence for compliance with international standards (BS5750/ISO9000)

Local/national labour market planning
23. analysing and quantifying skills availability within local labour markets
24. monitoring national and local skill supply shortages
25. providing training/learning guarantees

Identifying individual/organisational training needs
26. specifying the skill/competence needs of an organisation
27. identifying individual learning needs
28. a format for individual action planning
29. identifying group/organisational learning needs
30. identifying previously acquired competence
31. developing a strategic view of future learning requirements
32. co-ordination of different human resource development processes

Structuring learning programmes
33. linking training to business objectives
34. linking training to national economic needs
35. increasing the relevance and credibility of training/learning programmes
36. allowing new learners to see the 'whole picture' in a simple and convenient format
37. enabling learners to match the relevance of off-job training programmes
38. broadening the scope and relevance of traditional skills-based training
39. identifying learning opportunities in the work environment
40. co-ordination of on and off job provision
41. development of learning contracts
42. development of specific learning objectives
43. development of knowledge content for learning programmes
44. specifying off-job content and learning processes
45. specification of required outcomes and targets for external training providers

46. monitoring external training providers
47. evaluation and selection of learning resources against organisational requirements

Delivering and evaluating learning programmes
48. a format for structured learning in the work environment
49. identifying progression routes for learners
50. providing clear goals for learners
51. highlighting opportunities for transfer between jobs/occupations
52. evaluating individual/group training programmes

Careers guidance and counselling
53. a basis for information and advice for people entering a first career/job
54. a basis for information and advice for people changing to new careers/job
55. assessing aptitude and potential for careers/occupational areas
56. identifying common and potentially transferable skills in different careers/occupations
57. analysis of local and national career opportunities in outcome terms

Assessing achievement
58. identification of assessment opportunities
59. specifying the methods and processes of assessment
60. a specification for formative assessment
61. *a format for the collection of evidence for National Vocational Qualifications*
62. a specification for summative assessment for other forms of public certification
63. a specification for internal assessment and appraisal
64. a format for joint review of learner progress
65. a format for individual review of progress/achievement
66. criteria for the recording of achievement
67. a specification for self-assessment
68. a specification for peer/group assessment

Development of publicly funded training programmes
69. assessing requirements for national and local training provision
70. assessing funding requirements for national training programmes
71. allocating funding for national training programmes
72. monitoring success of publicly funded programmes
73. providing coherence for national provision of qualifications
74. development of formal assessment systems
75. monitoring and assessing priorities for the development of new qualifications
76. *development of National Vocational Qualifications*
77. *updating of National Vocational Qualifications*
78. providing criteria for equivalence between national and international qualifications

Table 15.1 Seventy-eight uses of occupational standards

standards, taken as a whole, are a reflection of organisational culture and values and identify both the outcomes required and the processes needed to achieve them. In Figure 15.1, this is represented by the dotted line which connects the goals to the standards. Organisations using national occupational standards should select those standards which best meet their needs and may wish to modify the national standards the better to reflect organisational goals and mission.

2. Standards can influence the design of all human resource development processes and systems as they provide a single set of specifications of what individuals and teams need to achieve. Thus, all human resource development systems, from selection, recruitment, planning training, reward systems, pro-

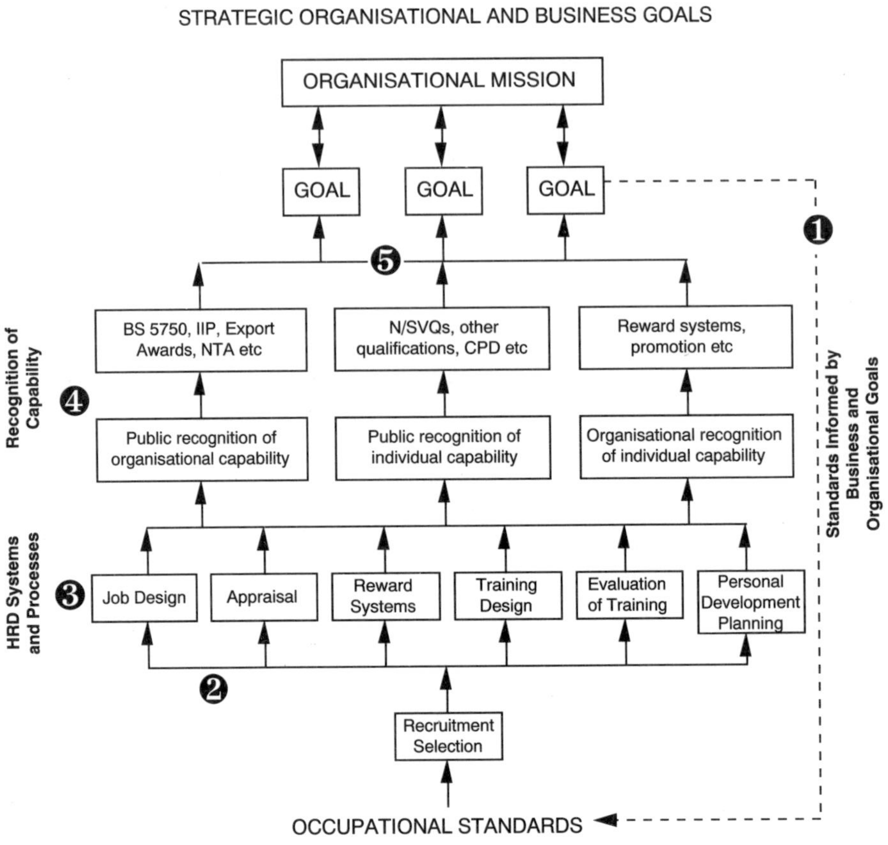

STRATEGIC ORGANISATIONAL AND BUSINESS GOALS

Fig. 15.1 Standards in organisations

motion and progression, appraisal and accreditation systems benefit from being based on the same set of outcomes and performance indicators. In addition, the coherence of the standards provides a vehicle for the total integration of human resource development systems.

3. Although the standards are influenced by organisational goals and, in turn, may be used to design human resource development systems, the standards by themselves are no substitute for strategic decision making. Decisions on the particular ways in which human resource management and development will be harnessed and deployed must still be made. The standards do not make the decisions, but they do provide useful and integrated specifications to improve human resource management and development.

4. Organisations themselves may recognise individual capability internally, or they may seek public recognition for individual employees (through NVQs and other relevant qualifications) or public recognition for the organisation's capability as a whole (such as through Investors In People for human resource

development and BS/ISO standards for the quality assurance of products and services). Systems of public recognition often impose constraints and conditions which the organisation has to take into account before committing itself to external accreditation. For instance, public accreditation of individual management capability would need to make use of the MCI standards and qualifications. Organisations would have to evaluate whether these national standards are sufficiently demanding for their managers or whether there may be other routes by which their competence could be recognised, such as through internal organisational processes. If organisations do choose to use the MCI standards and wish to access public certification for their managers, this will influence not only the standards which they use but also the human resource management and development processes which they put into effect, such as those for training and accreditation. Organisations which decide to concentrate solely on internal forms of recognition will have greater freedom of choice in the human resource management and development systems they choose, but may find they are unable to attract a range of suitable applicants who themselves are seeking some form of public recognition of their capability.

5. The mediating effect of external systems is shown in Figure 15.1 by the arrows which lead through the three systems for recognising capability before impacting on the achievement of organisational goals.

This model suggests that standards and qualifications are not an immediate, off-the-shelf panacea for organisational problems. They must be integrated into existing and planned human resource development strategies and plans and are only useful if they support strategic aims and goals – and there is no guarantee that they will. As we have repeatedly suggested throughout this book, many standards and qualifications are extremely limited in scope and merely reflect current activity. Such standards will be of little use to organisations wishing to change and develop to meet anticipated future needs.

However, if organisations do believe that standards can make a positive contribution to their human resource development strategy, there are obvious benefits to be gained. Perhaps the most important benefit is that the adoption or development of standards draws together and integrates different human resource development processes. Rather than having different methods and systems for defining learning needs, developing job descriptions and reviewing individual performance, the same set of performance indicators can act as a benchmark for all three.

We have identified six human resource development systems and processes which may benefit from the application of occupational standards. For the first five, we describe the purpose of the systems or processes, the problems which are reported with existing systems and the advantages and benefits which can be gained from the use of standards. For the sixth, reward systems, we offer some general comments, since this is an area in which there is very little evidence of development.

1 RECRUITMENT AND SELECTION SPECIFICATIONS

Purpose

To describe what potential candidates will need to be able to do, or have the potential to do with training.

Problems with existing systems

Recruitment can be a very hit-and-miss affair, leading, ideally, from job description to recruitment specification to advertisement, initial selection of applicants, selection processes, assessment and final selection. At each stage it is important that the same message is being given to selectors and candidates. Considerable time and resources can be wasted when descriptions and specifications are vague and imprecise. At worst, an inappropriate candidate can be selected (or conversely, the candidate may accept an inappropriate job) because the quality of information available to both candidate and selector is inadequate.

Advantages and benefits of using standards

Designing recruitment and selection systems against standards enables organisations to clarify the requirements of the post and attract the best candidates. As standards comprised different levels of detail they are ideally suited for extracting information for different audiences. Job descriptions and their related advertisements can be based on unit or element titles to provide potential applicants with clear descriptions of the range of work which the job entails and the outcomes which are expected. Standards can also be used to structure the application form to ensure that sufficient information is provided at the initial screening stage to allow the organisation to identify those applicants who are most likely to be suitable for the post and hence be invited through to the next stage. The unit and element titles, together with their related performance criteria and statements of range, can be used to identify the evidence which it is necessary to collect in order to design fair and just selection processes and which acts as a benchmark for making selection decisions. Selectors can be encouraged to seek out real evidence of the criteria rather than rely on vague generalisations from experience or 'what if' questions. Once the selection decision has been made, post-selection feedback to unsuccessful candidates can be structured around the criteria. For those employed there is the advantage that the first stage of personal development planning has taken place during the selection process and there is a firm basis for determining induction and other training needs.

Standards-based specifications should improve the quality of the information available about expected job performance and relevant achievements, for both candidate and selector – which means that there should be a better chance of the most appropriate person being selected.

The **benefits** of using standards in recruitment and selection can be summarised as:

- Precisely phrased adverts have the potential to attract the right people to the job and excite their interest.
- Detailed job descriptions sent with application forms will allow individuals to self-assess their suitability for the post, encouraging those with something to offer the organisation and discouraging those who are hopeful rather than capable, thus reducing the cost to the organisation by weeding out those of little immediate relevance.
- Candidates can be encouraged to present evidence that they have met such standards in the past or have the capability to reach them in the future.
- Standards provide a format for referees and encourage more relevant reports on performance.
- Selection designers have specifications against which to design a selection process which will collect valid and reliable evidence of competence from applicants.
- Interviewers have a specification which helps structure relevant and clear questions and the candidate has something tangible against which to ask questions.
- The evidence gained in the selection process can be used in personal development planning for the new employee and in structuring feedback for the unsuccessful.

2 JOB DESIGN AND JOB DESCRIPTIONS

Purpose

To describe the expected performance of job holders and the inter-relationships between different jobs.

Problems with existing systems

Job descriptions can be difficult to keep up to date, particularly in fast-changing environments. There is also the perception that expectations are the minimum required by the job description. In many organisations mere lip-service is paid to job descriptions, which are treated as little more than a necessary evil. Job descriptions are rarely related to any other documentation which concerns performance and often languish in drawers, only to be taken out and dusted when the job holder leaves and a recruitment specification is needed.

Job design can be equally fraught with problems. Often overwhelmed with tradition and current practice, or too closely engineered by task-based design systems, job design can easily fail to take full account of the complexity of work roles (as expressed by the Job Competence Model). Job design often also fails adequately to express required performance outcomes of individuals or to describe how an individual's contribution relates to the organisation as a whole, leaving some individuals to feel isolated or out of touch.

Advantages and benefits of using standards

Standards describe defined and realistic expectations, so they are a useful source for developing job descriptions and planning job design. The main benefit is that standards are written in distinct functional units. Each unit has a set of elements to which are attached the criteria for effective performance. This means that the outcomes of entire departments or the whole company can be described. And from this holistic picture, those parts which form the individual's job description can be selected, allowing the individual to see general requirements and those parts which are their responsibility, and from this they can identify their own contribution. Using this approach, each individual's job description can be viewed as a part of a whole, each job can be seen in relation to all other jobs within the department and everything can be related to the organisation's mission. The interconnections between jobs may be further examined by considering the impact of the Work Environment component of the Job Competence Model.

By using standards, functional units can be added and removed as job functions change or as the organisation shifts its focus and moves into new markets. Since standards are written in broad outcome terms they are less likely to outdate as markets and technology change. Units and elements developed nationally have built-in mechanisms for updating, so if organisations are using national standards they can update their job descriptions as the national standards are reviewed and amended.

The **benefits** of using standards in job design and job descriptions can be summarised as:

- Job design is based on clear and realistic expectations expressed in terms of performance.
- The unit structure of standards and the ability to apply standards to the performance of individuals and organisations shows the relationship between the parts (the job) and the whole (the department or function).
- The interrelationship between the whole and the parts allows individuals to see their own contribution to organisational outcomes and the value they add to the organisation.
- The unit structure facilitates rapid changes in job structure.
- Job descriptions become more flexible and easier to update and change.
- By making use of the different levels of detail within standards, job descriptions can be linked to personal development planning and appraisal.

3 IDENTIFYING LEARNING NEEDS AND PERSONAL DEVELOPMENT PLANNING

Purpose

To describe the gap between what it is necessary for people and departments to achieve and what they can currently do, so enabling individual goals to be set and plans to be agreed for meeting those goals. For individuals, this process offers opportunities to plan their own progress.

Problems with existing systems

The identification of learning and development needs can take many formats from lists of skills and tasks to descriptions of the personal qualities required. Too often, individual development needs are translated into the need for a particular training course which may bear little relation to the outcomes required. One of the key tasks which face those who are developing personal development plans is how to balance individual aspirations and goals with the needs of the organisation and the ability to meet current quality imperatives.

Advantages and benefits of using standards

Standards, because they are based on outcomes, relate individual performance requirements to those of the whole department or organisation. The progression opportunities open to individuals can be negotiated and planned, taking into account organisational needs as well as individual preferences and aspirations. Identifying learning and development needs based on standards allows clear judgements to be made which are consistent with job descriptions. Rather than get caught up with the detail of skills and department-specific tasks, the standards provide links with other parts of the organisation so that learning and development needs reflect organisational needs as well as those of the department and individual. Individuals are also provided with the tools for self-assessing their own strengths and weaknesses and can become more active participants in the process through the use of transparent benchmarks of performance. Identifying learning needs against the needs of the workplace also brings into consideration alternatives to traditional routes for learning, such as development through on the job project work.

The **benefits** of using standards in identifying learning and personal development planning can be summarised as:

- Descriptions are provided which combine and show relationships between individual and organisational requirements for performance.
- Negotiation over work roles and the identification of progression routes is facilitated.
- A common language is provided for job holders and those undertaking the analysis of learning needs.
- Individuals are given specific goals.
- Consideration of a range of learning opportunities is facilitated, including those linked to the achievement of organisational outcomes.

4 TRAINING PROGRAMME DESIGN AND EVALUATION

Purpose

To describe what people need to be able to do and identify methods and processes for supporting achievement.

Problems with existing systems

Training programmes can vary enormously in style and content, even within the same organisation. The programme may be based on a range of different perspectives such as a syllabus (listing things that need to be learned in sequence), skills hierarchies or personal qualities. It would not be unusual for apprentice training to be expressed as a sequential syllabus of basic skills, job training to be task based, supervisory training to be a list of topics (like law, discipline, etc) and management training to be a set of personal qualities (like leadership, team building). This is confusing to users, and can inhibit progression because the learning model seems to change as you progress within the system. Training can also lose touch with the key business purpose of the organisation, particularly when it is topic based. It is easy for specialist trainers to develop programmes which incorporate 'everything that there is to know about ...' or 'the thing I am most interested in at the moment is ...' rather than identifying precisely what people need to be able to achieve and the training inputs and processes which will lead most effectively to the desired outcomes.

Evaluation of training can also be very varied. At its most basic, participants are given the ubiquitous 'happy sheet' which invites scores against a number of different factors. Action planning activities offer more in the way of evaluation by developing learning contracts for participants to take back to the work environment, but such contracts are not always well structured or followed through. Participants are often left to translate what has been learnt on the course into the realities of their day-to-day work.

Advantages and benefits of using standards

Standards describe what should happen in work roles. Starting from that premiss, the training programme becomes an analysis of what inputs and processes will most effectively enable individuals to achieve those outcomes. The unit structure encourages a systematic approach to training, and the functional- and outcome-based format maintains links with the aims and business objectives of the organisation. Standards can accommodate, in more precise and achievable terms, the personal qualities which dominate much of management training, but they express them in terms of tangible outcomes.

Training programmes based on standards have evaluation potential built in from the design stage. Because the training activity is predicated on the gap between what people are expected to do and what they can do, the standard provides an index of success to judge performance before and after the training programme which can be followed through and sustained in the work environment by self-assessment and reviewed during appraisal interviews. This allows assessments to be made of improvements in performance after training and can also link with existing assessment processes and appraisal systems.

The **benefits** of using standards in training programme design and evaluation can be summarised as:

- Training is linked with organisational and individual outcomes and business performance.
- Learning facilitators can link the design and content of training directly to the needs of the individual and their current strengths and weaknesses.
- Training can be part of an integrated approach when combined with personal development planning and appraisal.
- A structured approach to learning and evaluation is encouraged.
- A common training format is provided for individuals at all levels of the organisation, enabling progression and recognising everybody's contribution to business goals.
- Learning objectives can be generated from performance criteria.
- An assessment and evaluation format is provided.

5 APPRAISAL

Purpose

To match individual performance to agreed expectations.

Problems with existing systems

Many appraisal systems are crude and subjective, with little more than a grading scale to assess job performance. Often, the actual criteria used in the grading remain hidden from the individual being assessed. The reasons for a particular grade being given can be hidden because there is no central reference point for the appraiser and appraised on which to agree. Appraisals can be treated like job descriptions, a necessary evil which is not taken seriously.

Advantages and benefits of using standards

Standards are a useful focus for appraisals because they are clear and specific descriptions of expected performance which are an agreed and understood benchmark for all involved in the process. They can also link directly with job descriptions, personal development plans and training programmes if the appraisal process is viewed as a central focus for supporting personal development.

The clarity of the units and elements offers clarity to assessment, which offers improved reliability and validity. Such clarity also enables the appraised to be more closely involved in the process. Being aware of their own strengths and areas for development, they are more likely to have a sense of ownership in the outcome. Through the use of standards, appraisal can become a constructive process whereby individuals are able to understand their contribution to quality outcomes and consider in partnership with the appraiser how they might improve their performance and progress. Appraisal can consequently be viewed as one part of the quality improvement and development cycle.

The **benefits** of using standards in appraisal can be summarised as:

- A common format for all parties is provided.
- Explicit, precise and fair benchmarks for performance are given.
- Those being appraised are encouraged to feel greater involvement and ownership, as they can self-assess their own strengths and weaknesses.
- There is greater validity and reliability in the appraisal process.
- Appraisal can be a constructive process through which individuals contribute to the assessment of their own performance and plan for how it may be improved.

6 REWARD SYSTEMS

Purpose

To match reward for performance to contribution to the organisation.

Reward systems are perhaps the most complex aspect of human resource management and the area most beset by traditional attitudes and values. The problems inherent in reward systems are too complex for us to describe in any detail and it would be foolish to suggest that standards can provide easy solutions to these problems.

The use of standards to underpin reward systems would appear to be an obvious application, although it is not particularly widespread, partly due to the fact that the Department for Education and Employment, perhaps quite wisely, has not promoted standards for this application because of the political sensitivities that might be aroused.

One sensitivity is the debate over whether individuals should be rewarded for what they are **able** to do or for what they are **required** to do in a particular organisation. This argument has a long history and applies equally to the selection of graduates who are often rewarded for their degree grade rather than their actual contribution. However, NVQs can throw this issue into sharp relief because a successful NVQ candidate has demonstrated competence in a work role. The question over whether this should automatically result in increased reward is still open to debate.

Reward systems also take into account the rarity of certain skills and capabilities. NVQs offer no easy resolution to this issue. They merely describe what the candidate can do, not what the capability is worth in the labour market. An NVQ will not offer a simple index of worth or value – that is still a matter which is subject to labour market demand and supply.

On the less controversial side, some organisations are looking to standards as a basis for reward systems because they appear to offer the possibility of identifying and indexing group contributions. This is particularly important as organisations move away from reliance on individual payment systems towards team-working environments. Standards also offer clearer descriptions of what constitutes required performance to recognised standards in other performance-related systems.

In summary, all we feel able to say about the applicability of standards to reward systems is that further experience is needed in this area before any lessons can be transferred to others.

16 In conclusion

This book has examined a strategy for developing the competent workforce for the next century. The basis of our argument has been that if the UK is to develop a competent workforce we need a vocational education and training system which prepares people fully for independent economic activity. In addition, we have argued that there are two more important purposes for any educational system: to empower people to play a full part as citizens in a democratic society and to enable them to develop their natural talents and capabilities to the fullest extent. Standards, as the specifications of quality in work roles, concentrate on the first of these purposes but do not ignore or exclude the other two. As we hope we have shown, developing citizens for active participation in a democratic society and enabling individuals to develop their natural talents is an imperative for the development of a competent workforce of the future.

Maximising individual capability is a necessary ambition for everyone in the population at every level of employment. Models which discriminate on the basis of status and position are not only profoundly undemocratic, they will also not serve our ambitions for economic development. The time is past when we could afford to support learning systems and processes which neglect the needs of the majority in favour of allocating most of the resources of education and training to further the interests of the few. The process of democratic development is not new to many progressive employing organisations which have developed human resource management and development approaches which are applicable across their workforce, linking the achievements of *all* individuals to those of the organisation.

Maximising individual flexibility in an environment of accelerating change is another imperative. The Job Competence Model illustrates the complexities which exist, potentially, in every work role. Individuals are increasingly required to take into account aspects of the work environment, handle contingencies, take responsibility for quality and balance, and prioritise a number of activities. Methods of work organisation where all variations are programmed out no longer fit the new organisations which have emerged in response to our changing economy. Jobs where individuals do not have to think for themselves and cope with environmental changes are not the model for the future.

In Chapter 1 we suggested that there are a number of strategic imperatives for the VET system:

1. a VET policy which is clearly related to the needs of the economy – so we need to know how we can create an economy which meets the needs of all citizens;
2. to articulate the roles and responsibilities of all those who have a stake in the development of vocational education and training;
3. to enable those stakeholders to play their part effectively by putting into place empowering processes for the development and implementation of VET.

We hope that in this book we have shown how the methods developed to deliver the original vision of the standards programme were designed for a purpose. They are not merely an elegant technical solution to an interesting problem. The methodologies, when applied in the way that they were designed and intended, are a contribution to a new strategy for vocational education and training.

The Job Competence Model expands our conception of occupational competence and suggests a universal method of describing competence which is independent of status and position. It offers a way of describing and embedding flexibility without regressing to lists of tasks with bolted-on common or personal skills.

Functional analysis helps us describe the expectations of employment across entire occupations. This holistic approach focuses on the outcomes which are required and shows the relationships between different outcomes. It also demonstrates that all the outcomes are essential ingredients in accomplishing the key purpose. This broad overview allows standards to be defined and developed strategically, concentrating on those work roles which are important for the future and suggesting combinations which may improve organisational effectiveness.

The related methodology of standards development and the systems and processes by which standards are implemented offer a new way of describing work roles. No longer confined by conflicting models of competence or different types of description, standards have developed from being a spin-off from conventional task analysis to accommodating all the aspects of competence suggested by the Job Competence Model. Standards, when appropriately negotiated and defined, give clear signals about requirements for future capability and offer a common set of descriptions to increase access and participation in the vocational education and training system.

Taken together, the new methods offer an approach which is capable of being:

- forward thinking and strategic;
- democratic;
- empowering and developmental.

Without constant vigilance and effective quality assurance, however, the methods easily can be appropriated and distorted to deliver the exact opposite of the beneficial characteristics described above. As we have seen, the methods are often used to devise systems which are:

- reflective of current and past practice;
- imposed with scant consultation on content and implementation (particularly with those to whom the standards will apply);
- conforming and instrumental.

So, in some senses, this book has charted the failure of a revolution. That is not to say that the objectives and changes which were hoped for are not possible, but it is clear that they have not been achieved as yet. Moreover, the objectives are constantly in danger of being undermined by bureaucratisation and short-term political expediency.

The Youth Training Scheme, which was one of the vehicles for the changes in methods and approaches, survived; but apart from rare centres of excellence it has failed to deliver its promise and remains at best a lowly regarded alternative to 'proper' education and training. The continued lack of adequate funding and unaddressed concerns about job substitution and issues of employment serve to undermine its credibility and claims to offer high-quality education and training.

The new standards which were to lead the revolution in both the design of VET and the recognition of competence have been implemented, but inadequately. The bare bones of the system are in place. Lead Bodies, and their emerging successors Occupational Standards Councils, do set standards for their occupational sectors. Many, however, lack the social partnership constitution which would allow them to speak with authority for all the stakeholders in VET. Some also lack a strategic focus, preferring to set standards which merely reflect current practices – practices which most political and economic commentators tell us are inadequate.

The National Vocational Qualifications developed from the standards are available in more sectors and in greater numbers than any previous qualifications. Previously unqualified workers are now able to access qualifications for the first time, and they are quite properly proud of their achievement and pleased that it has been recognised. Serious gaps in the provision of qualifications have been filled. Some coherence has been built into the system to replace the previous chaotic and irregular coverage of occupations.

But at what price? The main cost, if we are to take the critics seriously, is a loss of quality. Some of these complaints are merely the death throes of traditionalists who appear to want a return to apprentices sitting at desks, learning theory, with scant regard for its relevance and use. But many criticisms strike true. Our own is quite simple. In the headlong rush to implement the new VET system, too much attention has been directed at *how* the revolution can be delivered, the institutions, procedures and processes; the issue of *why* we are doing this has been sorely neglected.

There is a danger that standards and NVQs may become just another instrument to support routine skills training. The purpose – to improve the skills and competence of the workforce – is lost in a sea of hasty compromises as institutions charged with delivering change give way to vested interests and revert to the status quo.

Standards are developed which ignore the need to identify future capability and the increased responsibilities and broad model of competence described by the Job Competence Model. Standards may describe little more than highly specific routine procedures offered as a series of options which allow employers to fit the NVQ to the limited demands of limited jobs.

For some, this really is too much – and it ignores the lessons of history. The claim is that employers will not support candidates and allow access for assessment if the NVQs are too broad and do not meet their current needs. This happens to be the case – now – but it is the case because that is the expectation which has been fostered by NCVQ and Department for Education and Employment. In fact there is ample evidence that employers have consistently been willing to invest in education and training which is considerably in excess of their specific needs. Any employer who sponsors candidates for degrees or MBAs is doing so. Any employer who invested in apprentice training up to the late 1970s knew that the apprentice would be trained in many outcomes and skills for which the employer had no immediate use. There is no lack of evidence that if certain outcomes and learning processes are valued they will be supported by employers in the full knowledge that they will not be of immediate use.

The expectation has steadily grown that NVQs are quick, easy and cheap. To some this can be seen as advantageous – a new quick fix. To others it denotes cheap and nasty, devoid of quality and rigour. NVQs are frequently referred to as 'mickey mouse' qualifications, derided by professional educators and delivered only with reluctance. The language of the standards is frequently criticised for its density and the assessment process for its vacuity. The gradual extension of the NVQ framework to cover 'high level' and professional occupations is met with alarm as the assumption is that this will drive down quality. So a system which was developed to improve the quality of the workforce by improving the quality of VET and qualifications becomes the very antithesis of this worthy aim.

The system is now rootless, having lost the essential connection with the aims and vision of the original New Training Initiative. The need remains – and is as true now as when it was first voiced in 1981 by the New Training Initiative: 'Britain needs a flexible and adaptable workforce to meet the uncertainties which cloud the future … firms and individuals must either adapt to change or become its victims'.

White Papers continue to emphasise the need for a competitive workforce as if 14 years of initiatives might not have been expected to have some impact on this situation. The latest of the long stream of White Papers tells us, as if it were a great discovery, never before realised, that 'to compete internationally, the UK needs a highly motivated and well qualified workforce'. And the White Paper was launched at the same time as the DTI introduced no less than 70 new initiatives to support its delivery.

The time for disconnected initiatives is now past. Developing a competent work-force requires action, backed by a clear strategy and linked to a commitment: to educate all our citizens and to develop a wealth-creating economy which concentrates on the justice of distribution as well as the efficiency of production.

Philosophers have previously tried to understand the world; the point, however, is to change it. (Karl Marx, from *Eleven Theses on Feuerbach*)

Appendices

Appendix 1   Examples of functional maps

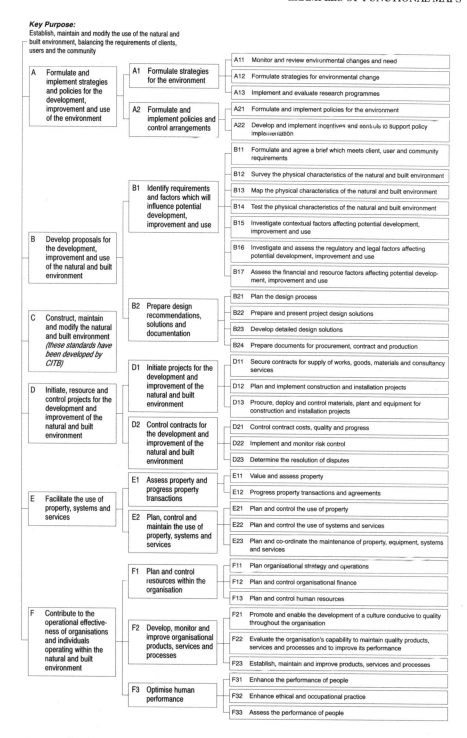

Key Purpose:
Establish, maintain and modify the use of the natural and
built environment, balancing the requirements of clients,
users and the community

A	Formulate and implement strategies and policies for the development, improvement and use of the environment	A1	Formulate strategies for the environment	A11 Monitor and review environmental changes and need
				A12 Formulate strategies for environmental change
				A13 Implement and evaluate research programmes
		A2	Formulate and implement policies and control arrangements	A21 Formulate and implement policies for the environment
				A22 Develop and implement incentives and controls to support policy implementation
B	Develop proposals for the development, improvement and use of the natural and built environment	B1	Identify requirements and factors which will influence potential development, improvement and use	B11 Formulate and agree a brief which meets client, user and community requirements
				B12 Survey the physical characteristics of the natural and built environment
				B13 Map the physical characteristics of the natural and built environment
				B14 Test the physical characteristics of the natural and built environment
				B15 Investigate contextual factors affecting potential development, improvement and use
				B16 Investigate and assess the regulatory and legal factors affecting potential development, improvement and use
				B17 Assess the financial and resource factors affecting potential development, improvement and use
		B2	Prepare design recommendations, solutions and documentation	B21 Plan the design process
				B22 Prepare and present project design solutions
				B23 Develop detailed design solutions
				B24 Prepare documents for procurement, contract and production
C	Construct, maintain and modify the natural and built environment *(these standards have been developed by CITB)*			
D	Initiate, resource and control projects for the development and improvement of the natural and built environment	D1	Initiate projects for the development and improvement of the natural and built environment	D11 Secure contracts for supply of works, goods, materials and consultancy services
				D12 Plan and implement construction and installation projects
				D13 Procure, deploy and control materials, plant and equipment for construction and installation projects
		D2	Control contracts for the development and improvement of the natural and built environment	D21 Control contract costs, quality and progress
				D22 Implement and monitor risk control
				D23 Determine the resolution of disputes
E	Facilitate the use of property, systems and services	E1	Assess property and progress property transactions	E11 Value and assess property
				E12 Progress property transactions and agreements
		E2	Plan, control and maintain the use of property, systems and services	E21 Plan and control the use of property
				E22 Plan and control the use of systems and services
				E23 Plan and co-ordinate the maintenance of property, equipment, systems and services
F	Contribute to the operational effectiveness of organisations and individuals operating within the natural and built environment	F1	Plan and control resources within the organisation	F11 Plan organisational strategy and operations
				F12 Plan and control organisational finance
				F13 Plan and control human resources
		F2	Develop, monitor and improve organisational products, services and processes	F21 Promote and enable the development of a culture conducive to quality throughout the organisation
				F22 Evaluate the organisation's capability to maintain quality products, services and processes and to improve its performance
				F23 Establish, maintain and improve products, services and processes
		F3	Optimise human performance	F31 Enhance the performance of people
				F32 Enhance ethical and occupational practice
				F33 Assess the performance of people

Fig. A1 The Construction Industry Standing Conference – Professional, Mangerial and Technical Occupations

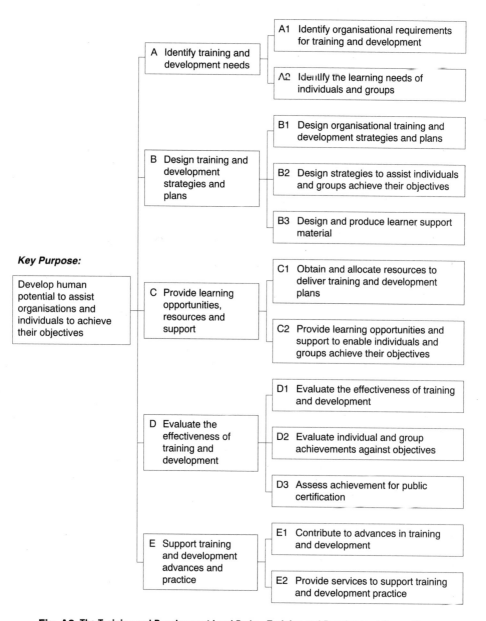

Fig. A2 The Training and Development Lead Body – Training and Development Occupations

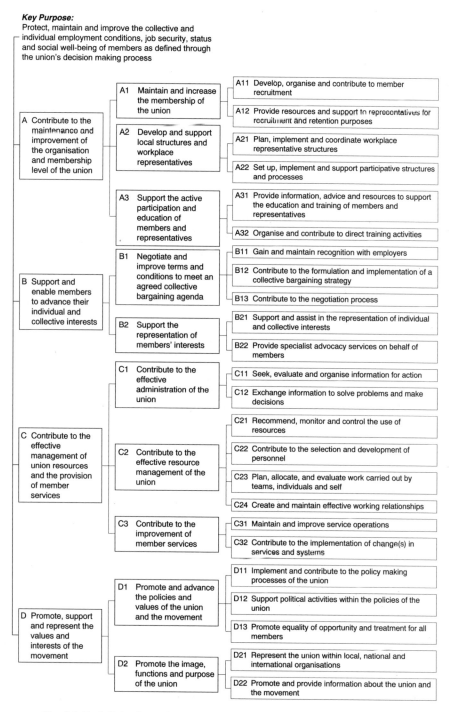

Key Purpose:
Protect, maintain and improve the collective and individual employment conditions, job security, status and social well-being of members as defined through the union's decision making process

A Contribute to the maintenance and improvement of the organisation and membership level of the union	A1 Maintain and increase the membership of the union	A11 Develop, organise and contribute to member recruitment
		A12 Provide resources and support to representatives for recruitment and retention purposes
	A2 Develop and support local structures and workplace representatives	A21 Plan, implement and coordinate workplace representative structures
		A22 Set up, implement and support participative structures and processes
	A3 Support the active participation and education of members and representatives	A31 Provide information, advice and resources to support the education and training of members and representatives
		A32 Organise and contribute to direct training activities
B Support and enable members to advance their individual and collective interests	B1 Negotiate and improve terms and conditions to meet an agreed collective bargaining agenda	B11 Gain and maintain recognition with employers
		B12 Contribute to the formulation and implementation of a collective bargaining strategy
		B13 Contribute to the negotiation process
	B2 Support the representation of members' interests	B21 Support and assist in the representation of individual and collective interests
		B22 Provide specialist advocacy services on behalf of members
C Contribute to the effective management of union resources and the provision of member services	C1 Contribute to the effective administration of the union	C11 Seek, evaluate and organise information for action
		C12 Exchange information to solve problems and make decisions
	C2 Contribute to the effective resource management of the union	C21 Recommend, monitor and control the use of resources
		C22 Contribute to the selection and development of personnel
		C23 Plan, allocate, and evaluate work carried out by teams, individuals and self
		C24 Create and maintain effective working relationships
	C3 Contribute to the improvement of member services	C31 Maintain and improve service operations
		C32 Contribute to the implementation of change(s) in services and systems
D Promote, support and represent the values and interests of the movement	D1 Promote and advance the policies and values of the union and the movement	D11 Implement and contribute to the policy making processes of the union
		D12 Support political activities within the policies of the union
		D13 Promote equality of opportunity and treatment for all members
	D2 Promote the image, functions and purpose of the union	D21 Represent the union within local, national and international organisations
		D22 Promote and provide information about the union and the movement

Fig. A3 Trade Union Sector Development Body – Professional Trade Union Officers

285

Appendix 2
Active verbs used to start statements of competence

Active verbs provide important information to users of occupational standards. In a functional analysis and a functional map the verbs may be used to suggest subsequent stages of analysis. For example, a statement like 'Prepare and present information to ...' may suggest a subsequent disaggregation into two statements, 'Prepare information ...' and 'Present information ...'.

In an occupational standard, the active verbs in the element title offer useful information about the content of the standard. Many users of standards do not wish to be exposed to the full detail of the standard – the performance criteria and the range indicators – so the phrasing of the element of competence title should give a clear indication of the coverage and content of the standard.

For these reasons it is important to choose the most accurate verb which best reflects the outcome which is being described. The verbs defined below are not intended to be exhaustive. There will be many verbs with a precise occupational meaning which may be used. However, it is useful to define all active verbs used within a set of standards to help users understand the focus of the standard.

adapt	modify or change
adjust	place in the correct relationship (*usually applied to control of equipment*)
advance	aid the growth or progress of
advise	recommend or suggest
advocate	speak on behalf of, to plead the cause of another
agree	concur or assent
allocate	apportion a share
analyse	separate into component parts
apply	put to use
assemble	put together the parts of
assess	determine the value of (*usually information or evidence*)
assist	offer or provide help
audit	review, examine and verify
brief	instruct or provide information
calculate	count or reckon mathematically

calibrate	adjust (*usually equipment or instruments*) against a specification
care	look after, tend or nurse
certify	verify or confirm
create	originate or conceive
chair	manage the process of a meeting
check	compare against a specification
coach	instruct or tutor for specific ends
collate	bring together and place in order
collect	assemble (*usually*) information
commission	identify and appoint others to perform a service
compare	identify similarity or dissimilarity
compile	collect together written material
conclude	settle or arrange finally
confirm	ratify or verify
constitute	set up or establish
contact	get in touch with
contribute	share or participate in
control	regulate or act in authority
convene	assemble or call together (*other people – usually a meeting*)
co-ordinate	organise into common action
create	develop from new
cultivate	prepare soil for plants
decide	determine, to resolve
defend	guard, protect or maintain against attack
define	fix the bounds or limits of
deploy	place for a purpose, to place strategically
design	form a plan, to contrive
determine	define limits, to resolve (*in contracts*)
develop	evolve to a more desirable state
draft	produce (*drawings or text*) in preliminary form
draw up	compose or put into shape (*often associated with contracts*)
empower	give power to, or share power with, to authorise
enable	provide with the means, knowledge or opportunity
encourage	help, inspire confidence
enlist	encourage co-operation
establish	(1) set up or create
establish	(2) place in a fixed position, to confirm
estimate	make a rough calculation usually without a measuring instrument
evaluate	determine the value of
finalise	put into final form, to complete
formulate	state or express in a clear or definite form

identify	find out, to establish identity
implement	put into practice
improve	make better
initiate	begin or originate
inform	impart knowledge to
inspect	examine
instruct	teach, to give guidance, to direct
integrate	make up parts into a whole
interpret	extract meaning from (*usually text*)
investigate	enquire or examine systematically
issue	put into circulation (*usually documents*), to give out for use
justify	prove or show to be right
lead	guide
maintain	preserve or retain in the same state
match	find an equal or counterpart
modify	change the form or quantity of
monitor	keep track of a process
negotiate	come to terms with others by conferring
obtain	succeed in getting, to gain or acquire
optimise	achieve the best balance between two or more competing parts
organise	arrange by planning and co-ordination
originate	create or bring into being
participate	have a share or take part
plan	formulate a scheme or method to achieve an objective
plant	place and secure plants in soil or growing medium
prepare	make ready, to put together resources
present	introduce formally
prioritise	place in order of rank or importance
process	engage in a series of operations or changes
procure	obtain (*goods and services*)
produce	bring into being
programme	plan a sequence of actions
promote	popularise, to advocate
propose	offer for consideration or acceptance
protect	shield from danger
provide feedback	return information to a source for control or alteration
provide information	offer facts and opinions to others
receive	take in or admit
recommend	introduce as suitable for acceptance
record	account for events (*usually in written form*)
recruit	identify and engage people
regulate	apply a control or rule

repair	return something to its optimum state
report	prepare and present and account (*usually formally*)
represent	serve as an authorised delegate or agent
research	investigate systematically
respond	reply, answer
review	look back over events, to critically examine
revise	examine and correct, to make an improved version of
schedule	plan, timetable or programme
secure	establish in safety, to obtain goods and services
select	choose one or more from several
service	perform duties and services
set	prescribe or assign
set up	make ready for use
specify	set down as a requirement
store	put away for future use
summarise	present a condensed version
supply	provide (*goods or services*)
support	promote the cause of, to provide resources
sustain	support, to maintain or keep going
synthesise	make a whole out of parts
teach	enable learning to take place
test	determine fitness for purpose
train	instruct and enable learning to take place
validate	ratify, confirm or substantiate
verify	assert or prove to be true
welcome	admit willingly, to receive with kindness or pleasure

Appendix 3

Evaluative terms used to qualify performance criteria

Evaluative terms are used in performance criteria to set the quality and level of performance expected. There are three formats for the use of evaluative terms. Those which qualify the noun take the adjectival form as in 'information is *accurate*'. Those which modify the verb take the adverbial form as in 'information is presented *accurately*'. In the glossary, these terms are presented in the format in which they most commonly appear. The third format is used where the outcome is intended either to produce a specific effect or to describe a state which should or should not occur as in 'presentations are *designed to* (promote goodwill)' or 'written copy is *free from* (discriminatory and offensive language)'.

The list of terms in the glossary is not intended to be exhaustive. Other terms which may be common to an occupational sector may also be used. However, it is useful to define all evaluative terms to help users understand the precise meaning of the criteria.

TERMS CONTAINED IN THE GLOSSARY

accurate
achievable
actively
adequate
agree
appropriate
alternative
capable of
capitalise
clear
clean
complete
conform
consistent

constraints of
constructive
correct
concise
credible
designed to
effective
emphasise
encourage
enhance
explicit
favourable
free from
fully

hygienic
justifiable
legible
likely to
necessary
maintain
maximise
minimise
observe
on request
optimum
persuasive
practicable
practical
preferred
politely
positive
promote

promptly
realistic
reasonable
regular
relevant
reliable
safe
schedule
secure
sterile
sufficient
suitable
support
systematic
up to date
valid
without delay

accurate
: a result which is within a prespecified tolerance. Applied to calculations and estimates which are approximations and to many manual operations. Often applied to written text or diagrams – limited variations are acceptable

- information is complete and *accurate* (adjective)
- total product costs are *accurately* estimated from the available data (adverb)

achievable
: possible within resource limitations

- recommendations and preferred options are *achievable* (adverb)

actively
: action which is proactive and encouraging

- participants are *actively* encouraged to make contributions to the discussion (adverb)

adequate
: sufficient for purpose

- *adequate* facilities and lighting are specified (adjective)

agreed
: a course of action, procedure or process which has the assent of at least two parties. The individual achieving the standard does not have to be one of the parties to the agreement

- negotiations follow *agreed* conventions (adjective)

- *agreed* notations and conventions are used in preparing reports (adjective)

appropriate | selecting from a range of possibilities, one or more of which would give an acceptable result in the circumstances

- the most *appropriate* facilities are selected to meet the requirements of the plan (adjective)
- the style and pace of communication is *appropriate* to the needs of the recipients (adjective)
- fragile items are handled *appropriately* (adverb)

alternative | used to describe the use of different items, processes or methods in cases where the normal item, process or method is unavailable (sometimes due to breakdowns)

- *alternative* methods of fixing are used in cases where normal fixing methods would cause an obstruction (adjective)

capable of | an action or option which is able to achieve a desired outcome

- the solution recommended is *capable of* restoring the system to an operational condition

capitalise | make the most of opportunities and resources available

- recommendations *capitalise* on the use of available resources

clean | self-explanatory. Often used in conjunction with 'free from' (see below)

- surfaces are visibly *clean* and free from dust and debris

clear | applied to text and speech – grammar and language conveys what is intended

- reports on variations are *clear* and accurate (adjective)
- safety signs and notices are *clearly* identified and positioned (adverb)

complete | applied to procedures, processes and documents – all operations have been undertaken and everything necessary or relevant has been included

- records are *complete* and accurate (adjective)
- surfaces are *completely* clean and free from debris (adverb)

concise | succinct and to the point

- summaries of discussions are accurate and *concise* (adjective)

conform   in accordance with accepted practice or conventions. Also used to indicate compliance with a set procedure

- technical solutions *conform* to recognised best practice in the sector/profession
- symbols adopted *conform* to standards drawing conventions

consistent   following a recognised and repeated pattern over a period of time. Also, conformance with good practice or procedures

- equipment use and operation is *consistent* with stated operating practice (adjective)
- safety equipment is used *consistently* (adverb)

constraints of   a limitation to action, usually in the form of a legal or other formal restriction

- appropriate materials are made available to participants within the *constraints of* copyright law

constructive   positive – used to describe feedback and responses

- feedback is *constructive* and designed to enhance the candidate's self-esteem

correct   correct is used when there is only one possible outcome such as a right or wrong result to a calculation or following a procedure in which there is no allowable variation. In most other instances, various degrees of variation and decision making are allowed, so 'correct' would not be the appropriate standard

- calculations are *correct* (adjective)
- gauges and instruments are *calibrated* correctly (adverb)

credible   outcomes which are plausible and reasonable

- recommendations describe *credible* courses of action to maintain conformance and quality (adjective)

designed to   with the intention to achieve a particular outcome

- presentations are *designed to* promote preferred recommendations in the most favourable manner

effective   the most appropriate means to produce the result required. Can also mean best use. The term 'effective' can be vague in some circumstances and more precise alternatives should be used

- the most *effective* use is made of available resources (adverb)
- an *effective* method is adopted (adjective)

emphasise   stress or highlight points made in discussions, presentations or arguments

- preferred options are *emphasised* and given additional weight in the presentation

encourage   used in interaction. To encourage means to invite and create opportunities for others to contribute or act in particular ways. Often used in criteria describing verbal feedback

- trainees are *encouraged* to identify their own learning needs
- all participants are *encouraged* to contribute to team discussions

enhance   improve

- the use of visual aids is designed to *enhance* the clarity of the presentation

explicit   clear and unequivocal – used in communication

- the criteria adopted are *explicit* and relevant (adjective)
- significant criteria are *explicitly* identified (adverb)

favourable   advantageous to the achievement of a preferred outcome

- legal precedents are selected which are *favourable* to the case (adjective)
- valid statistical information which *favours* the argument is presented and emphasised (adverb)

free from   a negative criteria which specifies that undesirable conditions have been eliminated

- drafts are *free from* discriminatory language
- the immediate working environment is *free from* hazards

fully   thorough and sufficient

- suggestions and recommendations are *fully* described and justified (adverb)

hygienic   a condition which minimises contamination – used in medical environments and food processing/preparation where it has a specific meaning

- instruments are in a *hygienic* condition prior to use (adjective)
- cooked and raw meats are completely separated and stored *hygienically* (adverb)

justifiable   usually applied to evaluation or the statement of a position

- the conclusions of the evaluation are *justifiable* in the light of the available evidence (adjective)

legible   applied to handwritten text or drawings – can be read by a competent user

- records are accurate and *legible* (adjective)
- draft sketches are annotated *legibly* (adverb)

likely to   increases the possibility of achieving a desired outcome

- materials and information are selected which are most *likely to* promote the argument
- the options most *likely to* achieve a successful solution are selected and recommended

maintain   act in such a way that an existing state is preserved and continued

- presentations to clients are conducted in a manner and style which *maintains* goodwill and trust

maximise   make best use of resources and opportunities when a single variable is important

- opportunities to reduce waste are *maximised*
- layouts are designed which *maximise* the use of materials

minimise   reduce the impact of an undesirable event or situation as far as is practicable

- wastage of materials and resources is *minimised*

necessary   essential, that which is required (could include an action, procedure, resources, etc)

- the resources *necessary* for team members to meet their agreed objectives are made available (adjective)

Note: the term 'where necessary' (as in 'additional resources are provided to team members where necessary') should be avoided in performance criteria because the use of the term in this context does not identify what a 'necessary' condition might be. In some instances it may allow the criterion to be omitted if the condition does not apply in a particular case. A more appropriate format is 'where resources are insufficient for team members to achieve objectives, sufficient additional resources are accurately estimated and made available'.

observe	conform to a procedure or code of practice

- health and safety regulations and guidelines are *observed* when cleaning moving machinery

on request	action which is initiated by a direct expression of needs by another party

- specialist information is provided *on request*
- facilities and resources which exceed agreed budgetary limits are only provided *on request*

optimum	the best balanced result, taking into account a number of factors which are likely to be different in each instance and where the range of possibilities may vary (different from 'maximised' where only a single factor is significant). Also used to describe outcomes which have to balance potentially conflicting needs

- *optimum* methods and processes are selected which best meet the criteria for evaluation (adjective)
- the products presented *optimise* the needs of the customer and the added value to the organisation (adverb)

persuasive	present an argument in a manner which is reasoned and is likely to influence a person or persons to change their position, view or attitude

- information and clearly associated arguments are presented in a *persuasive* manner (adjective)
- data and statistics are presented in a manner which is most likely to *persuade* the audience of the validity of the case (verb)

politely	within agreed and accepted norms of address and speech

- customers are greeted *politely* (adverb)

positive	to give a clear and explicit expression of support and assent

- policy decisions are *positively* supported
- the preferred option is *positively* recommended

practicable · options or solutions which are possible and workable within given circumstances (see also 'practical')

- a range of *practicable* options are identified, compared and contrasted (adjective)

practical · options or solutions which are the most realistic and workable within given circumstances (see also 'practicable')

- the most *practical* option is identified and promoted (adjective)

promote · encourage the adoption of a particular option or position (similar to and often used in conjunction with 'positive')

- agreed courses of action are *promoted* to staff and colleagues
- the preferred option is positively recommended and *promoted*

preferred · where the standard is based on the preference or choice of others, which may vary widely. Often used in interaction

- the client's *preferred* form of address is used (adjective)
- reports are submitted in a format which conforms to the user's *preferred* style and layout (adjective)

prompt(ly) · as soon as is possible or practical, taking into account other demands and priorities

- results of analyses are passed on to colleagues *promptly* (adverb)
- *prompt* warning is given to users about known problems and contingencies (adjective)

realistic · valid in light of available data. Rational and capable of justification

- recommendations and predictions are *realistic* in terms of the analysis and the data available (adjective)

reasonable · consistent with logic, well founded. Also, balanced and moderate

- conclusions are *reasonable* in the light of the data available (adjective)
- *reasonable* alternatives are offered which are likely to offer a resolution to the dispute (adjective)

regular · conforming to a procedure. Also, evenly-spaced and periodic

- *regular* maintenance schedules are followed (adjective)
- service provision is *regularly* monitored and checked for consistency and quality (adverb)

relevant   clearly and logically related to the desired outcome

- *relevant* previous cases are selected for evaluation. (adjective)

reliable   applied to processes or methods – a reliable method is one which will generate the same result on different occasions given the same circumstances

- a *reliable* analysis method is selected (adjective)

safe   in a condition which minimises potential damage to self, people or other objects. Includes the proper use of safety equipment and clothing

- equipment is restored to *safe* working condition following cleaning and maintenance operations (adjective)
- barriers to protect the public are moved and erected *safely* (adverb)

schedule   complete an activity or process before a deadline

- designs are completed to *schedule*

secure   can be used to mean safe or maintaining confidentiality

- records are stored in a *secure* location (adjective)
- fixings are positioned and fastened *securely* (adverb)

sterile   specific meaning in medical/care occupations – part of an index of cleanliness: 'clean – hygienic – sterile'. Used where objects or instruments are in direct contact with human or animal tissue or where there is a risk of cross-infection.

- instruments used for invasive procedures are maintained in a *sterile* condition prior to use (adjective)

sufficient   enough, without being too much, for the purpose in hand

- *sufficient* materials are available to meet anticipated production demands (adjective)

suitable   of a type and/or in a state which will produce the intended effect – very similar to 'appropriate' but usually more closely targeted

- plant and equipment are specified which are *suitable* for the production of the required products

support used in interaction, normally in counselling and guidance situations. To support means to be sympathetic to the needs of the recipient and to offer facilities and opportunities to solve problems

- guidance and *support* is offered to staff who are experiencing personal or work problems

systematic consistent and rigorous application of a procedure or process, usually in line with known rules and stages

- analysis criteria are *systematically* applied to the data (adverb)

up to date containing the most recent information or amendment available. Usually used to describe written records

- records of inspections are accurate and *up to date*

valid applied to a choice made from alternatives. Valid means the choice is one which is capable of producing the desired outcome

- *valid* statistical techniques are applied (adjective)
- a *valid* analysis method is chosen and applied (adjective)

without delay a more rigorous specification than 'promptly'. Used where the factor concerned takes precedence over all others. Often used to describe action in emergencies

- when alarms sound, premises are evacuated *without delay*
- in cases of medical emergency, help is summoned *without delay*

Appendix 4   Glossary of terms

This glossary contains definitions of terms and acronyms used in this book. Another useful source of definitions of terms used in vocational education and training can be found in Levy *et al. A Guide to Work Based Learning Terms.*

GLOSSARY OF TERMS

accreditation
assessment
Awarding Bodies
certification
competence/competencies
competent
core skills
criterion referenced
disaggregation
element of competence
evidence
evidence specification
functional analysis
functional unit
inference
iteration
Job Competence Model
key area
key purpose
key role
Lead Body
level (of NVQ)
National Council for Vocational Qualifications (NCVQ)
National Vocational Qualification (NVQ)
occupational competence

occupational standard(s)
Occupational Standards Council (OSC)
outcome
output
performance criteria
range indicators
range statements
statement of competence
task
task analysis
Scottish Vocational Education Council (SCOTVEC)
Scottish Vocational Qualification (SVQ)
unit of competence
work-based learning
work role

accreditation	the process of endorsing qualifications developed by awarding bodies against the NVQ criteria. Awards which meet the criteria are accredited and able to use the title National Vocational Qualification (or Scottish Vocational Qualification) and are allocated to a classification and level in the NCVQ framework of qualifications
assessment	the process of obtaining sufficient reliable and valid evidence about an individual's competence and making judgements of that evidence using explicit (predetermined) criteria. Evidence may be performance based or knowledge based. It is critical that the standard determines the evidence that is to be collected rather than the criteria being determined by the assessment methods and instruments which are used
Awarding Bodies	(also examining bodies) Organisations which offer assessment, validation and certification services. Awarding bodies may be specialised organisations (eg RSA, City and Guilds, BTEC, SCOTVEC) or Lead Bodies, or consortia which often comprise the Lead Body acting in partnership with a specialised Awarding Body. Only Awarding Bodies may make submissions to NCVQ. If Awarding Bodies or consortia do not include the Lead Body, NCVQ will require that the proposed qualification has the endorsement of the Lead Body
certification	the process of formally recognising that individuals are competent in one or more of the units of competence that

comprise an NVQ. Certification endorses the assessment of competence within a formal recording structure

competence/
competencies

(1) an underlying characteristic of a person which results in effective or superior performance. This refers to specific behaviour and may be expressed as a motive, trait, skill, aspect of self image, social role or body of knowledge which is applied. Widely used in American and UK literature on management training.   (2) the tasks which people perform. Used in the USA to describe a number of professional activities (mainly in the teaching profession).   (3) the term originally used to describe an element of competence ('a competence') in the first version of Technical Advisory Group Guidance Note 3 (Employment Department) and also used in the Youth Training Scheme (competence objective) for the same purpose. Superseded by the terms 'outcome', 'standard' and 'element of competence' because of the confusion caused with versions (1) and (2) above.   (4) the limits of authority and capability of an organisation – eg 'the competence of the committee' means the remit and authority of the committee. Widely used by the institutions of the European Union.   (5) an archaic term used to describe a person's means or wealth

competent

as in 'a competent person'. In this context, competent means the ability to perform to a standard. Particular sectors and industries often have an implicit concept of what competent performance means for particular occupational groups. Consequently, 'competent' is often taken to imply a minimum level of performance across a very narrow range of activities, such as in the use of the term 'barely competent'. By contrast, the concept can also mean the ability to meet 'best practice' requirements

core skills

a term used to describe a set of skills which are believed to be, or have been shown to be, central to performance. There are numerous core skill lists which can include quite different core skills. Within this book most of the discussion relating to core skills is in relation to the ESF/MSC study on Core Skills for Youth Trainees

criterion
referenced

used to describe assessment systems which are based on the judgement of evidence against independent and predetermined criteria in which the only possible outcome is the candidate being judged to be competent or not yet competent. Criterion–referenced systems do not allow for graded performance or alphanumeric marking systems

disaggregation   a process used in functional analysis to separate functions. Statements from the analysis are separated by the application of one or more disaggregation rules

element of competence   the smallest part of a statement of competence that can be formally assessed in an NVQ. An element of competence is a subdivision of a unit of competence. An element of competence must be stated with a high degree of precision to avoid ambiguity and must include performance criteria to indicate the standard to which the outcome described by the element needs to be demonstrated. In addition, range statements describe the contexts and variations over which the element will apply. The element title, plus the performance criteria and range statement is an occupational standard. A standard may describe only outcomes which are the sole responsibility of an individual to achieve

evidence   information about candidate performance which is collected, collated and assessed to make an overall judgement of competence. There are only two types of evidence: performance (what the candidate can do) and knowledge (what the candidate knows). The quality of evidence is judged against the criteria of validity (is it the right kind of evidence?), reliability (is the evidence accurate?) and sufficiency (is there enough evidence to make a safe judgement of competence?). The processes of evidence collection are also judged against the criterion of cost effectiveness (or added value) which requires that the costs of collecting and judging evidence should equate with the value of the information it offers to potential users of the qualification (often employers)

evidence specification   a clear description of the evidence which could be collected by a candidate to demonstrate competence. Evidence specifications vary widely in interpretation but should detail the quantity and type of evidence which is necessary to make a safe inference of competence for each element of competence within an NVQ. The most developed evidence specifications describe product evidence (tangible evidence which can be examined or inspected – what is done), process evidence (evidence about how something is done – usually concerned with interactions or the application of particular methods), knowledge of principles and methods (which enables competence to be extended to new and unfamiliar situations) and knowledge of facts and data (which are needed to underpin performance)

functional analysis	an analysis process used to develop occupational standards as far as a functional unit. A 'holistic', system-based analysis approach used to analyse whole occupations in terms of outcomes and the purposes of work activities, rather than specific activities, procedures and methods. The approach was developed to provide a methodology to identify occupational standards. Although the names may be similar, functional analysis is quite different from Functional Job Analysis and Functionalism. Its strength lies in a 'top-down', broad economic view taken in analysing the purpose and outcomes of work activity rather than detailing current activities found in tasks or jobs. Although more usually applied to entire sectors of the economy, functional analysis can also be applied to specific roles and organisations
functional unit	the final level of detail in a functional analysis which represents an outcome which an individual would be expected to achieve either alone or as a member of a team
inference	the process of drawing conclusions about existing and potential competence from the evidence available. In most assessment systems it is not possible or practicable to collect all the possible evidence against every criterion and for all the range of contexts required. Assessors must extrapolate (judge) that the sample of evidence presented is sufficient to infer total competence as defined by the element of competence
iteration	the process of constantly checking the overall coherence and structure of a functional analysis, which usually involves modifying statements at different analysis levels
Job Competence Model	a model of occupational competence which proposes four different components of competence: technical expectations, the management of contingency, the management of a number of activities to achieve overall goals and objectives, and the management of the interface with the wider work environment
key area	the functional areas identified at the first level of disaggregation in a functional analysis

305

key purpose	the unique contribution which an occupational sector makes within society and the economy. The key purpose is the starting-point for a functional analysis and often contains statements which infer the ethics, values and tensions which underpin occupational practice
key role	an area of responsibility in an occupational sector which describes the purpose of jobs in the sector rather than job descriptions, titles or activities. A key role is a level of detail in functional analysis one stage 'up' from functional units. A key role is a group of coherent functional units which forms part of the functional analysis process
Lead Body	an organisation or group of organisations which is recognised by the Department for Education and Employment as having the authority to set national occupational standards for a defined occupational area. Lead Bodies are increasingly joining together to form Occupational Standards Councils, which are responsible for developing national occupational standards across a broad spectrum of occupations
level (of NVQ)	an NVQ level is a description of general characteristics of work roles which define a hierarchy of achievement. All National Vocational Qualifications are assigned to a level in the NVQ framework. There are five levels (1 to 5) in which level 1 represents foundation or entry level occupational achievement and level 5 represents senior managerial and professional roles. 'Level' does not refer to general intelligence, grades of achievement or existing jobs. The level concept is intended to provide for progression through qualification structures
NCVQ	The National Council for Vocational Qualifications. A government sponsored body which has the remit to produce a coherent framework of qualifications, based on occupational standards developed by the employment sector. Qualifications are accredited if they meet a number of criteria which include relevance, open access, equality of opportunity and rigour of assessment. A qualification which is accepted becomes a National Vocational Qualification (NVQ) or Scottish Vocational Qualification (SVQ) in Scotland and is assigned to a level and area within the NVQ framework.

NVQ	National Vocational Qualification. A qualification based on standards developed by a recognised Lead Body which meets the criteria of the National Council for Vocational Qualifications (see also – SVQ). An NVQ is a selection of units of competence from an endorsed set of occupational standards to which an assessment process has been attached
occupational competence	the ability to perform whole work roles to the standards expected in employment. There are many definitions of competence ranging from the simplistic view of performance of limited tasks to the more holistic approach which encompasses the ability to manage the many components of the job or role within complex social and work contexts. This broader view is described by the Job Competence Model. Confusion occurs because the term often carries connotations of a minimal level of ability rather than best practice
occupational standard(s)	the level of performance required for the successful achievement of work expectations. Occupational standards are intended to specify best practice in a particular employment sector. Standards are expressed in the form of element of competence titles, associated performance criteria and range indicators (range statements, which are specifications for assessment, are developed when the standards are incorporated into qualifications). Standards are developed through a process of functional analysis. Standards may be 'reflective' – merely reflecting current requirements, or 'strategic' – focused on changing future requirements
Occupational Standards Council	see Lead Body
outcome	a term which describes the result of work activity rather than the activities or tasks which lead to the result. There are tangible and intangible outcomes. An intangible outcome is the result of a cognitive or interactive process – eg a decision, an action. A tangible outcome would be the physical result of an activity – a product which can be physically examined. Occupational standards are phrased as outcomes to accommodate changing methods and activities and to show commonality between activities and tasks which may be phrased differently but which produce the same result

output	the tangible and measurable result of activity – often confused with the term 'outcome'
performance criteria	the criteria which specify the quality or level of performance necessary for the successful achievement of a standard. Performance criteria are developed by identifying the critical outcomes and processes which demonstrate that a standard has been achieved. They are used as indicators by which to judge an individual's competence and provide an essential link to assessment
range indicator	the different contexts over which a standard is designed to apply. The range indicator is illustrative. Range indicators and range statements consist of a number of dimensions (such as customer, information) which describe variations in the application of the standard. Each dimension has a number of classes (eg customers: retail; wholesale) which describe critical differences which significantly alter the performance of the standard
range statements	range statements specify the range of applications and contexts over which an element of competence applies within an NVQ. The range statement is a specification, not a description of alternatives or examples. For example, if a range statement involving an analysis process describes different types of analysis method, such as manual systems and computerised systems, then a candidate must be competent in working with both systems to the level of performance detailed in the performance criteria
statement of competence	(1) the title and the units of competence of an NVQ. (2) used to describe the structure of statements in functional maps and elements titles. All statements of competence should include an active verb or verbs, an object and a conditional statement if this clarifies the context. For example, the statement 'Survey the physical characteristics of a development site' has the following structure:

Active verb	*survey*
Object	*the physical characteristics*
Condition	*of a development site*

task	a description of work activity which specifies timescales, sequences and procedures
task analysis	a method of analysing work activity. The processes of task analysis are associated with work measurement and control

systems and tend to be organisationally specific

SCOTVEC	The Scottish Vocational Education Council. SCOTVEC has two major roles. The first parallels that of the NCVQ as the accrediting body for SVQs and GSVQs in Scotland. SCOTVEC is also an awarding body which offers its own awards throughout Scotland. The awards comprise SVQs, GSVQs and other vocational qualifications such as National Certificate units and Higher National Certificates
SVQ	Scottish Vocational Qualification. The Scottish equivalent of an NVQ, accredited by the Scottish Vocational Education Council (SCOTVEC)
unit of competence	a unit of competence is a group of related elements of competence which have credibility as a recognised unit of achievement in an occupational sector. A unit is the smallest grouping of standards which is acceptable for separate accreditation within a qualification. A unit may be described as the point at which the individual becomes responsible for the outcome described
work-based learning	work-based learning has been defined as: 'Linking learning to the work role and having three inter-related components, each of which provides an essential contribution to that learning process. These three components are: structuring learning in the workplace, providing appropriate on-job training/learning opportunities, and identifying and providing relevant off-job learning opportunities'. (Levy, *The Core Skills Project and Work Based Learning*)
work role	an area of responsibility within an occupational sector which describes the purpose of jobs in the sector rather than the job descriptions, job titles and activities.

ACRONYMS

CBI	Confederation of British Industry
CISC	Construction Industry Standing Conference
CSC	Care Sector Consortium
DFE	Department for Education
DfEE	Department for Education and Employment (formed in 1995 from the amalgamation of the DFE and ED)
ED	Department of Employment

ED:TEED	Department of Employment: Training, Education and Enterprise Division
ESF	European Social Fund
ET	Employment Training
EU	European Union
GNVQ	General National Vocational Qualification
MCI	Management Charter Initiative
MSC	Manpower Services Commission
NCVQ	National Council for Vocational Qualifications
NTI	New Training Initiative
NVQ	National Vocational Qualification
PALS	Plants, Animals and Land Sector Consortium
TA	Training Agency
TC	Training Commission
TDLB	Training and Development Lead Body
TFW	Training for Work
TOPS	Training Opportunities Programme
TUC	Trades Union Congress
TUSDB	Trade Union Sector Development Body
SASU	The Standards and Assessment Support Unit
SCOTVEC	Scottish Vocational Education Council
SVQ	Scottish Vocational Qualification
YHAFHE	Yorkshire and Humberside Association for Further and Higher Education
YOPS	Youth Opportunities Programme
YT	Youth Training
YTS	Youth Training Scheme

Bibliography

Bannister, N. 'Networks tap into low wages', *Guardian*, 15 October 1995.

Beaumont, G. *Review of 100 NVQs and SVQs. A Report Submitted to the Department for Education and Employment.* No publisher, place of publication or date given, but assumed to be: London, Department for Education and Employment, 1996.

Burke, J. (ed.) *Outcomes and the Curriculum*, Lewes, Falmer Press, 1995.

Callender, C., Toye, J., Connor, H. and Spilsbury, M. *National and Scottish Vocational Qualifications: Early Indications of Employers' Take Up and Use*, Brighton, Institute of Manpower Studies at the University of Sussex, 1993.

Caple, T. and Mitchell, L. *Assessment of Management Competence at Work*, Bristol, NHS Training Directorate, 1992.

Care Sector Consortium *National Occupational Standards for Care: Based on the work of the Integration Project*, Luton, Local Government Management Board, 1992.

Channell, J. and St. John, M. J. with Deignan, A., Mansfield, B., Coulthard, M. and Sinclair, J. *Languages Issues in Standards Development and N/SVQs. Project Report for the Department for Education and Employment.* Birmingham, The Language Technology Research and Development Unit, 1996.

Chartered Association of Certified Accountants *Standards for Auditors*, The Chartered Association of Certified Accountants, 1992.

Christis, J. *The sociology of work stress and wellbeing. An environmental risk approach*, Pb 75665, Amsterdam, Nederlands Instituut voor Arbeidsomstandigheden, 1995.

Christis, J. *Sociotechnics, learning and the quality of labour*, paper given at the Invitation Conference 'Skill formation, on-the-job learning and on-the-job training', Amsterdam, 1995.

Confederation of British Industry *Quality Assessed – The CBI Review of NVQs and SVQs*, London, The Confederation of British Industry, London, 1994.

Confederation of British Industry Training Task Force, *Towards a Skills Revolution*, The Confederation of British Industry, London, 1989.

Construction Industry Standing Conference *Occupational Standards for Technical, Managerial and Professional Roles in the Construction Sector*, London, Construction Industry Standing Conference, 1994.

311

Crosby, P.B. *Quality is Free: The Art of Making Quality Certain*, London, McGraw-Hill, 1978.

Dale, B. and Oakland, J. *Quality improvement through standards*, Cheltenham, Stanley Thomas, 1991.

Department of Education and Science *Education and training for the 21st Century*, London, *HMSO*, 1991.

Employment Department *Guidance Note 1. A code of practice and a development model*, Sheffield, Employment Department, 1988.

Employment Department *Guidance Note 2. Developing standards by reference to functions*, Sheffield, Employment Department, 1988.

Employment Department *Guidance Note 3. The definition of competences and performance criteria*, Sheffield, Employment Department, 1988.

Employment Department *Guidance Note 4. The characteristics of units of competence*, Sheffield, Employment Department, 1988.

Employment Department *Guidance Note 5. Assessment of competence*, Sheffield, Employment Department, 1988.

Employment Department *Guidance Note 6. Verification and monitoring of assessment*, Sheffield, Employment Department, 1988.

Employment Department *Guidance Note 7. Project management, standards and NVQ/SVQ development*, Sheffield, Employment Department, 1988.

Employment Department *Guidance Note 8. Consulting on standards: establishing the national applicability of draft standards*, Sheffield, Employment Department, 1988.

Employment Department *Training for Employment*, Sheffield, 1988.

Fennell, E. (ed.) *Competence and Assessment Special Issue No 1*, Employment Department, 1989.

Fennell, E. (ed.) *Developing Assessable Standards for National Certification*, Sheffield, Employment Department, 1991.

Finegold, D. and Soskice, D. 'The failure of training in Britain: analysis and prescription', *The Oxford Review of Economic Policy*, 1988.

Further Education Unit, *Towards a Competence-Based System*, London, Further Education Unit, 1984.

Harvey, D. and Brown, D. *An Experiential Approach to Organisation Development*, New Jersey, Prentice-Hall, 1992.

Hayes, C., Fonda, N. *et al. Training for Skill Ownership*, Brighton, Institute of Manpower Studies and Manpower Services Commission, 1982.

Hodkinson, P. and Issitt, M. (eds) *The challenge of competence: professionalism through vocational education and training*, London, Cassell Education, 1995.

Hutton, W. *The State We're In*, London, Cape, 1995.

Hutton, W. 'Wealth of happiness may be in store', *Guardian*, 8 November 1993.

Jessup, G. *Outcomes: NVQs and the Emerging Model of Education and Training*, Lewes, Falmer Press, 1991.

Kilmann, R. *Beyond the Quick Fix*, California, Jossey Bass, 1984.

Labonte, R. 'Health promotion and empowerment: reflections on professional practice', *Health Education Quarterly*, vol. 21:2 summer 1994, 253–68.

Levy, M. *The Core Skills project and Work Based Learning – An overview of the development of a new model for the design, delivery and accreditation of vocational education and training*, Blagdon, Manpower Services Commission and the Further Education Staff College, 1987.

Levy, M. with Edmond, N. Mathews, D. and Oates, T. *A Guide to Work Based Learning Terms*, Blagdon, Training Agency and the Further Education Staff College, 1989.

McKiddie, T. 'Personnel NVQs: preparing for take-off', *Personnel Management*, February 1994.

Management Charter Initiative, *Senior Management Standards*, Management Charter Initiative, London, 1995.

Manpower Services Commission *Core Skills in YTS: Manual Part 1*, Sheffield, Manpower Services Commission, 1984.

Manpower Services Commission *Core Skills in YTS: Manual Part 2*, Sheffield, Manpower Services Commission, 1984.

Manpower Services Commission *The New Training Initiative – An Agenda for Action*, Sheffield, Manpower Services Commission, 1981.

Manpower Services Commission *SASU Note 16: Guidance on Designing Modules for Accreditation*, Sheffield, 'Standards and Assessment Support Unit of the Manpower Services Commission' 1986, (mimeo).

Manpower Services Commission *Youth Training Scheme: Guide to Scheme Design and Content*, Sheffield, Manpower Services Commission, 1984.

Manpower Services Commission and the Department of Education and Science *Review of Vocational Qualifications*, London, 1986.

Mansfield, B. 'Competence – two views', *Research and Development Series No. 3 Components of Occupational Competence*, Harrogate, PRIME Research and Development Ltd, 1988.

Mansfield, B. 'Design, learning and accreditation', in B. Mansfield, *The YHAFHE Certification Project: A Selection of Papers*, Leeds, Yorkshire and Humberside Association for Further and Higher Education, 1986.

Mansfield, B. 'Deriving Statements of Competence', in E. Fennel (ed.), *Development of Assessable Standards for National Certification*, Employment Department, 1991.

Mansfield, B. and Horton, P. *Work Based Assessment and its Certification*, Leeds, Yorkshire and Humberside Association for Further and Higher Education, 1986.

Mansfield, B. and Mathews, D. *The Components of Job Competence*, Bristol, Further Education Staff College, 1985.

Martin, S. 'A futures market for competencies', *People Management*, 23 March 1995.

Miller, R.B. 'Task taxonomy: science or technology', in W.T. Singleton (ed.), *The human operator in complex systems*, London, Taylor and Francis, 1967.

Mintzberg, H. *The nature of managerial work*, New York, NY, Harper and Row, 1973.

Mitchell, L. (ed.) *Vocational Education and Training Issues: Number 7: Shaping Tomorrows' Enterprises*, Harrogate, PRIME Research and Development Ltd, 1993.

Mitchell, L. and Cuthbert, T. *Insufficient Evidence: The Final Report of the Competency Testing Project*, Glasgow, SCOTVEC, 1989.

Mitchell, L., Mansfield, B. and Leigh, A. 'Understanding Knowledge': the Final Report of the 'Identifying and Accrediting Relevant Knowledge in the Building Society Sector' project, published as *Research and Development Report No. 4*, The Standards Methodology Unit, Department of Employment, 1990.

Moss Kanter, R. *When Giants Learn to Dance: Mastering the Challenge of Strategy, Management and Careers in the 1990s,* New York, NY, Simon and Schuster, 1989.

Munn, P. and MacDonald, C. *Adult Participation in Education and Training*, Edinburgh, Scottish Council for Research in Education, 1988.

National Council for Vocational Qualifications *NVQ Criteria and Guidance*, London, National Council for Vocational Qualifications, 1995.

National Council for Vocational Qualifications *The National Vocational Qualification Framework*, London, National Council for Vocational Qualifications, 1987.

Paper Federation of Great Britain, *Dry and reel paper and board by machine process*, NCVQ ID: U1018460, Paper Federation of Great Britain,

Parsons, T. *The social system*, Glencoe, Ill. The Free Press, 1951.

Parsons, T. *The structure of social action*, New York, NY, McGraw-Hill, 1937.

Peters, T. *Thriving on Chaos: Handbook for a Management Revolution*, London, Macmillan, 1988.

Plants, Animals and Land Sector Consortium *Common Units with associated information: Piloting/Field Testing Draft*, Kenilworth, ATB Land-base, 1995.

Prescott, B. 'Competence analysis flow chart – a step by step method for trainees to analyse their work activities using core skills', *Training and Development*, August 1985.

President of the Board of Trade, the Chancellor of the Exchequer, the Secretaries of State for Transport, Environment and Employment, the Chancellor of the Duchy of Lancaster, and the Secretaries of State for Scotland, Northern Ireland, Education and Wales by Command of Her Majesty, *Competitiveness: Forging Ahead*, London, HMSO, 1995.

President of the Board of Trade, the Chancellor of the Exchequer, the Secretaries of State for Transport, Environment and Employment, the Chancellor of the Duchy of Lancaster, and the Secretaries of State for Scotland, Northern Ireland, Education and Wales by Command of Her Majesty, *Competitiveness: Helping*

Business to Win, London, HMSO, 1994.

PRIME Research and Development and KAP Associates, Standards for Quality Managers. *Draft Occupational Standards and Knowledge Specifications*, PRIME Research and Development and KAP Associates, 1992.

Scottish Education Department *16s–18s in Scotland: An Action Plan*, Edinburgh, Scottish Education Department, 1983.

Scottish Education Department *16s–18s in Scotland: Guidelines on Curriculum and Assessment*, Edinburgh, Scottish Education Department, 1984.

Skills and Enterprise Network 'Planning for the 21st century: a summary of labour market and skill trends 1995/96', *Network News*, Nottingham, Employment Department, January 1995.

Smale, G. and Tuson, G. *Empowerment, Assessment, Care Management and the Skilled Worker*, NISW Practice and Development Exchange Series, London, HMSO, 1993.

Stewart, R. *The Reality of Management*, London, Heinemann, 1986.

Trades Union Congress, *Bargaining for Skills*, London, Trades Union Congress, 1992.

Trades Union Congress *National Standards for Full Time Trade Union Officials*, London, Trades Union Congress, 1993.

Training and Development Lead Body *Standards for Training and Development*, London, Training and Development Lead Body, 1992.

Training and Development Lead Body *TDLB Implementation Guide*, London, Training and Development Lead Body, 1992.

Wilson, R. 'Skill needs to the end of the century', paper presented to Skill Focus National Conference 'Future Skills Demand and Supply: Trends, Shortages and Gluts', York, December 1994.

Index

Coaching and Mentoring

Nigel MacLennan

The coaching/mentoring approach is probably the most effective way of helping others to achieve optimum performance in the workplace. Dr MacLennan's book covers the entire subject from basic skills to designing and implementing a tailor-made coaching and mentoring system. He starts by explaining the nature of achievement and the factors that determine it, and then introduces a seven-stage model that will enable managers and supervisors to encourage their people to develop their skills. He examines the problems commonly encountered and shows how to overcome them or, in some cases, turn them to positive account.

The book is interactive throughout, using cartoons, humour, self-assessment questions, case studies and illustrations to reinforce the text. A particularly valuable feature is a set of checklists that together summarize the key elements involved.

Coaching and Mentoring is, quite simply, a comprehensive manual of the best methods known today of helping people to succeed.

Gower

Assessment and Development Centres

Iain Ballantyne and Nigel Povah

Assessment and development centres have been established for some years as an effective method for selecting and developing people. Recent dramatic growth has led to increased demand for guidance on how to run them. This new book, by two of the UK's leading specialists in the field, will go a long way towards meeting that need.

It looks at the entire process, from the underlying concepts to the most effective methods of validation - not forgetting the organizational politics involved. The main objectives of the book are:

- to establish a thorough understanding of the principles and practice of assessment centres
- to provide sufficient knowledge to enable practitioners to run their own events in a professional manner
- to help readers to recognize when they may need to call on outside expertise
- to equip readers to ask pertinent questions of any prospective advisers.

Assessment and Development Centres represents a practical approach which is sure of a warm welcome from HR professionals.

Gower

Developing Your Business Through Investors in People

Norrie Gilliland

- What does Investors in People involve and how would it benefit my organization?
- How can I make sure our training and development activities will help achieve our business objectives?
- How can I encourage employees to "take ownership" of the business?
- What are the options for training and developing my people and how do I determine the most appropriate?
- How do I prepare for IIP assessment?

These questions are typical of managers involved, or expecting to be involved, in Investors in People. They and many others are addressed in this timely new book. Drawing on his experience of working on Investors in People with more than fifty organizations, the author describes the business benefits of developing employees through systematic communication, involvement and training.

He examines the IIP national standard in detail and outlines numerous ways of meeting it, showing how to align training and development with business objectives, how to assess individual development needs and highlighting the role of managers in the process. The intensely practical text is enlivened by cartoons, checklists and real-life examples.

For managers in every kind and size of business, for HRD specialists and for consultants, Norrie Gilliland's book represents the best available source of reference and guidance in an area too often regarded as complex and forbidding.

Gower